information & communication technology

for **WJEC** GCSE

Peter Vickers

Hodder Murray

A MEMBER OF THE HODDER HEADLINE GROUP

The Publishers would like to thank the following for permission to reproduce copyright material:

Photo credits
p.3 b PhotoDisc; **p.3** t, **29, 42, 44, 46, 57, 156, 189, 190, 195** b, **197, 198** t, **199** t, **200, 204** r and **205** t Steve Connolly; **p.12** Janine Wiedel Photolibrary/Alamy; **p.13** © Royalty-Free/Corbis; **p.14** Ferruccio/Alamy; **p.15** Getty Images; **p.16** © Royalty-Free/Corbis; **p.18** Peter Dejong/AP/Empics; **p.23** © John Turner/Corbis; **p.24** t PA/Empics, b Ace Stock Limited/Alamy; **p.35** © Jon Feingersh/zefa/Corbis; **p.47** Spencer Grant/Science Photo Library; **p.61** t Martyn F. Chillmaid/Science Photo Library, b David J. Green/Alamy; **p.63** educationphotos.co.uk/walmsley; **p.64** © Owen Franken/Corbis; **p.68** David Parker/600-Group/Science Photo Library; **p.70** © Royalty-Free/Corbis; **p.75, 78, 79, 80, 147** and **159** Peter Vickers; **p.117** Maximilian Stock Ltd/Science Photo Library; **p.119** ImageState/Alamy; **p.123** Emil Pozar/Alamy; **p.124** Photodisc; **p.129** Ed Young/Science Photo Library; **p.130** © BMW AG; **p.131** © BMW AG; **p.132** ImageState/Alamy; **p.140** AJ Photo/Science Photo Library; **p.144** © Serra Antoine/Corbis Sygma; **p.155** Volker Steger/Siemens AG/Science Photo Library; **p.157** Access Keyboards Ltd; **p.160** Isaac Newman/Alamy; **p.176** t Action Press/Rex Features, b Helene Rogers/Alamy; **p.177** James King-Holmes/Science Photo Library; **p.188** Esa Hiltula/Alamy; **p.191** Scenics & Science/Alamy; **p.194** Scenics & Science/Alamy; **p.195** t PhotoDisc; **p.196** t Geoff Oliver/photographersdirect.com, b © Royalty-Free/Corbis; **p.198** b © Royalty-Free/Corbis; **p.199** b © Royalty-Free/Corbis; **p.201** © Royalty-Free/Corbis; **p.204** l © Royalty-Free/Corbis; **p.205** b Hewlett Packard; **p.206** mediacolor's/Alamy; **p.207** Helene Rogers/Alamy; **p.215** Transtock Inc./Alamy; **p.228** Belkin; **p.262** Rex Features.

Acknowledgements
p.37 © 1996-2006, Amazon.com, Inc. and its affiliates; **p.39** © 2005 National Westminster Bank Plc. All rights, save as expressly granted, are reserved; **p.40** www.chatdanger.com, Childnet International; **p.41** Copyright © Brian Buckley, 1997-2006; **p.44** © Sky 2006; **p.56** Frenchtutorial.com; **p.59** © 1998-2006 QVC Inc/QVC; **p.136** Printed with permission of Mathemedics, Inc./Easydiagnosis, http://easydiagnosis.com; **p.139** Londontheatrebookings.com.

Every effort has been made to trace all copyright holders, but if any have been inadvertently overlooked the Publishers will be pleased to make the necessary arrangements at the first opportunity.

Although every effort has been made to ensure that website addresses are correct at time of going to press, Hodder Murray cannot be held responsible for the content of any website mentioned in this book. It is sometimes possible to find a relocated web page by typing in the address of the home page for a website in the URL window of your browser.

Hodder Headline's policy is to use papers that are natural, renewable and recyclable products and made from wood grown in sustainable forests. The logging and manufacturing processes are expected to conform to the environmental regulations of the country of origin.

Orders: please contact Bookpoint Ltd, 130 Milton Park, Abingdon, Oxon OX14 4SB. Telephone: (44) 01235 827720. Fax: (44) 01235 400454. Lines are open 9.00 – 5.00, Monday to Saturday, with a 24-hour message answering service. Visit our website at www.hoddereducation.co.uk

For files that support all activities marked with please visit www.ict4wjecgcse.co.uk

© Peter Vickers, 2006
First published in 2006 by
Hodder Murray, an imprint of Hodder Education,
a member of the Hodder Headline Group
338 Euston Road
London NW1 3BH

Impression number   5 4 3 2 1
Year   2010 2009 2008 2007 2006

Cover photo © Royalty Free/Corbis
Typeset in 11/14 pt Memphis Light
Printed and bound in Italy

A catalogue record for this title is available from the British Library

ISBN-10: 0 340 90784 3
ISBN-13: 978 0 340 90784 9

Contents

SECTION

Information technology: Use and impact on society

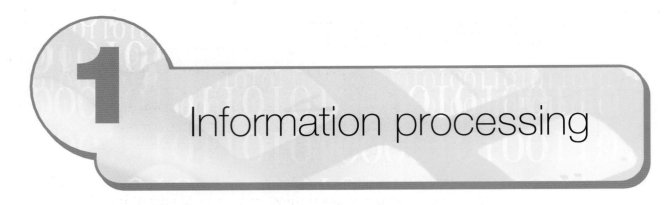

1 Information processing

1.1 Data, information and knowledge

Data consists of raw facts and figures.

Here is an example of some data:

| 17 | 17 | 18 | 20 | 20 | 21 | 22 | 22 | 23 |

These are just numbers in a sequence and have no meaning.

If we are now told that these are readings in °C taken from a temperature sensor in a classroom, and were taken at hourly intervals, then the data becomes information.

Data + Meaning = Information

Computers process **data** to produce **information**.

Computers process data. That is what they do. We give data to a computer. It processes the data and gives us back information. This data processing may involve organising the data, sorting it in some way or performing calculations on it.

Knowledge can be deduced from this information. We now know that the room has become warmer, and over the 8-hour period the increase in temperature has been 6°C.

Numbers are just one type of data. Data can be of other types such as words, pictures, videos or sounds. A computer will process any of these types just as easily.

If the information produced by computers is going to be useful, then the data that is used must be good quality data. A lot of time and effort is spent in making sure that no incorrect data gets into a computer system. There is a saying among computer users:

GIGO: Garbage In, Garbage Out.

GIGO – Garbage In, Garbage Out

This means that if you give a computer incorrect data then it will produce incorrect results. Many problems that arise with the use of computers are not caused by the computer but by the data that is used. People tend to blame computers for mistakes but it is usually the fault of the person who collected or entered the data.

1.2 Why use ICT?

ICT: Information and Communication Technology is the study of how data is collected, stored, processed and distributed.

ICT, which stands for Information and Communication Technology, is the study of the ways in which information is collected, how it is stored, what processing can be done on it and the different methods by which the information can be sent between computer users. It is also a study of how the information is used at the workplace or home.

As with most technologies there are good things about ICT and there are some not so good things and we will look at both the advantages and disadvantages of using ICT.

Figure 1.1 *Old methods of storing and distributing data are being replaced by ICT methods.*

Advantages of using ICT:

- When data is stored using ICT it will need less storage space. The old ways of storing data on sheets of paper or record cards and filing them away in filing cabinets are now being replaced by methods of storing data on computer systems.
- Data stored using ICT can be kept more secure. The data can be encoded so that, if it gets into the hands of unauthorised people they will not be able to understand or use it.
- If data is stored on a computer system, then it can be accessed quickly. This means that finding data is much faster.
- Back-up copies of data stored on computer systems can easily be made and these can be kept for security reasons. If data is accidentally destroyed then it can be replaced by the back-up copy.
- Data stored in a computer system can be changed easily. It is more difficult to alter text that has been printed on paper.
- Processing data is much faster on a computer.
- Fewer staff are needed, but they must have the necessary ICT skills.
- Data can be presented in a large number of different ways. Information may be displayed as printed text or in tables of data. Charts may be drawn to illustrate some information. Pictures or moving videos may be shown or presentations consisting of a number of slides may be used. Computers can also output sounds or music.
- Data stored on a computer network can be accessed by any other user on the network.

Computers can send data from one computer user to another in just a few seconds even if the users are in different parts of the world. This speed of communication is an essential element in many business systems.

Disadvantages of using ICT:

The disadvantages are much harder to find, but there are some…

● The cost of equipment can be high. Many businesses or people may not be able to afford to buy the computers and all the associated equipment.
● Difficulties may arise because people do not know how to use the equipment. A business may have to spend time and money on training its staff so they can effectively use a computer system.
● Viruses or hackers may damage data on computer network systems.

There are clearly more advantages than disadvantages so many businesses are now using ICT to improve the services that they offer to their customers.

Advances in ICT have caused many changes in the way businesses and organisations operate. We now see computers helping with management decision-making or planning financial budgets. There are fewer staff employed but they are better trained in the use of ICT. Marketing in many cases has become global and businesses can advertise their goods all over the world using the Internet.

> 02
> Businesses have been able to expand their operations worldwide.

1.3 Data security

> 03
> Organisations spend a lot of time trying to minimise the possibility of incorrect data getting into their computer systems.

Almost every business that uses ICT stores some data. It may be data about the items they sell, the details of their customers or their sales figures for the last year. Whatever the data is, it is vital that there are no errors in it. Mistakes in the data may result in inappropriate decision-making or loss of sales.

Incorrect data becomes even more critical in systems that store personal data. How would a customer feel if a bank told them they had less money in their account than there actually was? What might happen if a patient in a hospital was given the wrong treatment on the basis of incorrect data? A person may be refused employment on the grounds of an incorrect criminal record.

■ Activity 1.1 Internet search

In March 2003 a person in Huddersfield had failed to pay his electricity bill so he was sent another one, together with a threat to take him to court if he did not pay it. He was rather shocked when he opened the bill to discover the amount he was being asked to pay!

Use the Internet [Suggested search: +"electricity bill" +Huddersfield +2003] to find:

1 The amount of his shocking electricity bill.
2 The amount of his original bill.

Do you think the problem was caused by the computer, or was it incorrect data that was input?

Can you find any other cases where the use of computers has led to ridiculous situations?

1.3.1 Errors

There are many different types of error that may occur and businesses and organisations need to make sure their data is secure. A business runs the risk of losing its customers if they lose confidence in the way it is run. A number of different methods are used to try to ensure the data is not corrupted and we will discuss these in the next few sections.

Errors may occur at a number of different stages in the data's existence.

- Data might be collected and recorded wrongly.
- Data might be entered into the computer incorrectly.
- Processing of the data may cause errors.
- Stored data is subject to security problems.
- When data is transmitted from one computer to another it could become corrupted.

Data capture forms and **questionnaires** must be carefully designed to minimise the chance of errors being recorded on them.

Possible Error	Solution
When data is first collected it may be recorded on a special data capture form or on a questionnaire. The person who records the data may make a mistake and write down the wrong data.	It is important that data capture forms or questionnaires are designed in such a way that errors are minimised. The questions must be unambiguous – there must be no doubt in the mind of the person filling it in as to what they are meant to enter. Boxes might be used on the form to make sure that data is entered neatly and not scribbled down so quickly that the writing is illegible.

After the data capture forms have been completed they are then taken to a computer operator who transcribes the data. This means that they type the data into the computer probably using a keyboard. There are other methods of doing this such as using a scanner, which we shall study later in this book.

Data **verification** checks for transcription errors (the errors made when the data is typed in).

Possible Error	Solution
Transcription errors may occur. The person typing the data into the computer may make a mistake and enter incorrect data.	Methods of data verification will be studied in more detail in another section (see Section 7.3), but the data must be carefully checked by eye or even double-keyed – entered twice into the computer, and only accepted if the two versions are identical.

Before the data is processed it is checked again to see if it is sensible data. This process is called data validation and makes sure that no 'freak' readings are processed by the computer.

There are many different methods of data validation and we shall look at a few here. You should use some of these in your coursework.

Data **validation** is used to check that data is sensible before it is processed. Typical validation checks are range checks, presence checks, format checks and the use of check digits.

Most database and spreadsheet programs allow the user to set validation rules so the data is checked when it is entered.

Possible Error	Solution
Invalid data is entered. This may have been caused by incorrect data being originally collected or by a transcription error.	Data validation methods may be used to check that the data is sensible data.
	Range Check: Numerical data is checked to see if the value lies within an acceptable range of numbers.
	Example: The month part of a date must lie in the range 1 to 12.
Missing data.	Presence Check: A check to see that data is not missing.
	Format Check: A check that the data is in the correct format.
	Example: A postcode must be two letters followed by a number, a space and then a number and two letters.
Transposition error – entering the digits in a number in the wrong order.	Check Digit: A calculation is carried out on the digits of a number to create an extra digit, which is then added on to the end of the number.
	The computer will check when the data is entered that the check digit is correct.

1.3.2 Accidental damage to files

Once data is stored on a computer system it is still not safe. It is all too easy for a user to accidentally destroy data.

It is important for an organisation to have a proper back-up strategy. A back-up of the data is an extra copy of the data stored somewhere different to the original. If a disaster happens to the data then the back-up copy can be used instead.

Back-ups need to be made at frequent intervals and when you do your coursework it is vital that you never have only one copy of your work. Make frequent back-ups and store them in different places if you can. Make sure you name the back-up copies carefully so you know which is the most recent. If you lose your work for some reason, then it will be possible to get most of it back without having to do it all again.

A business may adopt the strategy of making a back-up of its data at the end of every day. The computer may be set to automatically store the data on tape overnight. The tapes for each day could be stored in a fire-proof safe in a different building and only re-used after a week has passed.

Back-up copies of important data need to be made frequently and stored in a different place to the original data.

Another way of protecting data from accidental deletion is to change the attribute of the file to 'read-only'. This is a setting that can be made on the computer, which means the file cannot be accidentally changed or deleted.

1.3.3 Viruses

VIRUS: A program which can copy itself from one computer file to another.

Stored data files may need to be protected from some types of malicious damage that are deliberately caused. The most common of these is a program called a virus.

A virus is a program which:

Special **virus-protection software** can be installed on a computer to protect the files from a virus. This will need to be kept up-to-date as new viruses appear all the time.

- can copy itself from one disk to another (e.g. by means of a floppy disk);
- can attach itself to an email so that it has the ability to spread from one computer system to another;
- can also cause damage to files stored on a computer's hard disk.

Each virus has a different name and can spread itself so fast that computers all over the world can be infected within just a few days.

Computer users need to protect their files from possible damage by a virus. The best way of doing this is to install special virus-protection software on the computer that not only will detect if a virus has been received but will also then try to remove it.

Figure 1.2 *The best defence against viruses is to install virus protection.*

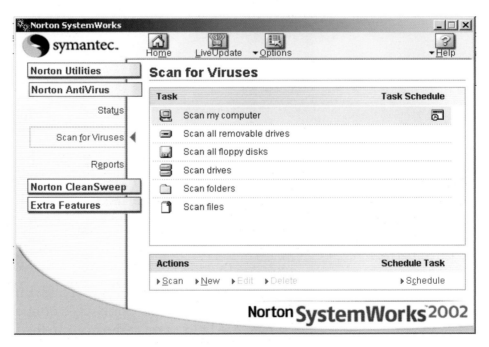

Here are some precautions to take to prevent infections by a virus:

- Try not to use a disk or memory stick on one computer and then transfer it to another computer.
- Do not open an email from a sender who you do not know. In particular, never open an attachment file that comes with it.
- Do not download data or software from the Internet. This is one of the main ways in which viruses spread.

● Run a virus check on a regular basis. Virus-protection programs can usually be set up to automatically check every new file before it is saved on your computer.

● Keep the virus definitions of your virus-protection software up-to-date to protect from new viruses. These definitions are used to identify viruses and the update can normally be done by downloading from the Internet.

...and don't forget to take those back-ups regularly in case files get damaged!

There are types of viruses called Trojans or Worms. Follow the steps above and you should not have to worry about them either.

■ Activity 1.2   Internet search

On Wednesday, 22 January 2003, a judge passed a prison sentence on the writer of the virus called Gokar.

Use the Internet [Suggested search: +Gokar +2003] to find:

1   Where did the writer of this virus come from?
2   What does this virus place in the Microsoft Windows directory of the infected computer?
3   What sort of virus is this and how does it spread?
4   What are the names of the two other viruses that he wrote?
5   How long was the prison sentence?

The GOKAR virus is said to have infected 27 000 computers in 42 different countries.

1.3.4   Hacking

HACKER: A person who gains unauthorised access to data stored on a computer.

Hacking has become a problem since networks have been developed. In particular, the Internet has allowed hacking to become a global problem. A hacker is someone who deliberately accesses data stored on a computer without authorisation.

Hackers may change the data to their advantage, or they may delete or damage the data. There have been a number of stories of people who have been sacked from jobs, hack into the company's computer and destroy the files out of malicious revenge.

Others may hack computers to gain data for criminal purposes such as blackmail.

Banks are frequently the targets of attack from hackers. Attempts are made to break into the bank's files or hackers may try to monitor files which are being sent to the bank in the hope of obtaining customer bank details and security information. Once they have that information they can pretend to be that person and withdraw money from their account or use their credit card to buy goods. It may be difficult to know how much hacking is happening, as banks are unwilling to admit to any failures in their security systems.

Organisations have to try to keep one step ahead of the hackers and devise ever more sophisticated methods of preventing them accessing their files. This is often seen as a challenge by hackers who communicate with each other over the Internet and often offer help with ideas of how to get past new security measures.

Protection from hackers:

- A system of passwords should be used. Each user enters a username and password when logging on to a system. Passwords need to be changed regularly and obvious passwords like dates of birth or pet names should be avoided. A user should never tell their password to anyone else.
- Users must log off properly every time they have finished using a computer.
- Computers should be switched off or disconnected from networks, particularly the Internet, when not in use.
- A call-back system may be used. The user calls into the system over a telecommunications link, and enters a username and password. The system then hangs up on the user and calls the user back on a predetermined number.
- To prevent important data being intercepted and used for wrongful purposes when it is transmitted down a network, the data may be encrypted. This means the data is coded so that a hacker will not be able to understand or use the data.
- A special type of software called a firewall can be used to prevent hackers from accessing a network.

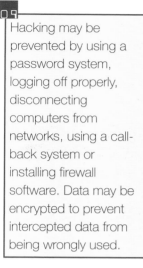

Hacking may be prevented by using a password system, logging off properly, disconnecting computers from networks, using a call-back system or installing firewall software. Data may be encrypted to prevent intercepted data from being wrongly used.

Figure 1.3 *Passwords – the best defence against hackers.*

■ Activity 1.3   Word processing (Easy)

Type the following into a word-processing program, format the text and print it out. (The font used here is Arial: Size 11 and the paragraph is fully justified.)

<u>The Good Hackers</u>
Not all hackers are bad! Hackers are now being employed by some organisations to '*hack the hackers*'. They call themselves '*ethical hackers*' or '*intelligence consultants*'. Their job is to track down the criminal hackers and bring them to justice.
Good luck to them!

Can you name five different types of text formatting used in this paragraph?

Summary

0.1 Data consists of raw facts and figures.

0.2 Computers process data to produce information.

0.3 People use information to produce knowledge.

0.4 GIGO – Garbage In, Garbage Out. If you give a computer incorrect data, it will provide incorrect information.

0.5 ICT stands for Information and Communication Technology. It is the study of how data is collected, processed, stored and distributed.

0.6 ICT methods require less human effort and produce faster and more reliable results than the traditional methods. It is easier to keep information secure. Businesses can usually improve their services to customers by using ICT methods.

0.7 ICT has had some impact on people. Fewer staff may be needed in some businesses. Staff may need to be trained to improve their ICT skills.

0.8 Data can be presented in many different ways, for example text, tables, charts, graphs, pictures, videos, sounds or music.

0.9 Data can be sent between computers on a network.

10 ICT costs may be high initially.

11 There are many different types of error that can occur. Businesses make great efforts to minimise the chance of errors occurring.

12 Careful design of data capture forms will cut down on data collection errors.

13 Data verification methods are used to minimise the risk of transcription errors.

14 Data validation checks are made to make sure the data is sensible. Typical validation checks are:
- range checks (making sure data falls within an acceptable range);
- presence checks (making sure no data is missing);
- format checks (making sure data is the correct type and format);
- check digits (extra calculated digits added to numerical data).

15 It is essential to take frequent back-ups of important data.

16 Viruses are small programs that can spread from one computer to another. They can be detected and prevented by installing special virus-protection software.

17 A hacker is a person who gains unauthorised access to a computer system. Prevention is normally done by using a system of usernames and passwords.

18 Data is often encrypted so that hackers cannot use it.

Practice questions 1

1 A solicitor's office has recently changed from a paper-based system of storing documents to an ICT system using computers and hard disks.

   a) Describe one advantage to the workers at the office. [1]

   b) Give one advantage to the firm of solicitors. [1]

   c) Give one disadvantage to the firm of solicitors. [1]

   d) How would the workers at the office make sure that there are no problems if a hard disk fails? [1]

2 When a new pupil joins a school, a form is filled in with all the details. The school secretary then enters the data into the computer system.

   a) Describe two possible sources of error that could occur. [2]

   b) How could each of these errors be prevented? [2]

Can you remember…?

1 What does GIGO stand for and what does it mean?

2 What does data verification check for?

3 What does data validation check for?

4 What are the four methods of data validation mentioned in this chapter? What does each method check?

5 What is a virus? How can you protect a computer against viruses?

6 What is a hacker? How can you protect a computer against hacking?

2 The implications of the use of ICT

2.1 ICT used by retail services

Shops are major users of ICT. When you go down to a supermarket to buy food or go to a travel agent to book a holiday, you will probably be served by someone using a complex computer system. Banks are another type of business that use computer systems to process your transactions, whether you are taking money out, paying in cheques or asking for a statement of your account.

2.1.1 Point of sale

Figure 2.1 *A POS terminal in a supermarket.*

The checkout tills in a supermarket or other large store are usually all linked to a computer that monitors the sale of items. The main computer will store data about the prices of all the goods and how many of each item remain in the shop. The till is often called a POS (Point of Sale) terminal.

The data is input usually with a barcode reader or a keypad. Items and prices are displayed on a small monitor (screen) and a receipt is printed on paper using a small printer.

2.1.2 Stock control

Stock is the name for all the goods a business has for sale or the items it uses in a manufacturing process. It is important that a shop does not have too many of any item. It may not be possible to sell them all and, in the case of supermarkets where items could be perishable, then they may go bad before they can be sold. Shops need to reduce this sort of wastage so they do not spend unnecessary money on goods they will be unable to sell.

If the shop has too few of any item then it may run out. Any customer coming in to the shop and wanting to buy that item will be

STOCK LEVEL: The quantity of a particular item in the shop or warehouse.

STOCK CONTROL: The management of stock levels. It is important that there is enough of any item to meet demand, but not so many that some are wasted.

disappointed if there are none left and may not return to that shop again. Not good business!

This is why stock control is so important.

The stock level of an item is the number of that item left in the shop. Each item has a re-order level set for it. When the stock level gets as low as the re-order level then more of that item will be ordered from the supplier. When the new stock arrives the stock level of that item is re-adjusted.

2.1.3 Automatic stock control

When a customer buys an item in a shop that uses a POS terminal, the sequence of events is as follows:

ITEMISED RECEIPT: A sales receipt showing the time and date of purchase, a list of the names and prices of all the items bought, as well as a total amount, the amount paid and the change given.

- The item being purchased is identified. This is usually done by reading a barcode but there are a number of other methods of doing this that are described in the next few sections.
- The data is sent to the main computer.
- The computer looks up the item in its database and sends details such as the description and price of the item back to the POS terminal.
- The description and price are displayed on a screen for the customer to see.
- When all items have been processed, the total bill is calculated and an itemised receipt is printed for the customer.
- The customer pays for the goods either with cash, by cheque or using a card.

2.1.4 Data capture

Computers get their data for processing using some method of **data capture**.

All data processed by a computer comes from somewhere. The method of obtaining this data is called data capture and it can be done in many different ways. The next few sections look at the most commonly used methods of data capture:

- barcodes
- OMR
- OCR
- machine-readable tags

2.1.5 Barcodes

Barcodes are used to identify items, especially in shops. A series of lines is scanned by a **barcode reader** and the code number is sent to a computer.

A barcode is a pattern of parallel black and white lines of differing thickness which represent coded data.

Figure 2.2 *A 13-digit barcode (4006501730572).*

The code is usually 13 digits long and consists of four sections:

- A two-digit code for the country the item was made in (e.g. 50 for the UK).
- A five-digit code for the manufacturer.
- A five-digit code which identifies the product.
- A check digit. This is used to make sure that the barcode is read correctly.

Figure 2.3 *An item being read by a barcode scanner.*

Note that the price of the item is not coded as part of the barcode. This is because barcodes are usually printed onto tins, packets or books and so are virtually impossible to change. Prices may vary between shops and sometimes the price needs to be temporarily altered for a sale or a special offer.

A barcode reader scans the barcode using a low-power laser beam and senses the pattern of reflected light. Sometimes the reader is built in to the surface of a terminal, and this is often called a **barcode scanner**. Hand-held readers are sometimes referred to as **barcode wands**.

> A barcode system in a shop provides a **fast service** for customers with **few mistakes** made. The customer gets an itemised receipt.

Advantages to the customer:

- The number of pricing mistakes made should be fewer than the old system where prices had to be keyed in manually.
- The process of serving customers is faster so there should be less time spent in queues.
- The customer is given an itemised receipt so they can check their bill has been properly calculated.

Disadvantages to the customer:

- The price is not found in the barcode. If a customer has picked up an item, it is impossible to see how much it costs without going back to the shelf where it came from to check the displayed price.
- Scratched or crumpled barcodes may cause hold-ups in the checkout queue as the barcode of the item may need to be entered manually.

> The shop management can use the records of sales to analyse patterns of spending and make effective and productive management decisions.

Advantages to the shop:

- There is no need to put a price on every item for sale.
- Automatic stock control means that people do not have to be employed to count the numbers of each item left on the shelves.
- All sales are recorded by the computer so sales patterns can be analysed and better management decisions made about sales promotions, or which items to sell.
- Fraud is minimised. It is not possible for the checkout person to enter a lower price at the till and pocket the difference.

Uses:

Barcodes are used in many different shops (e.g. supermarkets, newsagents and clothes shops, to name a few), but they are also used in other places. Libraries use them to identify and track books, and they can also be found on the membership cards of the borrowers.

You may also have seen barcodes on baggage labels at airports or on the shirts of marathon runners to identify them quickly at the finishing line. Hospital patients may have bracelet tags with barcodes printed on them. There are many other uses of barcodes but all have the same thing in common: to quickly identify a single item.

■ Activity 2.1 Internet investigation

Biology researchers have managed to place very small barcodes on the backs of bees so they can study their flying and mating habits. A laser scanner reads the barcode every time a bee enters or leaves the hive.
Find out more about this.

2.1.6 Optical mark recognition

OPTICAL MARK RECOGNITION (OMR): A means of detecting marks made on a sheet of paper such as a form. The forms are easy to fill in and the reader can input data from the forms very quickly.

Optical Mark Recognition (OMR) is a method used to detect the position of small marks on a sheet of paper. A pre-printed sheet is marked with small lines using a pencil or pen and then it is fed into an **Optical Mark Reader**, a machine that uses reflected light to sense where on the sheet the marks have been made.

Uses:

Some schools use OMR sheets to take daily registers of pupils. The sheets have a list of the pupils and a mark is drawn on the sheet against each pupil's name in one of two columns according to whether that pupil is present or absent.

The National Lottery uses OMR to read the lottery tickets that players have filled in. Each of six numbers is marked with a line on the ticket.

OMR is also used for multiple choice examinations. Each question has a number of different possible answers and the candidate has to put a mark on the correct one.

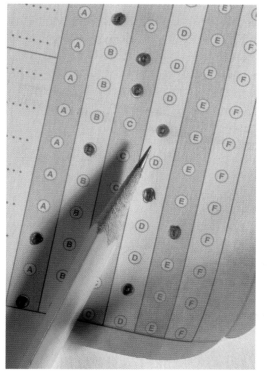

Advantages:

● OMR provides a fast method of filling in forms.
● Using OMR machines is a fast method of reading the data on the forms. The data will usually be input directly into a computer for processing.

Disadvantages:

● Forms can be large if they have to offer many options.
● People who are not used to filling in the OMR forms may not do it correctly and the reader will not be able to read the marks.

Figure 2.4 *An OMR form used for a multiple-choice examination.*

2.1.7 Optical character recognition

Optical Character Recognition (OCR) senses the patterns of light reflected off the surface of a sheet of paper with characters printed or written on it. The patterns are compared with stored data and the nearest match for each character is input to the computer.

OCR software has to be able to recognise letters in a wide variety of fonts, sometimes including handwritten characters.

Uses:

A scanner can be used to scan images of printed text into a computer. OCR software then converts these images into text that can be edited with word-processing software. This process can save a lot of typing!

OCR can also be used on handwritten characters provided they are carefully written.

Electricity bills may be calculated and printed by a computer on special forms and sent out to the customers. There is a tear-off section of this form at the bottom that is sent back together with a cheque payment for the bill. The details on this tear-off section are scanned and read using OCR, and the computer then credits the customer's account with the amount paid.

Advantages:

● It is faster to scan a document into a word processor than to type it.

Disadvantages:

● Accuracy can be poor especially if the printed text is faint or if the font is not a common one. Scanning handwritten characters may produce a lot of errors.

2.1.8 Machine-readable tags

Sometimes in shops, items such as clothes have tags attached to them. These tags have coded data on them that identify the item and these are removed at the checkout and stored. At the end of the day, the tags are placed in a machine which automatically reads the data from the tags and records the sales on the computer. The data may be stored on the tag as printed characters, a barcode or as patterns of holes.

OPTICAL CHARACTER RECOGNITION (OCR): A means of reading text directly from paper using a scanner and placing it into a word-processing document. This can save a lot of time, as there is no need to type the text.

MACHINE-READABLE TAGS: Tags that have data encoded on them that identify the item to which they are attached. A machine can automatically read these tags.

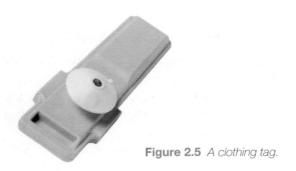

Figure 2.5 *A clothing tag.*

Uses:

Shops might use tags to identify the items to which they are attached. The tag is removed when a customer buys the item and sent to a machine that reads all the tags at the end of the day. The data is processed and stock levels are automatically adjusted.

Advantages:
- Automatic stock control.
- The tags may be kept and stored as a record of the day's sales.

Disadvantages:
- Too much handling by customers may damage the tags.
- Not a real-time system. The data is only updated at the end of the day, so data is not always up-to-date.

■ Activity 2.2 Internet investigation

Schemes are now in operation where pets can be tagged with small microchips placed just under the skin. If the lost pet is found, the tag can be scanned and the data from the tag can be looked up in a centralised database to find the owners.
  Find out more about this.

2.1.9 Portable data entry

A **Portable Data Entry Terminal** (PDET) may be carried around and used to enter data either by keying or using a built-in barcode reader.

The PDET can later be connected to a computer and the data downloaded. Some portable data entry terminals use a wireless connection to download.

Uses:

Data about items in a shop or a warehouse may be gathered, such as the number of each item still in stock.

Data about packages sent out on vans or lorries can be logged from the depot.

Traffic wardens can enter data about parking tickets issued.

Advantages:
- A PDET allows more flexible data collection. Users can walk round and collect data from different areas or buildings.

2.1.10 Touch-sensitive data entry devices

Some devices work by a user touching them. The position where the device is touched is sensed and used as data.

A **touch screen** might have a menu displayed on it. The user selects an option by touching the screen at one of a number of predefined positions.

Touch screens are often used at places where devices such as a mouse or a keyboard may get stolen or damaged. There are no loose or detachable parts.

TOUCH SCREEN: A user-friendly method of selecting options by touching the screen. The user does not need to be an expert in ICT.

Figure 2.6 *A Touch Screen being used in a museum.*

Uses:

Touch screens are often situated in places where members of the public can use them. For example, they may be found in museums, banks or doctors' surgeries. The screen may offer information about a museum or explain to a customer the services the bank can offer. Some touch screens are used in doctors' surgeries to allow a patient to register their attendance without needing to see the receptionist.

Touch screens can often be seen in restaurants or bars. Each item a customer buys is touched on the screen and the total bill is calculated and displayed.

Advantages:

- Low-level ICT skills are needed.
- Little possibility of damage or theft.

Disadvantages:

- If the touch screen is used a lot it may become dirty and difficult to read.

2.1.11 Automatic shopping system

AUTOMATIC SHOPPING SYSTEM: A system that uses computers to control stock levels. They keep track of all sales, find out what items are running low and send out orders to suppliers.

Most large shops and supermarkets now use a computer system to control their operations, and many of the jobs that used to have to be done by people are now done automatically. This means that the shop does not need to employ so many workers and therefore the wages bill is kept low.

Shops sell goods, but they also have to buy them in the first place from a number of different suppliers. As long as the money coming in from sales is greater than the money going out in purchases or bills, then the shop will make a profit and remain in business. Much of the job of the computer system is to make sure that the balance of sales and orders is maintained.

The shops will have an automatic **stock control system**. Every sale that is made is recorded and used to adjust the stock levels. This is an example of a **real-time system** and the data is always up-to-date.

RE-ORDER LEVEL: This is the quantity of an item that the stock level can fall to before more of that item is ordered from the supplier.

Each day the computer will search through the database of stock to find out which items have stock levels that have fallen below their predefined re-order levels. More of these items will need to be ordered from the suppliers and in some systems the computer does this automatically with no need for humans to do anything.

Some systems use the daily sales figures to automatically re-order stock from the suppliers. This means that stock levels are always maintained at the same level for each item. When new supplies are delivered the stock levels for these items are adjusted.

The computer system will do more than run an automatic stock control system. The sales transactions can be analysed and patterns of spending may be revealed. For example some items such as sunglasses may sell better in the summer months than in the winter, so more of them will be needed in stock in the summer. Wellington boots, however, may sell better in the winter months.

Volumes of sales may also have changing patterns and management decisions may have to be made about employing more staff at different times of the year or on different days of the week.

Some shops offer **loyalty schemes**. The customer may earn a number of loyalty points for each purchase they make at the shop. When enough of these points have been collected the customer may be rewarded with gifts or 'money-off' vouchers.

The customer may have a **loyalty card** that is used for identification. The computer can collect information from the POS terminal about how much the customer has spent and calculate loyalty points that are then added to their loyalty account.

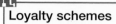

Loyalty schemes reward regular and high-spending customers and provide data about spending patterns.

Advantages to the customer:

- Automatic stock control will mean there are no shortages of any of the items for sale.
- Stock levels can be kept low so the goods will be fresher (particularly important in a supermarket).
- A loyalty scheme means goods may be bought cheaper using vouchers or points.

Advantages to the shop:

- Sales patterns can be analysed and used to make appropriate management decisions.
- Fewer employees are needed to run the stock control system.
- Customers remain loyal and do not go to other shops to do their shopping.

2.1.12 Online booking

ONLINE BOOKING SYSTEM: A system that allows enquiries about availability and bookings to be made and paid for using the Internet.

It is possible these days to walk into a travel agency and make enquiries about holidays. The computer used will be linked to a larger system using the telephone system or through the Internet. The customer can find out if a holiday they want is available on a particular date, and then they can book it.

Details of the customer and the holiday will need to be input. This is usually done using an on-screen form displayed on the monitor. The computer will carefully check the data before the holiday is booked and the details stored in the travel company's database. The booking needs to be processed immediately to stop any other customer trying to book the same holiday.

It may also be possible for the holiday-maker to pay for the holiday on the computer using a credit or debit card.

Online booking systems are now used for plane, train or bus journeys, cross-channel ferries or the Eurotunnel, theatre or cinema seats, hotel rooms, car rentals and so on. The list is very long and gets longer every year.

Practice questions 2.1

1 POS systems are often found in large stores and supermarkets.
   a) Where in a supermarket might you find a POS terminal?   [1]
   b) Name two input devices you would find at a POS terminal.   [2]
   c) Name two output devices you would find at a POS terminal.   [2]
   d) Describe two advantages to the customer of using a POS system.   [2]
   e) Describe two advantages to the supermarket of using a POS system.   [2]

2 Some shops operate loyalty schemes where customers receive points for goods they buy. With some schemes, when enough points have been earned, the customer receives vouchers to be spent in the shop.
   a) Describe one advantage to the customer of a loyalty scheme.   [1]
   b) Describe one advantage to the shop of operating a loyalty scheme.   [1]

3 Shops and manufacturing businesses need to have an effective stock control system.
   a) How does an automatic stock control system work in a large shop?   [3]
   b) Give two reasons why it is important for a shop to have an effective stock control system?   [2]

Can you remember…?

1 What does OMR stand for?
2 What does OCR stand for?
3 Would you use OMR or OCR for:
   a) scanning a typed document into a word processor;
   b) reading data from a lottery ticket?
4 What is the main advantage of using a PDET device to record data?
5 Why might a touch-sensitive screen be used in a busy shopping arcade?

2.2 Banking systems and money

Banks are some of the biggest users of ICT. Nearly all banking processes are performed by computers.

Banks are another major user of ICT technology. Computers now do nearly all the processing of money transactions, not only in this country but also all over the world. They were one of the first types of organisation to computerise their processes and banking systems are now global.

Here are some things a bank customer can do:

● Open a new account. There are different types of account on offer with a variety of benefits.
● Deposit money. The customer can put money into any of the accounts.
● Withdraw money. Money can be removed from any of the accounts.

- Pay bills by cheque.
- Ask for a statement. This will show the details of all the most recent money transactions that have been made.
- The customer may be given a debit card. Items can be bought at shops or on the Internet using this card.
- There are many other services that banks offer; too many to list here. Services such as arranging overdrafts or borrowing money, changing money from one currency to another (e.g. pounds to euros), sending money overseas and so on.

2.2.1 What part does ICT play in a banking system?

When a customer opens an account with a bank, their details are stored in the bank's large database. This database will also store details of all the money transactions the customer makes. This will allow the bank to print out statements at regular intervals and send them to the customers to keep them informed about how much money they still have in their accounts.

Every time a customer uses a cheque or a card to pay a bill, the bank has to move money around from one account to another. This is all done automatically by computer these days and no actual money is involved.

A very important job that ICT has to undertake is that of making sure that there are no breaches of security. The computers will need to check very carefully that no fraud or theft takes place in any parts of the system.

> One of the main tasks of a bank's computer system is to prevent or detect fraud.

■ Activity 2.3 Discussion

In 2003, fraud on UK credit and debit cards cost over £1 million every day. People with cards must take every precaution to stop them from being stolen. To fight back against this, a system of 'chip and PIN' cards is used.

What precautions need to be taken if you use chip and PIN credit cards?

2.2.2 Bank cheques

Cheques are used to pay money to someone else, such as when paying a bill. A book of cheques is given to a customer by a bank when they open an account. When payment is to be made, the cheque is filled in and given to the person being paid. They will then give it to their bank for processing.

When a cheque is written, there are five items that need to be filled in:

Figure 2.7 *There are five things to be filled in when writing a cheque.*

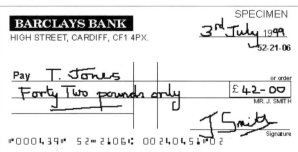

- the date
- the name of the person (or business) being paid
- the amount in words
- the amount in figures
- the signature.

2.2.3 Magnetic ink character recognition

At the bottom of every bank cheque there are some special characters printed. This is a special font used by banks and the ink used is special ink that can be magnetised.

There are three items of data encoded at the bottom of every cheque:

- The **cheque number**. Each cheque in the book has a different number.
- The customer's **account number**.
- The branch **sort code**. Every branch of each bank has a unique number to identify it.

The bank prints a fourth number after it has received the cheque, which is the amount of money.

A bank may receive a large number of cheques in a day, and they all then get sent off to a central clearing house.

Magnetic Ink Character Recognition (MICR) is the process which reads the data from these cheques and inputs it to the computer. The MICR reader magnetises the ink as the cheques are fed into the machine and sensors detect the pattern of the electromagnetic field around them. Some clever science at work here, but the machines can read a large number of cheques very quickly and provide automatic input for the computer system to process all the cheques.

Uses:
MICR is really only used by banks to read data from cheques. The technology is not really appropriate for other applications mainly because of the high costs of setting up the system and buying the hardware needed.

Advantages:
- A large number of cheques can be read very quickly.
- Crumpled or dirty cheques can still be read. It will make no difference to the readability of a cheque if ink or coffee is spilled all over it!
- The characters are difficult to forge.

Disadvantages:
- The equipment is expensive. MICR systems need special readers and also printers that use the magnetic ink.
- Only a very limited number of characters can be used.

2.2.4 Electronic funds transfer

When a shopper pays for goods in a large supermarket or shop, there are a number of different ways this can be done:

- cash
- cheque
- credit card
- debit card
- vouchers.

MAGNETIC INK CHARACTER RECOGNITION (MICR): This is a method of input used by banks to read data from bank cheques. It is a fast method of processing cheques but the equipment is expensive to set up.

We are still not ready for the cashless society, as we still need money for small payments such as taxi fares or vending machines.

ELECTRONIC FUNDS TRANSFER AT POINT OF SALE (EFTPOS): A system that allows payments to be made by swiping a card through a reader. Computers then automatically transfer money between bank accounts.

People are using cash less and less as the need for carrying cash diminishes. There are now more convenient methods of making payments, but we still need cash for things such as 'pay and display' parking machines at car parks, vending machines or bus and taxi fares.

Some people do not trust other methods and still prefer to use cash. There are privacy issues here and cash does not leave any trace of what has been bought or who bought it. Unscrupulous marketers cannot then use the information to send junk mail or make unwanted advertising phone calls.

Customers may write cheques to pay for goods but this can be a slow method and there may be a limit to the value a cheque can be written for, even with a guarantee card.

Electronic Funds Transfer at Point of Sale (EFTPOS) is a method of using cards at POS terminals to make payments for goods bought. The card may have a magnetic stripe embedded in it containing information about the customer's account. The checkout assistant will swipe the card through a magnetic stripe reader that reads the data stored on the card. (See also Section 2.2.7.)

Figure 2.8 *A card being swiped through a magnetic stripe reader.*

The POS terminal is linked to the shop's main computer and sends it details of the customer's account and the amount to be paid. This computer contacts other computers, which then make the appropriate money transfers.

Credit card: The money is transferred from the credit card company's account to the shop's bank account. The credit card company will then bill the customer for the amount transferred and the customer will need to arrange payment.

Debit card: The money is transferred directly from the customer's bank account to the shop's bank account. The customer will see the payment on their next bank statement.

Some stores have their own cards and these operate in the same way as credit cards.

One major problem with using cards is that of card fraud. Magnetic stripes are easily copied and there have been many cases of criminals making copies of credit cards and using them to buy goods. This is why it is important to keep your cards safe and not let them out of your sight when using them in shops. Banks and credit card companies are often unwilling to admit to the full scale of the problem, as it will affect people's willingness to open accounts if they think they may not be secure. To combat this fraud, the technology is moving on to smart cards.

Smart card: The card has a very small microchip embedded in it. A large amount of data can be stored on this chip: much more than on a magnetic stripe. The card is also a lot more difficult to copy. Data about the customer's account may be stored on it but it can also be used to store details about how many points the customer has gained in a loyalty scheme.

Figure 2.9 *A chip and PIN payment device. The card is swiped through the slot at the top.*

A 'chip and PIN' scheme cuts down on card fraud. **Smart cards** are used and customers have to verify payments by entering their Personal Identity Number (PIN).

Many stores now use 'chip and PIN' schemes for card payments. A smart card is used which also stores details of a customer's PIN. A PIN is a Personal Identity Number and needs to be typed in on a keypad to verify a card transaction instead of signing a receipt.

2.2.5 Automatic teller machine

Bank customers are given plastic cards when they open accounts. These cards have several different purposes such as guaranteeing cheques up to a certain value, or they may be used as a debit card when buying goods. They may also be used in an automatic teller machine (ATM). These are the devices that can often be seen in the walls outside banks, shops or petrol stations and are sometimes called 'hole-in-the-wall' cash machines or 'cash points'.

Figure 2.10 *An ATM – Automatic Teller Machine.*

An ATM is simply a computer terminal that is linked directly to the bank's computer system.

There are a number of services that can be requested at an ATM. Here are some things you can do using an ATM:

AUTOMATIC TELLER MACHINE (ATM): A device that allows customers to withdraw money without visiting a bank. Other services are available. A cash card is needed to use it.

- Withdraw cash from your account.
- Print a balance. This is the amount of money left in your account.
- Print a small statement. This will show details of the last few transactions that have been done.
- Order a new cheque book.
- Change your Personal Identity Number (PIN).

The sequence of events when a customer wants to take money out of the ATM is given on page 25.

1 The customer pushes their cash card into the card reader slot. The card has a magnetic stripe that stores data about the customer's bank account.

2 The customer enters their PIN using a keypad. The ATM checks to make sure the customer is the correct owner of the card. If the PIN is not correct, the card will be rejected and no further action takes place.

3 The customer enters the option required, in this case 'Withdraw cash'.

4 The customer selects the amount of money to be withdrawn.

5 The money is dispensed through another slot. The hidden part of the ATM is a safe that stores large amounts of cash. Special sensors check the notes as they are issued to make sure they are not too worn or folded. The sensor can also measure the thickness in case two notes are stuck together.

6 A receipt is printed on a small printer if it is requested.

Advantages to the customer:
- ATMs are always open: 24 hours a day, every day.
- ATMs are always nearby. They can usually be found outside large supermarkets, petrol stations or banks. You are never very far away from one if you are in a town.
- The service is fast so there are never very long queues.

Disadvantages to the customer:
- Banks offer more services.
- There can be problems with the ATMs such as the cash running out at busy times like bank holidays, or a cash card may be rejected if it is damaged and the card reader in the ATM cannot read it.
- A customer who forgets their PIN cannot use the ATM.

Advantages to the bank:
- Fewer customers will come into the bank so they do not need to employ so many staff to serve them.
- It is an automatic computer-controlled system so checks can be made to prevent customers withdrawing cash if they do not have enough in their account.

Disadvantages to the bank:
- ATMs are expensive to buy and install.

2.2.6 Home banking

As more and more people are becoming Internet users, the number of people managing their financial affairs from home is increasing. It is now possible to do a wide range of bank transactions from home. (See also Section 2.3.9.)

Make sure nobody sees your PIN when you enter it at an ATM.

HOME BANKING: An Internet or telephone banking service. Money transactions can be carried out at any time of day or night from the comfort of your own home.

2.2.7 The 'cashless society'

For some time now there has been talk about the 'cashless society': a time when people will not need to carry money around with them and all transactions will be done using electronic means. All purchases will be done using credit or debit cards at EFTPOS terminals and all bills paid using a home banking system.

The benefits of this would be enormous. Theft of money would immediately be eliminated. There would be no bank robberies. Attacks on shopkeepers and cashiers would stop and the streets would become safer as muggers would disappear and drugs would no longer be sold on the streets. People would not have to carry cash around with them or go to the ATM or bank to withdraw more when they ran out.

You might be wondering why this has not happened yet. Well, the truth is that not everyone wants it to happen. People like to feel cash in their pockets or purses and it is certainly faster than using cards to pay for some small items.

There are also privacy concerns that we have already mentioned (see Section 2.2.4). Cash payments leave no evidence, whereas payments by card can be traced to the person paying the card and where and when the payment was made.

It is not yet economically sensible for small payments to be made using cards. The equipment needed and the cost of setting up the system is too great for people such as taxi drivers or bus operators. Soft-drink-vending machines and car parking machines would need to be altered to accept card payments and this would be an expensive operation.

Practice questions 2.2

1 A person is using an ATM (cash point) to withdraw some money.
  a) What two data items must the person enter? [2]
  b) Give two advantages of using ATMs to withdraw money rather than going into a bank. [2]
  c) Give two problems that might occur when using an ATM to withdraw money. [2]
  d) Give one advantage to the bank of using ATM machines. [1]
  e) Apart from withdrawing money, describe two other things a person can do at an ATM. [2]
2 MICR is used to read data from bank cheques and use it as computer input.
  a) What does MICR stand for? [1]
  b) What three items of data are preprinted at the bottom of a cheque? [3]
  c) Give two advantages of using MICR over other methods. [2]

Can you remember...?
1 What are the five things you have to write on a cheque?
2 What is a bank statement?
3 What is a bank balance?
4 What are the two main types of plastic card? What is the difference between them in the way they work.
5 What does EFT stand for? How does it work?

6 What does PIN stand for?

7 State two things you should never do with your PIN.

2.3 Communications services

There have been no inventions in recent years that have had more impact on the way we live than the Internet. It has changed the way we work, the way we perform daily tasks such as shopping or banking, and it has even had an effect on the ways in which we spend our leisure time. Some people have found it easy to make changes but there are many who have not yet been able to adapt to using the Internet or are changing their ways only very slowly.

The Internet has made our lives easier in many ways. Tasks can now be performed from home that used to require travelling to the shops, post offices, banks or other places of work, but it has also caused new problems. The Internet has created new types of criminal, who use the Internet for theft, damage or fraud. We now have to protect our computers from viruses and hackers, as well as our houses from thieves and burglars.

2.3.1 The Internet

A computer network is a number of computers that are connected together by cable or the telephone network, and are able to exchange data. The Internet is a global network of computers that can communicate with each other. Any computer on the Internet can connect to any other and then send or receive data.

> **THE INTERNET:** A global network of computers. All computers on the Internet can communicate with each other (i.e. send or receive data).

There are now very few businesses in this country that are not linked to the Internet and a large number of home users are also connecting to it as the cost of connection comes down and people see the benefits of being a part of the biggest network in the world.

The types of network you will find on the Internet include:

- Commercial networks: shops, banks, broadcasting services.
- Government networks: parliamentary departments, local government.
- Educational networks: universities, schools.
- Private networks: set up by individuals.

■ Activity 2.4 Internet investigation

The Internet (originally called ARPANET) was developed in the USA in the late 1960s because the US Defense Department wanted a military communications network in the event of war. In the late 1980s, Tim Berners-Lee invented the World Wide Web and use of the Internet as we know it began. The first commercial website was launched in 1993.

The Internet has now become a network of more than 100 million computers, with over 50 million websites. It is still growing!

Find out more about the growth of websites on the Internet. If you can find statistics, enter them into a spreadsheet and draw a graph to show the rate of increase.

2.3.2 Internet hardware and software

Any computer can be connected to the Internet if it has the appropriate hardware and software installed, but in general you will need to use the services of an Internet Service Provider (ISP). An ISP will have powerful computers called servers that are permanently connected to the Internet.

There are a number of competing ISPs available and some of them are free but most charge for use of their services. This charge may be a set monthly fee or it may be based on how much you use the Internet. The free ISPs are financed by advertising. An ISP will provide you with the software to be installed on your computer.

When you want to use the Internet, your computer connects to one of the ISP's computers. You will probably then need to enter a username and a password. If it is accepted, the ISP will link your computer to their server, which then provides a link to the Internet.

The other software you need to install on your computer is an Internet browser. There are many of these but the main ones are Microsoft Internet Explorer and Netscape Navigator.

There are a number of different ways that a computer can access the Internet.

Dial-up:

To link a computer to the telephone system you will need a modem. This is a device that makes sure that the digital signals the computer uses are compatible with those of the telephone lines. The computer is connected to the modem which is then connected to a telephone socket, although sometimes the modem is internal and hidden inside the computer. You may hear the modem dialling and connecting to the ISP's computer.

Figure 2.11 *Two microcomputers linked over the Internet.*

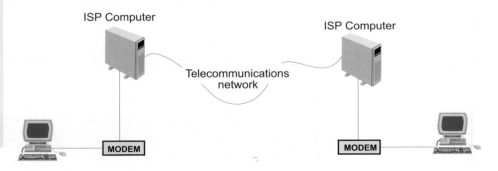

> To use the Internet you must subscribe to an Internet Service Provider (ISP). The ISP has servers that are permanently connected to the Internet.

DIAL-UP NETWORKING:
A means of connecting a computer to an ISP's computers using the telephone system via a modem. Speeds are slow.

MODEM: (*Modulator–demo*dulator) The hardware required to convert digital signals from a computer into analogue signals that can be sent down a telephone line. The modem also converts telephone signals back into digital signals that can be used by a computer.

Figure 2.12 *An external modem.*

The speed a modem sends and receives data is measured in kilobits per second (Kbps) or megabits per second (Mbps). The greater the speed of the connection, the faster you will be able to browse websites on the Internet or download data from them.

Integrated Services Digital Network:
Integrated services digital network (ISDN) is a faster method of connecting to the Internet, which uses a nationwide network of digital connections. The system uses digital signals (already compatible with the computer signals), so there is no need for a modem.

If a company wants to use ISDN to connect to the Internet a special cable will need to be installed. ISDN lines are now being replaced by faster methods such as ADSL.

Asymmetrical Digital Subscriber Line:
Asymmetrical Digital Subscriber Line (ADSL) uses the existing telephone lines to connect to the Internet. The technology allows very fast connection speeds. Downloading data is much faster than uploading, which makes this very suitable for applications such as web browsing.

ADSL links can be left permanently connected to the Internet, which improves the speed of access to websites and allows email messages to be delivered as soon as they arrive. Some web pages are automatically refreshed after a given time interval and this allows businesses to constantly view data such as share prices.

Cable:
Many homes have a cable connection for television and these can also be used to connect to the Internet.

2.3.3 Using the Internet

In the next few sections we will discuss different ways in which the Internet can be used:

- Browsing: searching for information.
- Email: sending messages to other email users.
- Online databases.
- Teleconferencing: holding meetings with people all over the world.
- E-commerce: using the Internet for buying and selling.
- Telebanking: banking from home.
- Web publishing: setting up websites.
- Chat lines: Communicating online with other computer users.
- Radio: Listening to programmes from worldwide stations or at a time other than when it was originally broadcast.

ISDN, ADSL and cable are fast methods of connecting to the Internet.

BROADBAND: A term used to describe fast Internet connections such as ADSL.

Unit 2 The implications of the use of ICT

2.3.4 Browsing

One of the main uses of the Internet is for finding information. There is a huge amount of information to be found on websites from news stories to share prices, from sports results to weather information and almost every other topic imaginable. But care must be taken! Some of the information to be found on the Internet is not always accurate and can often be out-of-date. It is better to check out several different sources of information and go to reputable websites.

Every website on the Internet has a unique Uniform Resource Locator (URL). This is an address where the website is to be found and can be entered into the address box of the browser. For example www.bbc.co.uk is the URL of the BBC website.

A complete URL has a prefix which shows the type of Internet resource you wish to use. If you do not use this the browser assumes you wish to view a website and places http:// at the beginning of an address. There are other types of page that can be displayed such as ftp:// (which is a resource that allows you to transfer files across the Internet).

Each page of a website will have hyperlinks. These allow you to navigate from one page to another. The hyperlink might be placed on a word or a picture and clicking the hyperlink with the mouse will cause the browser to display a different web page.

If you do not know the address of the website you want to display, there are powerful search engines which can help you such as Google, Yahoo!, Ask Jeeves and many others. If you go to the website of a search engine and type in keywords (i.e. what you are looking for) it will list a large number of links which might be useful. Just click on any of these to navigate to the website. It is better to be specific about what you are searching for if you are not going to be given a list of links that is too large.

Web browsers may offer other facilities:

- A list of 'favourites'. If you find a website that you wish to use frequently, then you can add it to a list of favourites for easy access.
- A 'history' of recently visited websites is recorded and can be used to display them again.
- A 'back' button which lets you go back to the website you have just visited.
- A 'home' page which you can set yourself. The home page is the website that is displayed when the browser is first opened. A button on the browser, when clicked, will return the display to that of the home page.
- A 'print' facility. It is usually possible to print a web page.

> **UNIFORM RESOURCE LOCATOR (URL):** A unique address that identifies a website on the Internet.

> **http** = Hypertext Transfer Protocol.
> **ftp** = File Transfer Protocol.

> Search engines such as Google help to find websites, but you need to be specific with your search.

2.3.5 Electronic mail

Electronic mail (email) is a system of sending messages from one computer user to another either on a local network or over the Internet. To use email, both users must be subscribers to the Internet and have email software installed. The most common email software is Microsoft Outlook Express, but there are many others.

> **EMAIL:** A system that allows a network user to send a message to another network user.

Every email user must have an email address. This is usually provided by the ISP and will look something like this:

john.smith@myprovider.co.uk

john.smith is the name of the user and **myprovider.co.uk** is the name of the domain used by the ISP to which the user is subscribed. Every email address is unique, which means that no two users will have the same email address and other people will not be able to read your emails. There is no problem with having more than one email address, and sometimes people use different email addresses for different purposes. For example a person may wish to use one email address from home and a different one from their workplace.

If you send an email to another person on the Internet, you need to specify the address of the person you are sending it to, and give the email a subject (a heading to indicate what the email is about). The subject you enter is what will appear on the list of emails of the person receiving your email. You type the actual message in a larger box underneath.

■ Activity 2.5 Spreadsheet and Internet

The challenge is to find a map of the floods in Panama that were reported in the news in December 2004.

1 Set up a spreadsheet with two columns as shown below.

Search keywords	Number of websites found
News	
News about floods	
News about floods in Panama	
"Panama Flood"	
"Panama Flood" +2004	
+"Panama Flood" +2004 +map	

2 Using the Internet, select a search engine and try each of the keyword searches in the table above, recording on the spreadsheet how many website links are found.

  If keywords are entered in quotation marks the search engine will look for websites that have those exact words in them. Most search engines allow advanced searches such as the last one in the table above. The search keywords in the last row mean: find all websites which have the words "Panama Flood" in them; they must also have the word '2004' in them and the word 'map'.

3 Can you find a map of the flood?

4 Add extra columns and use other search engines.

Figure 2.13 *A typical email screen.*

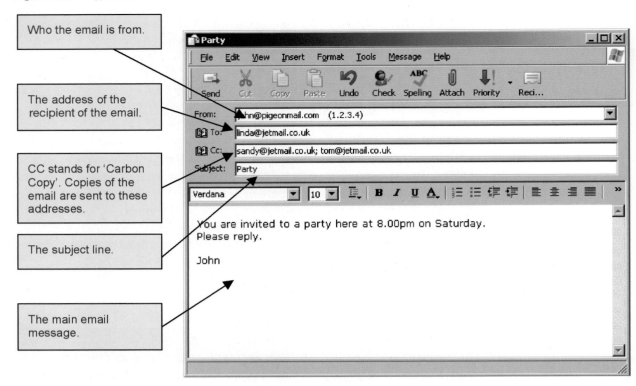

Who the email is from.

The address of the recipient of the email.

CC stands for 'Carbon Copy'. Copies of the email are sent to these addresses.

The subject line.

The main email message.

Once you have typed your message, you need to send it. If you are not connected to the Internet, it will be placed in your 'outbox', where it will stay until you connect. This is one of the most important advantages of emails: you can collect and send your messages at a time that suits you.

You can also choose when you receive your messages. This has the advantage over the telephone which interrupts what you are doing and demands immediate attention, no matter how inconvenient that is.

When you log in to your computer and open the email program, a connection is made and any emails waiting for you are downloaded. Any emails in your outbox are uploaded to your ISP's computer, which will then transmit them to the computer of the recipient's ISP, where they will be stored until they log in and download them.

Figure 2.14 *John sends an email to Jane.*

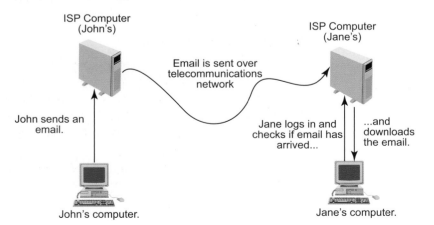

Email programs generally have the following facilities:

- **Address book:** This allows you to store the email addresses of people you may wish to send emails to, and sort them into alphabetical order. Email addresses can often be long and difficult to remember and the address book offers a convenient way of storing them and searching through the list for a particular address. When you create a new email, you can select one of the addresses stored in the address book without having to type the whole address.
- **Inbox folder:** The emails you receive are stored in the inbox folder, but you can create your own folders, and rules can be set for the program to know which folder to store the emails in when they are received. For example, you can set a rule for the program to store all emails from a friend's address in a separate folder.

When you see an email in the inbox, you can open it and read it or print it out, but you can also reply to it and write a message back to the sender, or you can forward it on to another email user's address.

- **Outbox folder:** This contains all the emails that are waiting to be sent. When a connection is made, this folder is emptied as all the emails are uploaded to the ISP's computer.
- **Sent item folder:** A record is kept of all the emails that you have sent.
- **Deleted item folder:** All the emails that you have deleted are stored in this folder until you choose to empty it, when they are permanently removed.
- **Multiple copies:** You can send the same email to a number of different addresses.
- **Attachments:** Any file that can be stored on a computer, whether it is a document, a picture, a sound file or a video clip can be attached to an email and sent to another user.

The sending of emails is now commonplace and is rapidly replacing the conventional methods of communication. The first task done when a person turns on a computer is often to 'check the mail'.

Advantages of email:
- Emails arrive within seconds. The postal service takes a day or two and is sometimes referred to as 'snail mail'.
- It is a cheap method of communication and there are no extra charges for sending emails.
- It does not matter if the recipient is online when the email is sent. It can be received at a time when it is convenient for them.
- An email can be sent to a number of different users at the same time.
- Files may be attached to an email and sent with it.

Disadvantages of email:
- Objects cannot be sent, for example you cannot send a birthday present by email!
- A large amount of emails received are unwanted. These are called **spam** and ISPs sometimes place spam filters on their computers to try to remove them.
- A paper document will need to be scanned before it can be sent by email.
- Some legal processes require original documents and will not accept scanned copies so these will have to be sent by conventional post.
- There is sometimes a limit to the size of an attached file, so very large files may not be sent.

Emails received are stored in the **inbox**. Emails waiting to be sent are stored in the **outbox**.

Spam: A term for unwanted emails.

Webmail

WEBMAIL: A means of sending and receiving emails using a website.

Figure 2.15 *Hotmail is an example of a webmail site.*

Webmail allows users to send and receive emails by visiting an online website. The computer hosting the website stores all the emails and they are not sent to your computer. The main advantage of this is that emails can be checked from anywhere in the world with an Internet connection. For example, you can check your emails if you are on holiday.

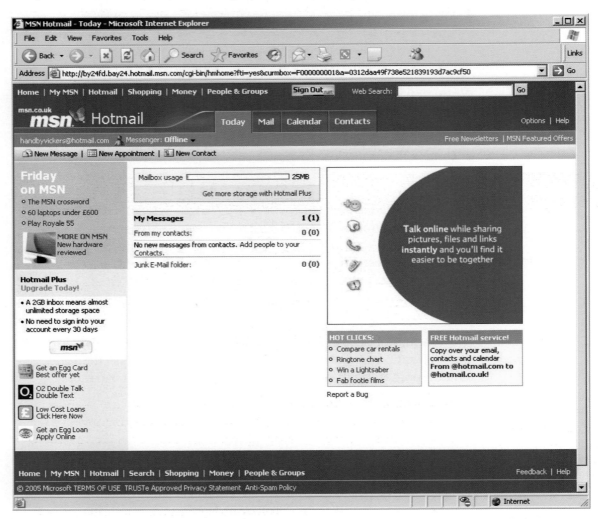

2.3.6 Online databases

2.6
Online databases can be accessed on Internet web pages to find information.

One of the main uses of the Internet is to find information. There are many people who need to find up-to-date information, including school pupils and college students. A doctor may want to find the latest information about an illness and its treatment, or a scientist may need to find out about the properties of a chemical.

There are a number of databases which can be used on the Internet and many of them are free to use. Some typical examples are:

● Dictionaries giving definitions of words, and thesauri that give alternative words with similar meanings.
● Dictionaries for translation of foreign languages.

- Medical databases with information about diseases and their treatments.
- Records of political papers and debates (e.g. Hansard: the daily proceedings in the UK Parliament – http://www.parliament.uk/hansard/hansard.cfm).
- Scientific records.
- Travel timetables for trains, buses or planes.
- Records of plants for gardeners and environmental work (e.g. a database of herbs can be found at http://herb.umd.umich.edu/).
- Records of 'most wanted' criminals or missing persons. These databases can be viewed from all parts of the world, which may help in finding these people.

Most online databases will have their own search facility so you can quickly find the topic you are searching for.

The main advantage of online databases is that you do not have to go and buy a dictionary or travel down to the local library to find what you need, but some of these databases are complex and it can be difficult sometimes and time-consuming to find exactly what you want.

Activity 2.6   Internet investigation

Use the Internet to find the English meaning of these foreign words:

- Teclado (Spanish)
- Boktryckare (Swedish)
- Ellenõrzõmûszer (Hungarian)
- Kiboko (Swahili)

… and the odd one out is?

2.3.7   Teleconferencing

TELECONFERENCING: A way of holding meetings between people who are not in the same room.

In most workplaces, meetings need to be held to discuss business strategies or make decisions, but nowadays some business employees may be many miles apart. They may even be in different countries around the world, and this makes it difficult to hold a meeting at short notice. It can also be expensive, both in travel costs and time, to move staff between company locations.

Figure 2.16 *A teleconferencing meeting.*

Teleconferencing, sometimes called **videoconferencing** if it includes video links, solves this problem. Meetings are held using computers linked to the Internet, and the participants can communicate with each other using microphones and speakers to talk, and cameras to see each other. Special videoconferencing software needs to be installed on all computers being used.

Advantages:

- It is not necessary for people to travel to the meeting. This would save time and there would be no need for expenses such as buying tickets or hotel accommodation. People can attend the meeting from their home or their office.
- Meetings can be called at short notice, and it does not matter where in the world the people might be, as long as they have access to a videoconferencing computer.

Disadvantages:

- Many people prefer to meet face-to-face with others when important decisions need to be made. Meetings held on computers lack the personal touch.
- The videoconferencing equipment needs to be bought. Microphones, speakers and video cameras are required on each of the computers and the necessary software installed.
- Although it is improving, the technology is not yet perfect and the sound and pictures may not be completely synchronised and may appear a little 'jerky'.

2.3.8 E-commerce

Most businesses now operate websites on the Internet, which act like shop windows allowing them to display details of the company and the goods they have for sale. E-commerce is the term used for 'electronically' buying or selling goods or services over the Internet and is becoming increasingly popular.

A buyer can navigate to the website of a business, browse the items offered for sale by looking at pictures and descriptions, and add the items they want to buy to a 'shopping basket'. When all items have been selected, the buyer then proceeds to a 'check out' where the details of the purchase are confirmed and the method of payment is chosen. This usually involves giving details of credit or debit cards and information about the address where the goods are to be delivered. The goods are then sent, usually within a few days, and delivered to the buyer's home. Most companies add a charge for delivery, or postage and packing.

> Shopping can be done from the comfort of your own home using e-commerce websites as long as you pay by card. Extra charges are often made for packaging and delivery.

It is possible to buy almost any item over the Internet these days, from books, CDs and DVDs to plants, insurance, computer equipment and even items you may buy at the chemist. The list is very large and increasing all the time as more and more companies set up e-commerce websites.

Advantages:

- The range of goods available is very large. Almost any item can be found for sale on an e-commerce site using search engines. Gone are the days when you might travel some distance to a shop to find that it does not stock the particular item you want.
- Shopping can be done from home, avoiding the need for the time and expense of travelling to the shops.
- Goods are delivered directly to the doorstep. Some items can be large, heavy or difficult to carry.
- A business operating an e-commerce website does not have to pay for premises such as an office or a shop.

Figure 2.17 *Buying goods is easy on the Internet.*

● Businesses can easily expand their market to anywhere in the world. Any person with access to the Internet can order an item from a website and have it sent to them.

Disadvantages:

● Sometimes there can be a wait of several days or weeks before an item purchased from an e-commerce site arrives. If you buy from a shop, you can have it immediately.

● You cannot touch or smell the goods you are buying. For example, it is sometimes not apparent from a picture what an item of clothing feels like (e.g. how soft or how heavy it is). Fresh food bought over the Internet may not be exactly the same as the picture displayed and it would be impossible to feel how fresh an item of fruit is. There is no way of telling what a bottle of perfume or a bar of soap smells like.

● Some people are worried about giving their credit card details over the Internet even though extensive precautions are taken by e-commerce companies to make sure the details are not intercepted. The details are usually encrypted (coded) before they are sent so they are meaningless to anyone else.

2.3.9 Telebanking

Many banks and building societies now have websites on the Internet where customers can carry out basic banking tasks. You will need to have an account with the bank and will be asked to register with them for use of their online services. They will issue a password that must be entered whenever the site is used, to make sure that customers can access only their own bank account. You may also be asked to enter a PIN (Personal Identity Number) for extra security.

Banks vary in their online services but the most common tasks which you can undertake are:

- View a statement of an account. This will display the most recent transactions and will give a balance (i.e. how much money is remaining in the account).
- Transfer money from one account to another. For example, money can be transferred from a current account to a savings account.
- Bills can be paid. This is done by transferring money from your account to the account of the business whose bill is being paid.
- Set up or alter standing orders or direct debits. These are payments to be made regularly.
- Apply for loans or mortgages.

Other services may include ordering new cheque books or applying for credit cards.

Advantages:
- Banking can be done from home, saving time and avoiding the need for travel.
- Greater control over financial matters. A customer can check the amount of money in an account every day.
- Banking can be done at any time on any day of the week.

Disadvantages:
- People are concerned about security. They are afraid that others may be able to hack into their account and transfer money, but banks take security very seriously and put many safeguards in place to stop these sorts of problems.
- A lack of the personal touch. Sometimes people feel more comfortable discussing banking matters with people rather than on machines.
- There are some banking services which are not available online.

2.3.10 Web publishing

The World Wide Web has become the main way of presenting information, not only for businesses but also for computer users at home. There are new websites appearing every day and others are being constantly updated.

Businesses use a website rather like a shop window, to display their goods and services and give information about the company and what it offers. Other organisations may present types of information such as travel timetables, book catalogues or educational material.

Some people create websites about themselves and their family, or about a topic they are particularly interested in.

28
Common banking tasks can be done from home. There is no need to travel to the nearest branch of your bank, and you can do the tasks whenever you feel like it!

29
Banks need dependable security measures.

Figure 2.18 *A typical site for home banking.*

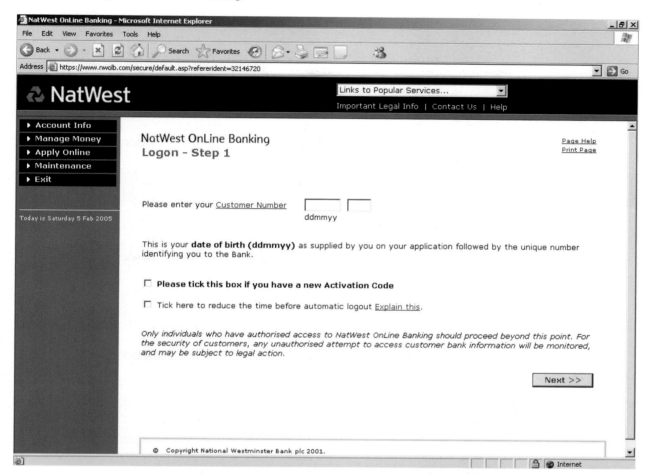

There are many programs available which may be used to create a website, and they operate very like a word processor. Text and graphics are combined and arranged on the page, and links are provided to navigate between the pages.

Designers of websites need to plan carefully the layout of each page and the way the pages are linked. It should be easy for a viewer to navigate around the site and find information they are looking for. Pages must be designed with the intended user in mind and the design must be appropriate to those users. For example, pages for children will need to be colourful and simple.

One way of publishing a website on the World Wide Web is to subscribe to a company which offers website space. Some ISPs offer their customers space to create websites, but there are other businesses on the Internet who charge according to how much space you want to buy.

If you create a website you will need to upload it to your web space and for this you will need a File Transfer Protocol (FTP) program. The program will establish an Internet link to the web space and upload the files you select.

FTP stands for File Transfer Protocol. You will need an FTP program to upload a page to a website.

2.3.11 Chat lines

It is possible for users of the Internet to log in to special chat websites and hold a real-time typed conversation with others. To manage this and make it easier for different people to find each other, there are special 'chat rooms' where users can arrange to 'meet'.

Users of chat rooms sometimes use special abbreviations to save time when typing, for example BCNU is short for 'Be Seeing You'. Similar abbreviations are often used when sending text messages on mobile phones.

■ Activity 2.7 Internet investigation

Here are some abbreviations used in chat rooms. Can you find out what they mean?

BBL	BTW	CUL
FYI	OTT	TNX
ROTFL	HHOK	NHOH
OIC	TTYL	BRB

Figure 2.19 *A website set up by ChildNet International to inform about the potential dangers of chat.*

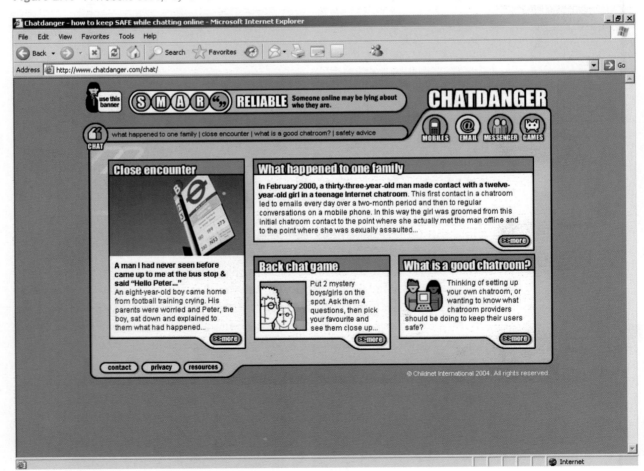

CAUTION:

You should exercise extreme caution when using a chat room. People may not be who they say they are, and you should never give anybody personal information such as your name, address, email or telephone number. It is never a good idea to arrange to meet somebody you have only chatted to online.

If anything at all makes you feel uncomfortable or worries you, then tell somebody about it – preferably a parent or teacher.

Beware! Chat rooms can be dangerous places.

2.3.12 Radio, music and video broadcasting

The Internet may also be used for entertainment. You can tune to a radio station from almost anywhere in the world and listen to their live broadcast as long as your computer has a sound card installed and speakers or headphones. You will also need some media playing software such as Real Player or Windows Media Player.

The speed of your Internet connection is an important factor when listening to radio or video broadcasts as a slow connection can cause the sound to frequently stop for a few seconds. This is because the feed is being played at a faster speed than the signal is being received.

Figure 2.20 *Radio is broadcast on the Internet from many countries of the world.*

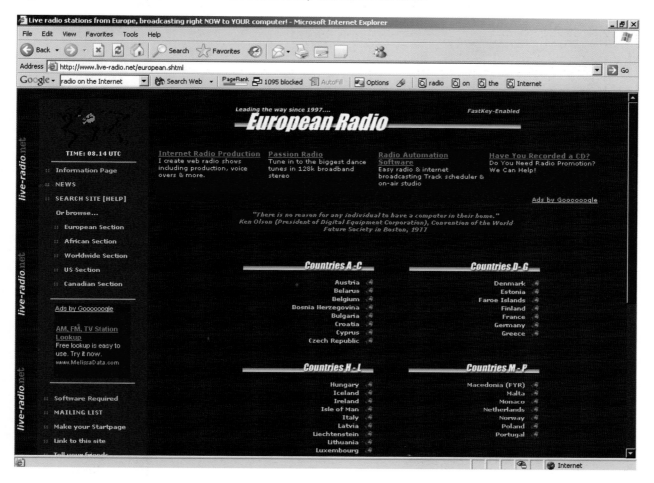

There are also a number of video broadcasting stations that can be received over the Internet, including many news stations and music companies, although these usually charge for their services.

2.3.13 Other communication services

There are other communication and information services that do not use the Internet. These include:

- fax
- voice mail
- teletext
- interactive digital television
- mobile telephones

2.3.14 Fax

FAX (short for facsimile): A means of sending scanned documents over telephone lines or the Internet.

A fax is a means of sending and receiving documents over telephone lines. The document is inserted into a fax machine and the number of the person to whom the document is to be sent is dialled. When a connection is successfully made, the machine scans the document and transmits it over the telephone system to another fax machine at the receiving number, which then prints out the document.

Some photocopiers also include facilities for printing or sending faxes. It is also possible to send a fax over the Internet using special faxing software and a scanner.

Figure 2.21 *A fax machine.*

Advantages:

- It is a fast method of sending copies of documents over great distances. If the document was photocopied and sent in the mail, it would take several days to arrive.

Disadvantages:

- The quality of the scanned document may sometimes not be very good especially if pictures are included.
- The document is not received in electronic format so it cannot be edited or immediately saved onto a computer.

2.3.15 Voice mail

A voice mail system allows spoken messages to be sent. It is frequently used as an answering service on phone lines. A caller may receive a recorded message if the line is busy and be given instructions on how to leave a message in the required person's mailbox or access other options available. It is often used in a large organisation to direct a caller to an appropriate extension that can deal with their request.

When it is convenient, the owner of the mailbox can listen to voice mail messages left by callers.

2.3.16 Teletext

Teletext is an information service provided by television broadcasters. Each page of information has its own number and can be viewed by pressing buttons on a remote control handset. All the pages are transmitted in sequence along with the television signal and after a short delay, when the requested page is received it is displayed on the television screen. There is a limit to the number of pages of information that can be stored because of this delay. Too many pages would mean an unacceptable wait for the viewer.

There are pages of information on news stories, weather forecasts, sports, share prices, TV listings and many other topics. A special font is used but graphics are very basic and made up from blocks of colour.

One important use of Teletext is to provide subtitles to TV programmes for deaf viewers.

The service is free but the viewer can only look at the information and cannot respond to it: it is a non-interactive service. The use of Teletext is lessening as there is far more information available on the Internet, which is an interactive system. However, it is conveniently available on TV sets.

Figure 2.22 *A Teletext page.*

2.3.17 Interactive digital television

There is a change happening to our televisions. They are becoming digital. This will mean better picture and sound quality, but another more significant change is that they are becoming interactive. This means that we will have a say in what we watch and be able to participate in quiz shows or questionnaires, surveys or games.

The services offered by the Internet will become available through our televisions and we will be able to send emails or buy items from the TV.

On some televised sports events you can select the camera angle that you want to view, or look at real-time statistics, and some news channels allow you to select which news story to watch.

INTERACTIVE: There is two-way communication between user and machine.

Figure 2.23 *Services available over the Internet are now being offered on interactive television channels.*

2.3.18 Mobile phones

Some mobile phones allow you to browse Internet pages or view small versions of web pages using WAP. The pages need to be small because the screens on mobile phones are small but information on news, weather, sports events, share prices and other areas of interest are readily available. It may also be possible to create your own pages.

Owners of WAP mobile phones are also able to:

WIRELESS APPLICATION PROTOCOL (WAP): A standard used by mobile phones to display web pages.

Figure 2.24 *A mobile phone.*

- send and receive text messages;
- send and receive emails;
- play games;
- listen to music or to the radio;
- take photographs and send the images to another person;
- capture short video clips;
- download different ring tones;
- use an installed memory chip for storing data.

Practice questions 2.3

1 Tom uses a WAP mobile phone to access the Internet.

   a) Give two problems that may arise when using a mobile phone. [2]

   b) Give one advantage of using a mobile phone over a standard landline phone. [1]

   c) Give two other services Tom may be able to use his mobile phone for. [2]

2 Sarah regularly sends emails to her friends.

   a) What is email? [1]

   b) Give two advantages of using emails rather than the normal postal service. [2]

   c) Give two disadvantages of using email. [2]

3 A small company wants to start selling goods using the Internet. One thing they need to do is to subscribe to an ISP.

    a) What is an ISP? [1]

    b) Give one other thing they need to do. [1]

    c) Give one advantage of selling goods over the Internet. [1]

Can you remember…?

1 What does URL stand for?

2 Name three things you can do when telebanking.

3 Give an advantage and a disadvantage of telebanking.

4 What is teleconferencing?

5 What must you never do when using a chat line?

6 When researching on the Internet, what software do you need?

7 Name five services available on the Internet.

8 Name two services available with interactive digital television services.

2.4 The electronic office

Nowhere has the impact of ICT been greater than in the office. The way that office staff perform their tasks and the skills they need to carry out their daily work have changed in recent years as an increasing number of businesses have adopted modern methods of storing and processing information.

One reason that the paperless office is still not a reality is because paper is a very reliable form of storing information.

Word processors have replaced typewriters and computer disks have replaced filing cabinets. Methods of communication have moved from the old mail services and telephones to emails, mobile phones, faxes and the Internet. The changes have happened quickly as the new technology develops and many office workers have had to retrain and upgrade their skills. The amount of paper is getting less as it is being replaced by electronic methods of communication.

The next few sections of this book look at the different ways that ICT can help office workers, and studies the hardware and software available to them.

2.4.1 Networks

It is now commonplace for computers in an office to be connected together to form a network. Each computer must have a network card and communications software installed in order for it to be able to use the network. A network interface card (NIC) looks like a small circuit board and generally slots into the main motherboard inside a computer. The card also has a slot into which a network cable can be attached. Once the computers are linked together they can share resources and communicate between each other.

Computers may be connected to form a **network**, no matter how far apart the computers are.

A computer that is not linked to a network is called a stand-alone computer.

Some networks connect computers in the same room, but some are much larger and may connect computers that are in different buildings or even in different countries. Computers on the same site may be connected by cable but if the computers are distant from each other then the telephone system is used.

Figure 2.25 *A network interface card.*

There are two main types of cable that are used on networks: metal wires made from copper and shielded with a casing, and fibre optic cables which use light and can be used over greater distances than copper cables.

Some offices may use a wireless network. This means that there is no need for cables, and the computers have special wireless network cards installed that can receive the signals transmitted by a wireless hub.

> **3 L**
> Wireless networks do not need expensive and unsightly cabling, but there is a limit to the distance the computers can be from the hub.

Advantages of networks:

- **Hardware can be shared**. For example, a printer on a network can be used by all the computers connected to that network. There is no need to buy a separate printer for each computer. The same applies to any other item of hardware on the network such as a scanner or a high capacity storage device.
- **Software can be shared**. A computer program may be installed on one computer on a network, but can be run on any of the other computers. This is generally not a good idea because the speed of running would be slowed down.
- **Data can be shared**. A database can be stored on one of the networked computers but can be accessed by a user on another computer. The computer where the database is stored is usually referred to as the **file server**. It is possible for several users to access the database at the same time.

  A number of different office workers may wish to work on the same file. If it is saved on the file server's hard disk then each worker can load the file from there, make any changes or additions and then save it back.
- **Networked computers can communicate**. Messages or files can be speedily sent from one networked computer to another.

Disadvantages of networks:

- The **high cost** of cabling and setting up.
- **Viruses**. Computers on a network can be liable to attacks from viruses if files are being sent between the computers. A virus can spread from one computer to another very quickly and precautions need to be taken to prevent this.
- **Hackers**. People may gain unauthorised access to files saved on a network server for malicious purposes.
- Sometimes a network **fails to work** properly and this can cause havoc in the office. Large networks can be very complex and will need to be maintained by skilled IT staff.

2.4.2 ICT in the office

The main uses of ICT in the modern office are for creating documents, storing and organising information, budgeting and decision-making. It is also widely used for communication.

> **3 S**
> Most business offices use computers and office staff need to have ICT skills.

Word-processing and desktop-publishing (DTP) packages are used to create documents that look professional. It is important that customers of a business are impressed with what they see and feel confident that their affairs will be dealt with in a professional manner. Letters and other documents convey an impression about a business which, if they are poorly presented, will not impress people, who may then take their business to rival companies.

Figure 2.26 *An electronic office.*

Information is stored using database software, and this should provide efficient ways of organising all the data so that it can be quickly retrieved when required. Old methods of filing papers were time-consuming and finding important information was often a slow process, requiring looking up card indexes and finding the correct folder in a filing cabinet. Much time and effort was spent in making sure that papers were filed correctly.

Networks and the Internet have had an enormous impact on the way office staff communicate. Documents and letters can be sent and received very quickly using emails and electronic files can be attached to these.

Companies advertise their services on websites and many buying and selling transactions can be carried out over the Internet. This has led to a globalisation of many businesses, expanding from one local office to reach out to potential customers all over the world.

2.4.3 Intranets

> Businesses and offices have intranets so that important and frequently-needed information is easily and quickly available.

An intranet is a private network, set up by a business or an organisation, that behaves like the Internet, but its web pages are only accessible to their own staff. The intranet looks and feels like a website. Pages of information are linked together using hyperlinks, and a browser is used to navigate around the site. The intranet is not directly connected to the Internet although it is possible to do so using special gateway computers, but these will need to run special firewall programs to protect the intranet from unwanted hackers or viruses from outside.

Intranets have become an important means of informing staff about company business. An intranet might have pages of information that staff may need to know and access, or it might have up-to-date company news or figures for monthly targets. Much of the intranet would have information about procedures to follow for office tasks, or Codes of Conduct (instructions to the staff about what they are expected to do and how they are expected to behave while at work).

Many schools have set up their own intranets, which hold useful information for the teachers and pupils about the school and the work they do. There may be pages of useful information for each subject taught in school, or calendars showing the main events in the school year. Pupil work may be displayed on the intranet for other pupils to see.

2.4.4 Software in the office

The software installed on the computers in an office will usually comprise of the items given on the following page.

- **Word-processing** or **desktop-publishing** programs for creating and managing documents.
- **Information handling** programs for storing and organising databases.
- **Spreadsheet** programs for data involving calculations.
- **Communications** software to allow communication between the computers, including email facilities.
- **Graphic design** software for creating and editing images.

2.4.5 Word processing

Many people have predicted a 'paperless office' where all documents are created on computers and sent from one person to another by email or other network methods, without needing anything printed on paper. Well, we are not there yet! The amount of paper in an office seems to have increased because of the ease with which documents can be printed. Fax machines are also users of large amounts of paper, and office staff feel safer if they have a printout of a document in case the computer hardware fails.

A word processor is used to create a document. Text is typed at a keyboard, but there are many advantages over the old method of using a typewriter. It is much easier to make changes and improve a document so it looks good when finished.

Documents can be attached to emails and sent to other people in the office, or anywhere in the world if there is an Internet link. They may be saved on a file server's hard disk if there is an office network, from where other staff can load them at any time.

Word processors also usually provide a spellchecker, which highlights words that it thinks may be spelled incorrectly. A large number of words are stored in the word processor's dictionary, and every time a word is typed, it will check to see if that word is in its list. If it is not, then it will show that word as a possible error and will suggest correct spellings. Words can be added to the dictionary at any time but the spellchecker is not foolproof: a word may be spelled incorrectly in a particular context, but if the incorrect word is a valid word in another context then no error will be picked up. For example there would be no spelling error shown in this sentence:

I here that you have gone two far this thyme.

Some word-processing packages include a grammar checker that will look for simple errors in grammar such as repeated words or missing commas. It is difficult to write a program that checks grammar, as the rules are so complex, so grammar checkers often give misleading advice.

Another facility that is usually available is a thesaurus. A word can be highlighted and the thesaurus will suggest a number of synonyms (alternative words with the same meaning).

Benefits of using a word processor:
- Documents can be created which **look professional** and pleasing to read. This will always impress a customer or another office member.
- A document can be **saved** and used at a later time. Once it has been created, it can be loaded and used as many times as is necessary.

Word processing software may include a spellchecker, grammar checker and thesaurus.

● **Editing** a previously created document is fast. It does not have to be completely retyped, but can be loaded and changed easily.
● **Multiple copies**. Once a document has been created, you can print as many copies of it as are needed.
● **Time saving** devices such as **macros** mean that documents can be created or edited quickly.

Mail merge

When a company wants to send a similar letter to a number of different people, it often uses a technique called mail merge. A large proportion of the junk mail we receive through our letterboxes daily is produced using mail-merge techniques. A database is used to insert data into copies of a specially prepared form letter. The process of mail merge is explained in more detail in Section 4.3.11.

2.4.6 Desktop publishing

Desktop publishing (DTP) is used to create complex documents that a word-processing program may not be able to produce. Publications like newspapers or magazines, brochures and advertisements are created using DTP.

Pages are created using frames, which may be positioned anywhere on the page. These frames contain text or graphics, and can be used to create a number of columns on the page.

The text that is to be used in the publication will usually have been prepared using a word processor and then imported into the appropriate frame on the page. Similarly, any graphics will have been prepared using a graphics package before being imported. The DTP program should only really be used to arrange the items on the page and for special effects.

Benefits of DTP:

● High quality professional-looking publications can be created which have impact.
● It is easy to edit the layout of a publication.
● The display is WYSIWYG.
● Publications can be made with a consistency of style. A company may have its own style for publications.
● It is possible to create more complex layouts than with a word-processing program.

WYSIWYG (WHAT YOU SEE IS WHAT YOU GET): The display on the screen is how it will look when printed out.

2.4.7 Spreadsheet

Spreadsheets are widely used in offices for any application that needs some calculations performed or some graphs drawn. For example, a spreadsheet could be used to plan the annual budget of a department in a business, so that the management know how much money they can spend on items such as advertising or whether they can afford to employ a new secretary.

The spreadsheet can then be used to investigate the best allocation of money by changing the numbers on the spreadsheet. Various spending plans can be looked at to see if the total amount to be spent is less than the full amount allowed.

Text, numbers and calculations are placed in a grid of rectangular cells called a worksheet. A spreadsheet may consist of a number of worksheets that are related to each other and interact.

Benefits of using a spreadsheet:

- **Automatic calculation**. Every time the content of a cell is changed, calculations are performed and other cells are updated if necessary.
- **Easy to edit**. Changes to the contents of the cells are easy to make. If the spreadsheet is done on paper it is much more difficult!
- **Graphs and charts** can be drawn using the data in selected cells. These have greater visual impact and are easier to understand than complex sheets of data. Trends and patterns are easier to see on graphs.

■ Activity 2.8 Spreadsheet (Microsoft Excel)

Download the file **budget.xls**. This is a simple budgeting spreadsheet for a newsagent. There are two worksheets to this spreadsheet:

- Budget: This calculates the overall net profit for the month.
- Wages: This calculates the monthly wages bill.

Use this spreadsheet to answer the following questions:

1 How much could the shop spend on marketing this month and keep its net profit at least £2000?
2 Could the shop hire another shop assistant and still keep the net profit over £2000?
3 If newspaper sales fell to £12 000 and they made one of their three sales assistants redundant, would the shop still show a net profit?

2.4.8 Information-handling software (Database)

All businesses need to store data of some kind. It may be the details of all their customers and the orders that have been placed to buy goods. It may be the details of their staff so that their pay can be calculated at the end of the pay period.

A computer uses a database to store information. Once the data has been entered, it can be edited, searched or sorted easily, or deleted if it is no longer needed.

A database provides facilities for organising the data in different ways such as sorting alphabetically, and there will be ways of finding information quickly. The main benefit of a large database is the fast speed at which information can be found.

The data stored in a database can be used in a number of different ways. It can be used to produce reports or exported to other applications such as spreadsheets or word-processing programs.

In an office environment, the database is usually stored on a network's file server so that every other user on the network can access the information and be able to update it.

> **DATABASE:** A database is an organised collection of related data. It is possible to add, edit, manage and retrieve data from a database. The structure of a database allows data to be found and used quickly.

> 3.8
> A database allows you to find information easily and quickly.

Benefits of using a database:

- **Fast access**. Finding data on the database is much faster than in a paper-based system where the data is stored on paper in filing cabinets.

- **Easy to edit**. Whenever data needs to be updated, a database makes it easy to find that data and to change it.
- **Validation**. There are ways of setting checks on the data as it is being entered to make sure that no inappropriate data gets into the database.
- **Reports**. Results of searches can be used to produce printed reports that may help the management of a business in their decision-making.
- **Sharing**. The database can be shared with any number of users on a network and any user can access and edit the data.
- **Security**. Passwords may be set so that no unauthorised user can access the database, which may contain personal and sensitive data.

2.4.9 Graphic design software

There are many software packages available that allow you to create and edit graphic images but they fall into two main categories:

- **Bitmap graphics**: Pictures are stored as a large number of pixels.
- **Vector graphics**: Pictures are drawn and saved as coordinates and mathematical formulae, making file sizes much smaller than bitmaps.

Graphics can be drawn using tools such as a paintbrush or flood-fill, they can be scanned from photographs, or downloaded from a digital camera.

Clipart images are often provided with a graphics package. These are small ready-made graphics that can be used and edited, or incorporated as part of a larger graphic. Many clipart images are cartoon-like in character but might speed up the development of a DTP publication. The Internet is a good source of a large number of clipart images and many of them are free to download and use.

Graphics can be saved in a variety of formats. Bitmap pictures can be very large when saved because every pixel in the picture is saved. Other formats (for example JPEG) use compression methods to reduce the size of the picture when stored. There will be a loss of detail but this should not be obvious to the human eye.

Some graphic design packages allow you to create animated graphics (graphics that move) for use on a web page. Animations consist of a sequence of still graphics that are displayed very quickly in succession.

Benefits of using a graphics package:
- **Simple editing**: Pictures can be easily edited (e.g. scratches can be removed from old photographs, red-eye can be removed from flash photographs).
- **Size changing**: It is easy to change the size of a picture. A graphic will take up less storage space if it is re-sampled to a smaller size in a graphics package than if it is changed on a DTP page.
- **Special effects**: Many graphics programs provide some special effects such as altering the brightness and contrast of a picture, colour filters, textures and many more.
- **Trial and error**: Pictures can be edited to see what they look like. If the desired effect is not achieved, a different method can be tried.

PIXEL: Short for *picture element*. The smallest amount of information displayed graphically on a screen. A single coloured dot.

Bitmap graphic files are large but can be compressed into other formats such as **JPEG** (.jpg) or **GIF** (.gif), for example for use on web pages, with little loss of quality.

Figure 2.27 *Clown with ripple effect and with bubbles effect.*

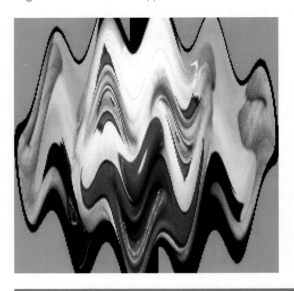
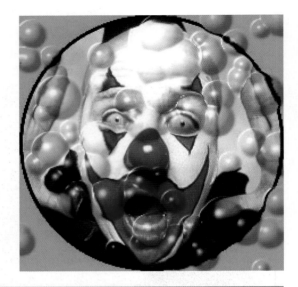

■ Activity 2.9 Graphics

Download the graphic **oldphoto.bmp**.

   This is an old photograph in need of some touching up. See if you can edit it so the scratches are invisible.

2.4.10 Developments in interfaces

Without a user interface we could not use the computer, but some user interfaces are easier to use than others.

There have been changes in the ways that people use computers over the years. An interface is where two things meet. The **Human–Computer Interface** (HCI) is the boundary where the user and the computer meet. It is commonly referred to as the **user interface** and it determines the way that the user interacts with the computer and gives instructions about what is wanted.

The design of the user interface on a piece of software takes into account the expected ICT skills of the users. Software companies design the user interfaces to make their programs as easy to use as possible, and they try to make the different programs they create as similar as possible, so that users are familiar with the way they work. For example, the Microsoft Office programs always have the 'File' menu first, and the 'Print' button always looks the same.

The main types of user interface are:

- **Command line interface**: Users type instructions using a special set of words and symbols. This is the interface used in the early days of computing and is really only suitable for skilled ICT users, as the instructions need to be known.
- **Menu interface**: A menu of options is displayed and the user selects one of them. This is more user-friendly than a command line interface as the options do not have to be remembered.
- **Graphical user interface (GUI)**: Small pictures are used to represent options that the user can select. Microsoft Windows uses a GUI (icons show the applications that can be run, and programs use buttons with pictures on them).

WIMP: Windows, Icons, Menus and Pointers. An example is the Windows operating system.

This is an example of a WIMP environment, where selections can be made by placing the mouse pointer over an icon or screen button and clicking the mouse button.

Figure 2.28 *Windows uses a GUI (Graphical User Interface).*

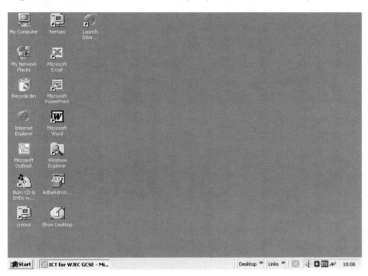

- **Voice interface**: A microphone is used, into which the user speaks a command to the computer. Sophisticated software analyses the voice pattern and executes the instruction given.
- **Special devices**: There are a number of devices for people who have difficulties using a computer or for small children. These include Braille keyboards that have patterns of dots embossed on the keys, and 'concept' keyboards with overlays placed on the keyboards. Touch-sensitive screens offer a non-keyboard method of selection.

2.4.11 Health and safety

There are a number of health and safety issues in the office environment. Many of these are to do with ergonomics (the study of a worker and the environment). Careful consideration must be given to the design of the chair, desk, computer, telephone and other equipment to increase efficiency and avoid discomfort, fatigue or health problems.

Common health problems include:

- **Back or neck strain**: Using a badly positioned desk, chair and computer for long periods can lead to aches in the back or neck.
  - Chairs should be adjustable and set at the correct height (forearms should be horizontal).
  - Take frequent short breaks and walk around.
- **Eye strain**: Poor quality monitors, poor lighting and long hours staring at computer screens may lead to eye problems.
  - Computer screens should be set at the correct distance – an arm's length away.
  - Monitors should not flicker or be turned up too bright. They should be able to swivel and be positioned at a comfortable angle.
- **Repetitive strain injury (RSI)**: Constant use of the joints in fingers, hands or wrists can lead to long-term pain or stiffness in the tendons. This is a common problem for office workers who spend long hours using a keyboard or mouse, and surgery is often undertaken to help alleviate the symptoms.
  - Use rests for wrists or arms.
  - Take frequent short breaks from typing or using a mouse.

Neck strain, eye strain and RSI are all preventable problems. Office managers must make sure that their staff are seated comfortably and properly so that these problems can be avoided.

- Perform hand and wrist exercises regularly.
- Relax. Grip the mouse lightly (tension can cause RSI).
- Position the keyboard and mouse at a proper distance and height, and make sure you are sitting comfortably.
- **Fitness problems**: Sitting for long periods at a computer desk can lead to fitness problems due to lack of exercise. Make sure you take plenty of exercise when not at work.

Practice questions 2.4

1 An office may have its computers on a network.
   a) What is a network?   [1]
   b) Give two advantages of using networks over stand-alone computers.   [2]
   c) Give one disadvantage of using networks.   [1]
   d) When an office worker logs on to the network, what two items of data
      need to be entered?   [2]
   e) Give one advantage of using a wireless network.   [1]

2 Here is a poster to advertise the next School Musical.

> School Musical
> Fame
>
> Wednesday May 12th
> to
> Friday May 14th
>
> Tickets available now.

The director sees the poster and uses a word-processing package to improve it.

> School Musical
> **Fame**
>
> Wednesday May 12th
> to
> Friday May 14th
>
> **Tickets available now.**

Give five facilities of the DTP package that have been used.   [5]

Can you remember…?

1 Name three types of user interface.
2 Name three types of health hazard for office workers using computers.
3 What does WYSIWYG stand for?
4 Name the two main types of graphic.

2.5 ICT in the home

'There is no need for an individual to have a computer in the home' – Ken Olsen, President of the Digital Equipment Corporation, famously said in 1977. Well, things have changed a lot since then, and it is now common for people to have a personal computer in the home, and there are plenty of good reasons for doing so. There are many homes that now have more than one computer and some even have a home network, where the computers are linked together.

There are other uses of ICT in the home than using personal computers and many homes have devices that are controlled by microprocessor control systems such as those used for controlling the heating. Some of the main reasons for having a computer at home, and how we should be using them, are looked at in the next few sections.

> The number of homes that have a computer is increasing every year.

2.5.1 Home learning

With a connection to the Internet, a computer becomes a very useful learning tool for pupils and students, and for almost anybody who has an interest they would like to pursue, or new skills they would like to learn.

Research can be carried out on the World Wide Web using browsers and search engines to find information, and assignments or homework can then be presented using a word processor, DTP program or even as a multimedia presentation.

The best way to learn how to use a computer program is to try it out and experiment with it. Much of your ICT studies will involve learning how to use word-processing programs, spreadsheets, database programs and DTP software. If the same programs are installed on your home computer as the ones in school, then it will be easier to learn the skills at home rather than in the classroom, where there may be more distractions.

COMPUTER-ASSISTED LEARNING (CAL): A way to learn a skill using a computer and interactive software on CD or DVD, or by using the Internet. Using CAL programs can be a more enjoyable way to learn than traditional methods.

Computer-assisted learning (CAL) uses interactive software to help teach a subject. For example, there are programs that help you to learn a foreign language. Words or phrases can be learned and their pronunciation can be listened to using speakers. Short tests are provided to check if the words have been learned, with feedback provided about how well you are doing.

Most CAL software is modular and you progress from one module to the next only if you achieve an acceptable standard in the knowledge tests. CAL software can be bought on CD or DVD but there are many websites that offer free learning.

Figure 2.29 *A website that teaches French.*

Advantages of home learning:

- You can learn from home (no travelling to evening classes).
- Learning can be done in your own time and at your own speed.
- There are often online chat rooms or discussion forums where others who are learning the same subject can exchange ideas or discuss problems.
- There is a wide range of learning courses available.

Disadvantages of home learning:

- Problems may not easily be solved, as there is no tutor to discuss them with. Students may feel somewhat isolated.
- There may be a lack of motivation if the student can select the frequency and times when learning takes place.

2.5.2 Leisure

ICT can be used for fun things as well as for work.

The major use of a computer in the home is for leisure and entertainment. This can take many different forms, and is probably more responsible for the increase in the number of homes having computers than the serious reasons!

2.5.3 Home publishing

DTP programs can be used at home to produce publications related to an interest or a hobby. For example, an archaeology enthusiast could produce a monthly newsletter or magazine about the activities of a local archaeological society to send to all its members, or a war game hobbyist could print a pamphlet giving the scenario and orders for a forthcoming battle.

Web pages can be produced for a website and displayed for other people with the same interests. A history enthusiast could produce a website about a period of history that he is studying, or a sports fan could publish pages concerning their club. There are many examples of this on the Web and the number of special interest websites is growing fast.

People who are interested in photography are using digital cameras to take photographs and publishing their pictures on the Internet. Even family photos can be placed on websites for relatives or friends to be able to see from anywhere in the world. Photographs can be downloaded from digital cameras and stored on a computer's disk, where they can be organised into albums and viewed on the monitor. Since pictures can use up a large amount of storage space, they are often saved onto a CD or DVD. Selected photos can be printed using a colour printer. This is much faster than the conventional way of waiting for a film to be developed, but the quality of printed pictures depends on the quality of the printer.

Some digital cameras allow short movies to be taken and these videos can also be downloaded and stored, or published on a website. Using publishing software, catalogues can be produced of all the photographs that have been stored, or of your music CDs or video DVDs.

LL
Special interest websites can be viewed by enthusiasts all over the world.

L5
Catalogues can make it much faster to locate an item such as a photograph or a track on a music CD.

LB
Interactive games use the Internet to link competing players in a real-time game.

2.5.4 Games

Computer games have become very complex, using realistic videos and sound clips. The main reason for this is the rapid increase in the power of computers. The processors have become faster which means that graphics can be displayed in greater detail, and digitally recorded sound gives a greater sense of realism. High quality graphics cards and sound cards help speed up the processing and increase the performance of the game.

Special dedicated consoles can be bought which, because they only play games and do very little else, produce a better quality of video and sound.

Games are usually bought on CD or on DVD but some websites are dedicated to interactive game-playing.

Many people are concerned about the time that children spend playing computer games and they see it as a form of addiction. The concern is that this solitary activity is preventing proper social interaction with others and limiting development of social skills. Children are becoming unfit as they

Figure 2.30 *A screenshot of a computer game.*

are not getting enough exercise, but then, as Bertrand Russell (a clever British mathematician) said, 'The time you enjoy wasting is not time wasted.'

Advice: Limit the time you spend on any computer activity... especially playing games!

2.5.5 DVD films

Because of the large storage capacity of a DVD it is possible to save the whole of a movie on one of them, and this can then be played on a computer and viewed on an ordinary monitor. The recording is made using digital data, which gives the film better quality than on a video.

DVDs also allow you to skip to a position in the middle of the film: on a video there is a lot of winding of tape!

Many film DVDs also include extra material such as still photos, behind-the-scenes stories or a short documentary on the making of the film and special effects used.

2.5.6 Computer art

You can practise painting with no wastage of material using modern graphics software.

Some graphics packages are very sophisticated these days and provide a large number of special facilities and effects such as the realistic use of paintbrushes or different types of crayon. One way of spending leisure time creatively is to draw or paint a work of art: if you don't like it you can throw it away without any wastage of paper or paint. Who knows? You may be an artist with hidden talent! Pictures that you are proud of can be displayed on a website for all the world to see and admire.

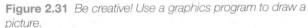

Figure 2.31 *Be creative! Use a graphics program to draw a picture.*

2.5.7 Interactive television services

INTERACTIVE TV: Television that allows the viewer to actively participate in a number of activities.

Some television broadcasters provide services for which the viewer has some input. They may include:

- Interactive games.
- Voting in simple surveys and displaying the current results.
- Interactive shopping.
- Pay-to-view movies. You can watch selected movies at a time of your choice and the cost is added to your monthly bill.

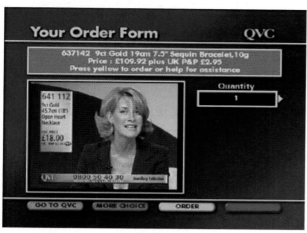

Figure 2.32 *One of the shopping channels available on digital television.*

- Sports channels that allow the viewer to select from a number of different cameras or look at game statistics.
- News channels where the viewer can select a video from a choice of news stories.
- Holidays may be advertised and the viewer has the facility to make a booking.
- Betting services.
- Email.

Caution should be taken as some of the services might have costs that may not always be apparent.

2.5.8 Music and sound

Play music while you use the computer, or watch videos when you finish your work.

If you have speakers attached to your computer you can use programs such as Microsoft Media Player or Real Player to play music.

Music tracks can be obtained from the Internet in a special compressed format called MP3, which makes the files smaller and faster to download even though there is some loss of quality compared with a CD. Music files can also be ripped from CDs and stored in MP3 format.

Music companies allow some free downloading of sample music, but most will charge for each track. The downloaded files can be saved on a computer's hard drive and then copied onto an MP3 player.

Musical instruments need a **MIDI** interface to connect to a computer.

MIDI: Musical Instrument Digital Interface.

For those more serious about music, there are software packages available which allow you to connect musical instruments such as keyboards, drums and guitars to a computer. You can then record the music you play, or even compose pieces of music and play them back through the instruments.

A number of different soundtracks can be recorded and then combined and edited using a program called a sequencer: a recording studio in your own home!

Microphones can be used to 'sample' sounds. This means that a recording of the sound is taken at a number of regular intervals and stored digitally. The greater the sampling rate, the better quality the sound will be but the size of the file will be larger. The sound can be edited, saved and used in multimedia presentations.

■ Activity 2.10 Sound

Download the file **noises.wav**.

Play the file and you will hear sounds made by five different objects. The initial letters of these objects spell a word we use often in ICT.

Can you name the objects and discover the hidden word?

2.5.9 Control systems

Another use for computers in the home is for controlling systems such as heating or alarm systems. These are examples of control systems and use a number of sensors attached to a computer through an interface. The sensors take regular readings of measurements such as temperature or sound and input them to the controlling computer.

The computer analyses the readings and decides whether any action is necessary. If action is needed, the computer sends out a signal to operate a device such as a heater or an alarm.

2.5.10 Environmental control

Figure 2.33 *A simple heating control system.*

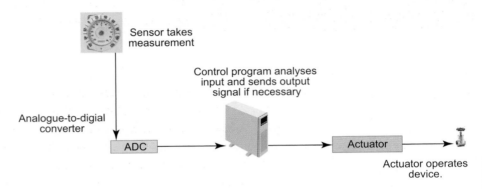

In a heating system, there is a sensor that takes regular readings of the temperature of a house. Temperature is an analogue measurement so it must be converted into a digital measurement to enable the computer to process it. This conversion is done by an analogue-to-digital converter (ADC).

When the computer receives the data, the control program will analyse the reading. If the reading is too low, the computer will send a control signal to an actuator that can turn a heater on. If the reading is too high, the computer sends a signal to switch the heater off.

A similar system could be used to control the temperature and humidity in a greenhouse. Sensors measuring the temperature and humidity are connected to a computer that can turn sprinklers on if the air is too dry, or open and close ventilators if the temperature is not within an acceptable range.

ACTUATOR: A motor that can operate a device when it receives a signal.

2.5.11 Alarm systems

PASSIVE INFRARED (PIR) SENSOR: A device for detecting movement.

A number of different sensors could be used in an alarm system in the home. Passive Infrared (PIR) sensors measure the infrared radiation of a room and can detect any changes caused by movement. Proximity sensors have two parts that activate a signal when they are separated, and can be used on windows or doors to detect when they have been opened. Pressure sensors can be placed under mats to sense when a person stands on them.

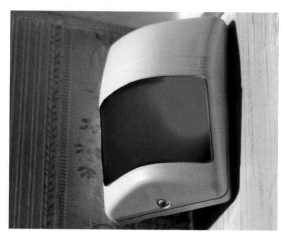

Figure 2.34 *A PIR sensor that is used in a computerised alarm system to detect movement.*

All of these sensors, if activated, send a signal to the controlling computer, which will output a control signal to an alarm device.

There is usually a short delay between receiving a signal and an alarm being activated, which allows the owner of the house time to switch the system off by entering a security code. If the security code is not entered then the alarm will sound.

When an intruder is detected, the system may activate a siren that makes a loud sound, or switch on the lights. Some alarm systems connect to an automatic telephone dialler, which sends a recorded message to the police.

2.5.12 Microprocessor control

50

> **Microprocessors** and microcontrollers are integrated circuits (chips) and they can be found controlling many household appliances.

There are many electrical appliances in the home that have microprocessors/microcontrollers in them and we are sometimes unaware of them, or we take them for granted. A microprocessor is just an integrated circuit (a 'chip') which can perform a lot of processing activities on very small circuitry.

An example of a device that has a microprocessor is a washing machine. There is a control program stored in it, which can run the different wash sequences set by the user. Once started, the washing machine does not need to be supervised because the program is run automatically, and will set the water temperature and go through the appropriate wash, rinse and spin cycles without any need for intervention.

Figure 2.35 *A microprocessor has very complex miniaturised circuitry.*

Devices that are controlled by a microprocessor are often called **embedded systems**. They have become possible because of the small size of the microprocessors, and the fact that programs (sequences of instructions) can be stored in them.

Some devices in the home that are controlled by microprocessors include:

- **Dishwasher**: A selection of different sequences and temperatures can be selected and a delay timer can be set. Some models have sensors that detect the amount of dirt in the water, and adjust the cycle accordingly.
- **Video or DVD recorder/player**: The time at which recording starts and ends can be set and the channels to be recorded are selected.
- **Microwave oven**: Different programs for different foods can be run.
- **Refrigerator**: Microprocessors control the temperature inside.
- **Mobile phones**: Phone numbers can be stored and text-messaging programs run.

- **Games consoles**: These are really small computers dedicated to playing games.
- ...and many more: television, HiFi system, digital camera, remote-control toys, etc.

■ Activity 2.11 Internet investigation

A glimpse of the future?

Find out what a **domotic system** is.

List five tasks that you would be able to use a domotic system for.

Practice questions 2.5

1 Computer use in the home has increased rapidly in recent years. Give an example of how a home computer user might use each of the following:
   a) spreadsheet [1]
   b) control software [1]
   c) desktop publishing [1]
   d) database. [1]
2 Computer games are often played by pupils at home.
   a) Give one reason why playing a computer game may be a good thing. [1]
   b) Give one reason why it might be a bad thing. [1]
3 People often use computers to learn at home.
   a) Give two advantages of home learning. [1]
   b) Give one reason why it might be difficult to learn at home. [1]

Can you remember...?

1 What does CAL stand for?
2 Name two sensors that may be used in a computer-controlled alarm system in a home.
3 What is an embedded system?
4 Give five examples of embedded systems in the home.
5 A control system may include an ADC. What is an ADC?
6 Why might an ADC be needed in a control system?

2.6 ICT in education

ICT in the classroom interests, motivates and helps make learning more enjoyable. It's true!

There are many ways that ICT can be used in the school environment, not only to help with the administration but also to help with learning. ICT helps to make education more interesting, giving pupils better motivation so that the whole learning process is a more enjoyable experience. If a pupil is motivated and wants to learn, then this will improve their attention span and help them concentrate better. You will learn more from an interesting lesson than a boring one!

Figure 2.36 *An Interactive whiteboard.*

Computers help to make the learning process more interactive, which means that pupils actively take part in their education. It is always more interesting to be doing something rather than just listening.

Interactive whiteboards (IWBs) are large white screens that can be seen by the whole class. They are connected to a computer and can be used like a large monitor. During a demonstration, a special pen is used like a mouse pointer to click on the IWB.

Pupils can use interactive software to learn about a particular subject. For example, a computer-aided learning (CAL) program can be used to help you learn a foreign language. A pupil can learn new words, hear them spoken, repeat them and be tested on how much progress has been made.

If a computer is connected to a network, pupils can exchange ideas or discuss and debate online. The Internet is a valuable resource and also provides other facilities like email and discussion groups.

> **COMPUTER-ASSISTED LEARNING (CAL):** A way to learn a skill using a computer and interactive software on CD or DVD, or by using the Internet. Using CAL programs can be a more enjoyable way to learn than traditional methods.

2.6.1 Benefits of ICT in education

Coursework

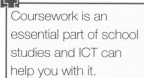

> Coursework is an essential part of school studies and ICT can help you with it.

There are many subjects for which pupils have to present coursework. Teachers provide guidance, but mainly you have to do the work on your own. This is where ICT can be of great help to you.

The **Internet** can help with research, and pages on the World Wide Web can be used to find information. Search engines can find relevant pages for you, but you have to be careful that the page is up-to-date and reliable. It is always better to check your information on several different websites and try to use well-known ones. There are several encyclopedias that have websites, and these often provide sound or video clips to illustrate topics.

A discussion group on the Internet (often called a **bulletin board** or a **forum**) can be helpful in getting ideas. A message can be posted and anyone who sees it can respond with their thoughts and ideas.

Email can provide contact with pupils in other schools in this country and abroad, and allow an exchange of ideas and help you to find out information from a current source. If you are learning a language like French, then corresponding with a pupil in a French school would be of great help in learning the language: and it would also help them improve their English!

DTP programs can help with the presentation of coursework. Publications can easily be produced with professional-looking layouts: an important factor when it comes to impressing the examiner!

Spreadsheets and **charts** can help organise numerical data for mathematical or scientific coursework. Tables of data can be copied and pasted into a document and graphs and charts can help to illustrate points.

Databases can be used to store data, sort it and produce reports by searching through the data in different ways. For example, research into family sizes in different sociological groups can be stored in a database. Reports can then be produced about whether the size of the family is related to the circumstances they live in.

Coursework can be a large piece of work. You need to make a backup of your work at frequent intervals, and preferably in different places in case the file gets lost or damaged in any way. If there is an up-to-date backup of your work, then there will be no crisis if one copy gets corrupted.

> Always keep an up-to-date backup of your coursework in case of computer problems.

2.6.2 Special needs

There are pupils in school that have physical problems or learning difficulties. ICT can help these pupils with their learning. There are specialist input devices such as Braille keyboards or speech recognition systems, and concept keyboards have special overlays that help a handicapped pupil to input data.

Figure 2.37 *A one-handed keyboard.*

For pupils who have difficulty typing there are word banks or prediction software, which offer choices of words or phrases that can be selected to speed up the production of text.

There are many programs to help pupils with learning difficulties improve their reading or writing skills, or help them with their basic mathematics so that they can be better included in classes for other subjects. These programs use colourful, exciting and interactive methods to help motivate the pupil and make learning an interesting experience.

2.6.3 Distance learning

It is possible to carry out studies from home or anywhere in the world using distance learning. This involves signing up for a course on the Internet and learning online, using web pages and other resources, and then taking online examinations, and hopefully gaining a qualification.

> **DISTANCE LEARNING:** A means of studying for a qualification such as a degree course at home, in your own time and at your own speed.

There are many colleges that now offer distance learning degree courses, and you are not limited to colleges in this country if an overseas one is offering the course you want to study.

Care needs to be taken to select a course from a reputable college, but there are great benefits in learning this way as you can select the time and place for learning and proceed at your own speed. There are many courses offered online and it may be easier to find one that suits your needs, rather than try to find a college that offers that course.

2.6.4 School events

ICT can help in the organising of school events. For example, your school may be performing a musical show at the end of the term, involving the school orchestra and pupils who are actors or dancers. Here is a list of some of the different ways that ICT can help:

- A **database** can be used to store details of all the pupils taking part, including the forms they are in and whether they are actors, dancers or musicians. This will make it easier to contact pupils.
- A **spreadsheet** can be created and used to help in the financial planning. The expected costs of the show can be entered and this can then be used to set the prices of the tickets and the programmes to make sure that the show makes an overall profit.
- **DTP** software can be used to design posters to advertise the show, the tickets and the programmes.
- **Word-processing** programs can be used to produce weekly rehearsal sheets showing the times of the rehearsals and which pupils are involved.
- After the show has taken place, a **website** can be created including pictures from the performance and a description of the development of the show, cast lists and any notable events that happened. This can be placed on the school intranet for all pupils to see.
- **MIDI** can be used with musical instruments.
- **Computer-controlled** lighting boards and sound systems can be used to run pre-programmed sequences of lighting effects or pre-recorded sounds.

2.6.5 Datalogging

DATALOGGING: A term used to describe the automatic collection of data from a number of sensors.

Computers can be used to collect data automatically from a number of sensors using datalogging. The frequency of the readings and the total length of time that readings are to be taken for can be set, and once started, the system does not need to be attended to.

An example of datalogging may occur in a science lesson, when readings from an experiment might need to be taken every 10 seconds over a total time of 20 minutes. These readings can then be processed to produce a graph to illustrate the experiment.

Another example may be the automatic collection of weather data from a school weather station. Readings may be taken at hourly intervals of the temperature, air pressure and wind speed and collected by a computer, stored and processed to produce statistics and graphs of the local weather patterns.

The benefits of using a datalogging system:

● Data collection is automatic. No intervention is necessary.
● Readings can be continuously taken over long periods and through the night if necessary.
● There is no chance of somebody forgetting to take a reading. Scientific experiments may be useless if a reading is missed out.
● The readings will be more accurate if a computer takes them, as there is no chance of human error.
● Sensors can be placed in situations where it is dangerous for humans to go. For example, wind speed sensors (anemometers) may be placed on the roof of the school.
● If needed, the readings can be taken very quickly. It may be necessary to do several readings every second from a number of different sensors for some scientific experiments and humans could not achieve this.

Disadvantage of using a datalogging system:

● If there is a fault it may go unnoticed for a long time.

Practice questions 2.6

1 Some pupils in a school may have handicaps or learning difficulties.
   a) Name two hardware devices that may help pupils with special needs.   [2]
   b) Give two ways in which a writer of educational software might try to motivate pupils with learning difficulties.   [2]
2 A pupil is preparing some coursework and needs to find out information about the topic she is studying. Give three different ways in which the pupil can use a computer to research the topic.   [3]

Can you remember...?
1 What is datalogging?
2 When datalogging is used in a science experiment, what two items of data need to be input to the program?
3 Give three benefits of using a datalogging system.
4 What is a bulletin board (sometimes called a forum)?

3 The impact of ICT

3.1 ICT in the workplace

No place has seen a greater impact from the use of ICT than the workplace. Offices and factories, shops and warehouses have all been affected by the development of ICT and the ways that people carry out their work have had to change. Most businesses have benefited from the change, but there are some people who have struggled to adapt to new practices.

The next few sections look at how the advancement of ICT has affected people at the workplace, what the benefits have been and what problems have arisen.

3.1.1 Employment

There have been some types of job that have disappeared, as they have become either unnecessary or have been replaced by computers and automated machinery. Some of the main types of job that have been lost are:

> **5 L**
>
> ICT has created many new jobs, but it has caused some unemployment as old-style, boring and repetitive or dangerous jobs have been lost.

- **Boring, repetitive jobs** in factories have been lost because the people who used to do them have been replaced by robotic machines. For example, people used to be employed in factories to hand screw tops into bottles of drinks as they passed slowly by on a conveyor belt, but now a robotic machine does this repetitive task.

- **Jobs in a hostile environment** have been replaced by robots. There are some places that are unhealthy or uncomfortable for humans to work in such as a factory where paint spraying takes place. The fumes from the paint are dangerous, so robots now spray paint onto the bodywork of cars in a car assembly plant, for example.

- **Old-style office jobs** such as typists and filing clerks are being replaced by computer systems that perform the same tasks more efficiently. For example, when a number of copies of the same document were needed, a team of typists would need to type them individually. Nowadays, a single worker can use a word processor to produce the copies in a fraction of the time.

- **Fewer people work in shops**. Supermarkets do not need to employ people to count the number of each item remaining on the shelf, as this is done nowadays using automatic stock control. People will need fewer shops as online shopping becomes more widespread.

- **Fewer people work in banks** because of automated systems like ATMs that perform many of the tasks of traditional bank staff.

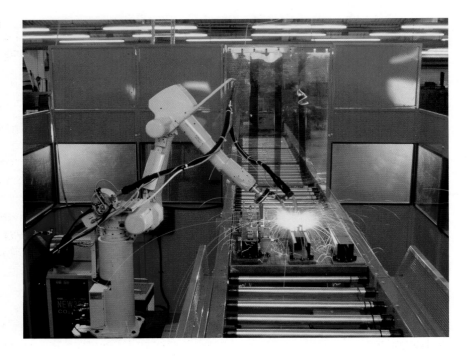

Figure 3.1 *Welding robots have replaced humans in some factories.*

Businesses generally have cut the number of staff working for them, mainly for economic reasons. By using ICT methods to carry out their business, they can do more work, increasing productivity and therefore the inflow of money, while being able to manage with fewer staff and cutting the outflow of money being paid as wages.

The good news is that there are a large number of new jobs that have been created because of ICT. Here is a list of some jobs that did not exist before the introduction of computers:

- **Computer programmer**: The software that is used by computers or robots needs to be written by programmers (sometimes called software engineers).
- **Systems analyst**: When a company wants to computerise its business or upgrade its existing system, then a systems analyst is called in to design the new system and start it working.
- **ICT technician or network technician**: Any school or organisation that has a large number of computers or a network needs a technician to manage the system and troubleshoot any problems.
- **Hardware designer**: All new hardware must be designed, prototyped and tested.
- **Website designer**: Every web page displayed on the World Wide Web needs to be designed and created, but also many need to be kept constantly up-to-date. For example, a web page that displays news stories needs to be updated every few minutes.
- **Database manager**: If an organisation keeps a database of information, then it will need to be designed, created and kept up-to-date.

In fact, there are now large manufacturing companies that produce computer hardware, and these will employ workers who carry out a wide range of jobs from production of the hardware to maintenance of the machinery used.

3.1.2 Retraining

We have seen that the introduction of ICT has caused some job losses but those jobs were the more undesirable jobs: the repetitive, boring or dangerous jobs. There are many new jobs that have been created, but these need different types of skills and therefore people have to be retrained so they can carry out these new jobs effectively.

ICT is constantly changing, so staff must be trained to use new equipment or new software, and they will need to make sure that their ICT skills are up-to-date. This is not easy and companies must offer training to meet the needs of the staff, so their businesses can be more productive.

Training can be done using the Internet or interactive CDs. Staff can learn at their own pace and do not have to travel to a college. Some companies produce their own CAL software, which makes sure the staff learn exactly the right skills to be able to carry out their work.

3.1.3 Changes in working practices

ICT has caused many changes in the way that work is carried out, particularly in the way that people communicate with each other. Here is a list of some of the changes that have taken place:

> ICT has changed the way in which we work, making life at work easier and ensuring maximum productivity.

- **Mobile phones** are being used more often because they can be carried around and used anywhere. People can be contacted on the mobile phone at any time, they do not have to be in the office.
- **Email** is used to send messages. There is less need to write a letter and post it in a letter box. If copies of a document need to be sent to another office, then they can be sent using a **fax** machine.
- The hours that people can work are extending because, for example, a **laptop** can be taken home or used on the train commuting to work, to catch up on unfinished tasks.
- Buying or ordering goods and materials can be done online over the **Internet** instead of sending an order through the post or having to visit a shop or warehouse.

3.2 Teleworking

TELEWORKING: Working from home (literally 'working at a distance'), using email and the Internet for communication. A teleworker can choose when to work and for how long.

An increasing number of people are working from home and using ICT methods to communicate with their place of business. This is called **teleworking**, and involves the use of email, the Internet, and fax machines.

Advantages of teleworking:
- No travel expenses.
- No time wasted in travelling to work.
- Flexible hours. The teleworker has greater choice of when and how long to work.
- Employers do not have to provide office space or facilities such as a canteen.

Disadvantages of teleworking:

● There is less social interaction and teleworkers may feel isolated.
● There may be more distractions in the home environment (e.g. infants, domestic jobs, callers, etc.)
● It may be more difficult for the management to check on whether work is being properly carried out.

Figure 3.2 *It may be difficult to motivate yourself working at home!*

3.3 Economic impact of ICT

> Companies that sell goods or services have increased their profitability by using **e-commerce** (i.e. buying and selling over the Internet).

Another effect that ICT has had on many businesses is that they have been able to offer their goods and services to people overseas. ICT has enabled them to advertise on websites, which can be viewed by anybody in any country in the world, provided they have a computer with Internet access. It has also allowed people to buy goods from companies overseas by ordering them through a website.

This globalisation of business has expanded markets, and allowed companies to streamline their operations so they can employ fewer people, decrease their expenses and therefore maximise their profits.

If people buy goods through a website, there is no need for the company to buy and equip as many shops, or employ managers and shop assistants to run them. Money will also be saved on heating and lighting bills and property taxes. Goods can be shipped directly from a warehouse to the customer's doorstep.

Globalisation is not without its critics and some say that rich countries are gaining at the expense of poorer countries whose shares of the global market are extremely small.

3.4 Codes of practice

> A **code of practice** makes sure that all customers get treated fairly and consistently.

A **code of practice** is a set of standards that a business would expect its employees to conform to.

It is not legally binding but the business may ask an employee to agree to it before starting their job, and so it could be grounds for dismissal if they were not obeyed.

It is always in the best interest of a business to treat its customers fairly and with due consideration or they will take their business elsewhere.

It ensures consistency of practice. All employees will conduct their business in a similar way.

3.5 Legal issues

The development of ICT has also created new types of crime.

The problem of hackers gaining unauthorised access to sensitive or important data has been tackled by the Government when they introduced the **Computer Misuse Act** in 1990. This defined hacking as a crime, and anybody caught accessing files that they are not entitled to on a network can expect to receive a fine or even a prison sentence.

This Act also makes the creation and spreading of viruses a criminal offence.

The increasing use of credit cards has led to an increase in computer fraud, where a criminal steals information about a person's card details and uses it to buy goods or withdraw cash from the owner's bank.

Identity theft is becoming a problem. Many people do not realise how easy it is for criminals to obtain personal data about us. They may watch us when we type a PIN at an ATM, or listen in to a conversation when we give our credit card number to a business. Receipts or statements that have our names, addresses or bank details can be retrieved from bins.

The Internet has become a favourite place for trying to get our personal details from us, and fraudulent emails may be sent asking for bank details. These criminals then pretend to be us, and can withdraw money from our bank accounts, apply for credit cards and create enormous bills, or purchase goods online without us even knowing about it.

To prevent identity theft:

- Never give out bank details or passwords on emails.
- Do not throw away receipts, bills or statements without tearing them up first.
- Check your bank and credit card statements regularly to make sure that there are no unexplainable transactions.
- Make sure nobody watches you when you enter a PIN at an ATM or other card authorisation device.
- Do not write down passwords.
- Change passwords regularly.

There is also a law that makes it illegal to copy software without the permission of the holder of the copyright. Software companies usually issue a licence when you buy a piece of their software, and include a special code number that has to be entered when the program is installed on your computer, to prove that it is a legal copy.

58
It is a criminal offence to hack into a computer, create a virus, or copy software which has a copyright.

IDENTITY THEFT:
Pretending to be someone else by using their stolen personal details.

59
It is illegal to run a copy of software that you have not paid for. You are breaching the Copyright, Designs and Patents Act. It is also illegal to download copies of music files that are not offered by the music companies.

Businesses or schools may wish to run a software package on a number of their computers. They need to buy a 'site licence', which allows them to install the program on a given number of computers on their premises.

Making illegal copies of software is called 'software piracy' and is difficult to prevent. It is a common practice because it is easy to do and because of the high cost of software.

It is also an offence to download copies of music files from the Internet, unless they have been offered by the music company that owns the copyright. This practice, however, is widespread and difficult for music companies to trace.

■ Activity 3.1   Internet investigation

Many of the crimes mentioned in this section carry heavy penalties for people who are found guilty. These may include large fines or even prison sentences.

Use the Internet to investigate the sentences that have been passed on people convicted of software piracy or copyright infringement in this country. What is the largest fine you can find for an individual? For a company?

Summary

- ICT has caused some jobs to be lost, but generally these are the boring, repetitive or dangerous jobs.
- Fewer people work in factories, offices, shops and banks.
- Many new ICT-related jobs have been created.
- The new jobs require new skills so people have had to be retrained.
- ICT changes very fast so people need to constantly be trained in new skills.
- The way people work has changed.
- Email and faxes have replaced letters in the post.
- Mobile phones are being used more for communication.
- Buying and selling is done over the Internet instead of in shops.
- Teleworking means people can work from home using the Internet and other ICT.
- Businesses can become global. They can expand their market to anywhere in the world by using e-commerce.
- Employees often are required to sign a Code of Practice: a set of rules stating how they are expected to work.
- Codes of Practice ensure consistency of practice: everybody gets treated the same.
- The growth of ICT has created new crimes.
- It is illegal to hack or create viruses.
- It is illegal to steal software (i.e. use it without buying it or paying for a licence).
- It is illegal to make copies of music or software. This is software piracy.
- Identity theft is a growing method of computer fraud. Guard against it!

Practice questions 3

1 Teleworking enables people to work at home by using the Internet and other ICT.
   a) Describe two advantages of teleworking to the employer. [2]
   b) Describe two advantages of teleworking to the employee. [2]
   c) Give one disadvantage of teleworking to the employee. [1]

2 Describe three ways in which the way people work in an office has changed with the introduction of computers and networks. [3]

3 The developments in ICT have caused some jobs to be lost but has also created new ones.
   a) State three jobs that have been lost. [3]
   b) State three new jobs that have been created. [3]
   c) The developments in ICT have also created new types of crime. State three new crimes that have been caused by ICT. [3]

Problem solving

4.1 Introduction

Pupils taking the GCSE course in ICT (Short or Full Course) will need to make sure their skills on the computer are good enough to be able to use a variety of different software packages. The next few sections are a guide only to the skills you need to achieve, but there is nothing like practice to master them properly.

Many of the practical exercises involve downloading files from the website mentioned at the beginning of this book, and using them to practise a variety of skills.

Remember: **Practice makes perfect**.

4.2 Graphics

Bitmap graphic files are large but can be compressed into other formats such as **JPEG** (.jpg) or **GIF** (.gif), for example for use on web pages, with little loss of quality.

COMPUTER-AIDED DESIGN (CAD): A software drawing tool utilising computers to assist designers create graphic designs of objects. CAD can be used to design cars, houses, kitchen layouts, aircraft, bridges, electronic circuit boards, etc.

A **graphic** is a **picture** (sometimes called an **image**).

Graphics software is used to create or edit an image, whether it is a picture for a school newsletter, a company logo to be placed on a letterhead, or even a family photo you are sending by email.

There are two main types of graphic:

- A **bitmap** graphic: A picture made up from thousands of pixels, which are individual coloured dots.
- A **vector** graphic: Made up from a number of objects such as circles or lines whose details are stored. These details may be their coordinates, colour, size, type of fill, etc.

A bitmap graphic tends to be much larger than a vector graphic when it is saved as a file, but is more appropriate to use for photographs. There are special formats that can be used when saving bitmap images that compress the picture into a smaller size with little loss of quality.

Vector graphics are used for images such as company logos or designs created with a computer-aided design (CAD) program.

Bitmap graphics usually lose quality when they are increased in size and they may become blurred. This does not happen to vector graphics whose size can be changed without any problems.

Figure 4.1 *A bitmap graphic would be used for a photo whereas a vector graphic would be used for a company logo.*

4.2.1 Creating a graphic

Graphics can be drawn freehand from scratch, but this is tricky using a mouse and can result in disappointing pictures. There are specialist hardware devices such as graphics pads that make freehand drawing and painting much easier.

Bitmap graphics may be input from a scanner or downloaded from a digital camera. You can use Microsoft Paint to create simple bitmap graphics. There are more complex graphics programs that provide better facilities, but we can do the basics with Paint.

Some graphics packages allow you to set the size of the graphic you want to draw and the colour of the paper (the background colour).

Drawing

There are three main tools for freehand drawing: pencil, paintbrush and airbrush. Each of these gives a different texture when used, and in most graphics packages there will be a large number of different textures and thicknesses of brush to choose from. Figure 4.2 shows the three different freehand drawing methods used in Paint.

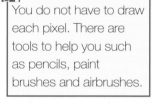

You do not have to draw each pixel. There are tools to help you such as pencils, paint brushes and airbrushes.

Figure 4.2 *The three freehand drawing tools of Microsoft Paint.*

Figure 4.3 *The design of a bedroom using some of the shape tools.*

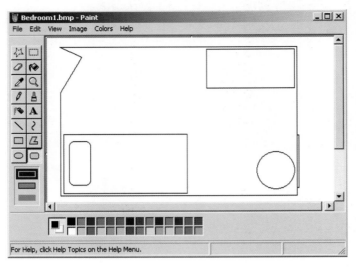

Figure 4.4 *Shapes and text have been added to the plan.*

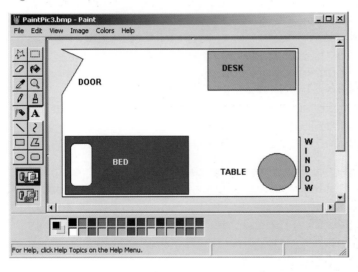

Figure 4.5 *A variety of textures have been used as fills for the shapes.*

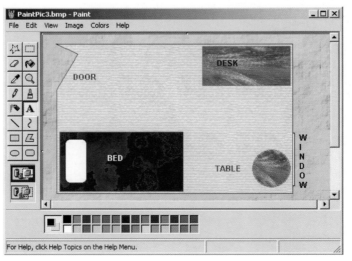

All three of these tools use the foreground colour to draw, unless the right mouse button is held down, when they use the background colour.

Lines and shapes

A number of tools for drawing shapes such as squares, rectangles, circles and ellipses are provided. The design of a bedroom shown in Figure 4.3 uses some of these shapes.

Text

Text can be placed anywhere on the graphic. The font style and size can be selected.

Fill

Fill tools use the colour selected to fill an enclosed area on the graphic.

Advanced graphics programs will offer a variety of different textures as fills. A texture has the look of a fabric or solid material, or it may be a coloured pattern. Figure 4.5 uses several different textures as fills for the shapes.

Clipart

Clipart saves a lot of time. There are many websites offering free clipart, which are small graphics that have already been drawn for you. You can include them in a graphic by copying them (right-click the mouse on the clipart image and copy), and then pasting them into your graphic (right-click and paste).

Figure 4.6 *Two clipart images that have been copied and pasted from an Internet website.*

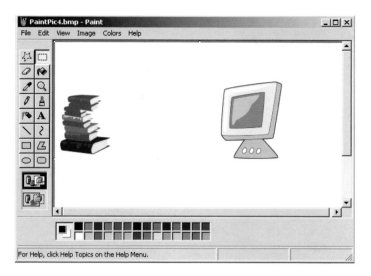

4.2.2 Editing a graphic

A bitmap graphic can be edited pixel by pixel. This can be a time-consuming and unrewarding process but is sometimes necessary. The program will allow you to zoom in and magnify a small area of the graphic until each pixel is visible. The colour of each pixel can then be individually changed.

Figure 4.7 *Zoom in to edit pixels.*

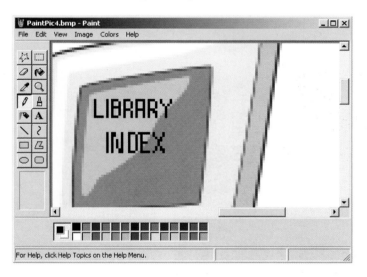

If you use clipart from the Internet, make sure that it is free and not protected by copyright.

Text and shapes can be added to complete the graphic. The finished graphic can be printed or saved before being imported into a DTP program as part of a larger publication.

Figure 4.8 *The completed graphic, ready for inclusion in a school newsletter, created using Microsoft Paint.*

4.2.3 Advanced techniques for bitmap graphics

If you have a favourite photo but the quality is not very good, it may be possible to improve it using a graphics package. If it is a printed photo, you will need to use a scanner to digitise it, so it can be loaded into your graphics program. Here are some examples:

The graphics software may have tools to allow adjustment of the brightness and contrast of the picture.

● The original photograph is too dark and needs to be brighter (Figure 4.9).

Figure 4.9 *Adjusting the brightness of a photograph.*

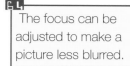

The focus can be adjusted to make a picture less blurred.

● The original photograph is out of focus and needs to be sharper (Figure 4.10).

Figure 4.10 *Sharpening the focus of a photograph.*

Adjusting **hue** values changes the amount of each primary colour that is shown in the picture.

● The colours of an original photograph may need adjusting (Figure 4.11).

Figure 4.11 *Changing the colour hues of the photograph.*

In advanced graphics software there will be many other special effects available. Figure 4.12 shows one where the corner of a picture is curled.

Figure 4.12 *An example of an advanced graphic effect.*

4.2.4 Advanced techniques for vector graphics

A vector graphic may be resized (made larger or smaller) without any significant loss of detail because it is stored as a set of mathematical descriptions. This is why fonts are usually stored as vector graphics.

A graphic can be resized by dragging one of its **handles** (the small squares at the corners and the middle of each side). It is important to drag one of the corner handles if you want to keep the correct proportions of the graphic, otherwise the picture will be distorted.

A vector graphic can be **rotated**. The angle, centre of rotation, and the direction of the rotation can be selected. It may also be reflected in a horizontal or vertical axis. Layering can be used to place one image on top of another. Many different images can be combined into a single graphic by layering them.

Figure 4.13 *A vector graphic can be resized by dragging one of the corner handles. It will be distorted if one of the other handles is used.*

Figure 4.14 *Three separate graphics have been combined into one.*

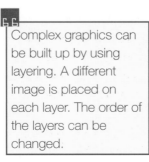

Complex graphics can be built up by using layering. A different image is placed on each layer. The order of the layers can be changed.

The separate parts of a vector graphic can be individually edited. Each graphic consists of objects such as lines, curves and filled areas, each of which can be changed without affecting the others. The objects can be grouped together or split apart when necessary.

Figure 4.15 *The colours of the roses have been changed without affecting the leaves or stems.*

■ Activity 4.1   Graphics

1   Draw and label a plan of part of your school. Include doors and stairs and colour the external areas appropriately (green for grass, grey for tarmac, etc.).

2   Download the file **sporty.bmp**. This is an outline of a person.

   ● Using a graphics program, draw a set of sports clothes on the outline (this could be football, netball or hockey kit, etc.).
   ● Add some accessories (e.g. ball, hockey stick, or other relevant equipment), and draw in a background.
   Try and get as much detail as possible into your image.

3   Design a new badge for your school.
   Search the Internet for a piece of clipart to start you off with the shape of the badge and use the painting tools to edit it.

4   Download the file **working.bmp**. Use bitmap graphic tools to paint in the colours. Let your artistic instincts flow!

4.3 Word processing

WYSIWYG (WHAT YOU SEE IS WHAT YOU GET): The display on the screen is how it will look when printed out.

A word-processing program is used to create a document that can either be printed or emailed as an attachment to another computer user. Many word-processing programs use a WYSIWIG approach to creating documents. There are many different programs available but one of the most widely used is Microsoft Word.

As software has developed, word-processing programs have adopted many of the functions previously only available in DTP programs.

4.3.1 Page layout

It is most important that care is paid to the layout of the page before even a word of text has been typed. When you create a new document, you will need to set up the following:

This is portrait:

And this is landscape:

Figure 4.16 *The page setup dialog box in Microsoft Word where you can set the page size and orientation.*

- The **size** of the page. This is the paper size you want the finished document to be printed on. Most printers use A4 paper and so pages should be set to A4 size (29.7 cm by 21.0 cm).
- The **orientation** of the page. There are two to choose from: portrait and landscape.
- The size of the **margins**: top, bottom, left and right margins may be set.

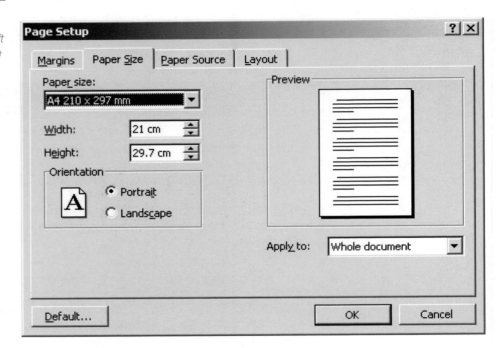

Once the page size and margins have been set, you are ready to start typing in the text, but before you do, select the font that you are going to use and the size of the text. There are many different fonts, each of which displays the text in a different style, and the choice of font will often depend on the document you are typing: Is it a serious piece of coursework or is it a fun message for your friends?

Word Processing   *Word Processing*   **Word Processing**

Word Processing   *Word Processing*   **Word Processing**

A good tip for making documents look good: **Do not use too many different fonts on the same document**. A document that has a lot of different fonts looks untidy and is difficult to read.

4.3.2 Entering and editing text

68

Text will always be entered at the position of the **cursor**. When a letter is typed, the cursor moves on.

69

There are two keys used for deleting text.
Backspace: Deletes the character to the left of the cursor or any highlighted text.
Delete: Deletes the character to the right of the cursor or any highlighted text.

Once all the layout settings have been made, you are ready to type in the text. Typing is not difficult but it needs to be constantly practised if you are to do it with speed. If you try to type too fast you will end up making a lot of mistakes and correcting them will slow you down!

The **cursor** is a flashing vertical line that indicates the place where the next piece of text that is typed will appear. You can move the cursor to a new position by clicking the mouse pointer or by using the cursor control keys (arrow keys).

If you type an incorrect character, pressing the **backspace** key will delete it, and the cursor will move back one space as well, so the correct character can be entered. There is also a **delete** key that removes the character to the right of the cursor.

To delete a word, double-click on the word to select it, and then press the backspace or delete key.

If you want to delete a whole block of text, you must **highlight** it first before pressing the backspace or delete key. Dragging the text cursor from the beginning of the block to its end does this, and the highlighted text will appear in reverse colour.

Figure 4.17 *Highlighted text will appear in reverse.*

The problem with Tom was that he never knew which way to turn once he had walked into the maze of tunnels. He could see the turnings but had absolutely no idea which one led to the exit, and there were no footprints showing on the dirt floor to indicate the passages down which he had already walked. Tom knew that this time he was really lost.

When you are typing, you do not have to worry about when you get to the end of a line, as word-wrapping will make sure that a new line is automatically taken at the right place, and that no word gets split between two lines.

Moving text

A block of text can be moved from one position in a document to another using '**cut and paste**'. This involves highlighting the text to be moved, cutting it, moving the cursor to the new position and pasting.

To repeat a section of text in another position of the document, use '**copy and paste**'. Highlight the text, copy it, move the cursor to the position of the new text, and paste.

70

You will find **cut**, **copy** and **paste** in the Edit menu in Word, but the shortcut keys are:
CUT – Ctrl X
COPY – Ctrl C
PASTE – Ctrl V

Cut, copy and paste can be done in nearly all programs and are some of the most useful tools for moving data around, not only text on a document but data such as graphics or tables of numbers can be moved or copied from one program to another. For example, you can copy a part of a spreadsheet and paste it into a document, or copy a graphic and paste it into a spreadsheet.

On some word-processing programs, such as Microsoft Word, you can highlight a piece of text and move it by dragging it with the mouse from one position in the document to another.

4.3.3 Formatting text

The format of text is the way that the text appears on the document. A section of text can be highlighted and the font or size can be changed, but there are several other ways of changing how the text is displayed:

> **?1** **Formatting** text makes a document easier and more pleasurable to read.

● **Text alignment**: Text can be aligned to the left, to the right or centred.

This block of text has been aligned to the left, which is the default alignment used by most word processors.	This block of text has been aligned to the right. This is needed for things like addresses at the tops of letters.	This block of text has been aligned to the centre. This is useful for such things as headings.

● **Justification**: If text is fully justified, it is spaced out so that each line of text is exactly the same length.

> This block of text has been fully justified. Each line is exactly the same length, and this gives a very neat appearance to text when it is printed in books.

● **Colour**: Text can be highlighted and the colour of the text, or the colour of the background, can be changed. For example, headings in a document can be displayed in a colour that stands out.

> **?2** **Borders** can be different patterns of lines, dots or dashes, or various thicknesses, or even can be made from small pictures.

● **Borders**: Blocks of text, or whole pages, can have borders around them. Here is a single **WORD** with a border.
● **Bold, italic and underline**: Sections of text can be emphasised by specially formatting them:

This is bold text.
This is italic text.
This is underlined text.

> **?3** The **numbers** can be displayed as Roman numerals (I, II, III, IV, …) or as letters (a, b, c, d, …).

● **Bullets and numbering**: Lists of text items can have bullets or numbers placed at the beginning of each item to make them easier to read. The shape of the bullets can be changed, or the style of the numbers.

❖ Bulleted item 1	1) Numbered item 1
❖ Bulleted item 2	2) Numbered item 2
❖ Bulleted Item 3	3) Numbered item 3
❖ Bulleted Item 4	4) Numbered item 4

- **Indent**: The first word of a paragraph is often indented (i.e. moved to the right). This can be done by using the **tab** key before typing the word.
- **Line spacing**: The distance between lines of text can be changed.

> This paragraph of text has the first word indented and is displayed using single line spacing.

> This paragraph of text has the first word indented and is displayed using double line spacing.

Figure 4.18 shows Microsoft Word's formatting toolbar where you can select the formatting options listed above.

Figure 4.18 *Formatting text can be done using the buttons on Microsoft Word's formatting toolbar. Make sure you highlight the text you want to format before clicking on the button.*

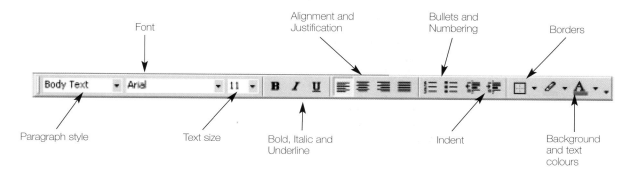

4.3.4 Tabulation

The **tab** key looks like:

To make lists of data items more readable, they are often placed in columns. A tab is the jump made by the text cursor when the **tab** key is pressed on the keyboard, and the lengths of these jumps can be set by dragging the tab stops along the ruler bar at the top of the page to the positions you want the columns to be.

Figure 4.19 *The tab stops can be dragged along the ruler to set the tab positions.*

Tab positions

If you need more precision, the distances of the tabs can be entered using the Tabs dialog box.

Once the tab stop positions have been set, it is easy to line up columns of data on the page, by using the tab key.

Mark	Thompson	10C
Thomas	Smith	10Y
Jane	Jones	10Y
Alice	Jenkins	10B

4.3.5 Tables

If the lists of data are to be displayed in a grid, then a table should be used. The number of rows and columns can be set, and dragging the vertical lines on the table can change the widths of the columns.

First name	Surname	Form
Mark	Thompson	10C
Thomas	Smith	10Y
Jane	Jones	10Y
Alice	Jenkins	10B

4.3.6 Styles

When creating large documents, such as your coursework documentation, it is a good idea to define some text styles. These make sure there is consistency in the way the document looks and makes it appear more professional. When setting a style (e.g. Headline), you can specify the font, size and colour to be used and any formatting of the text, including line spacing.

4.3.7 Headers and footers

A **header** is a section of a page that appears at the top of every page of a document when it is printed, and a **footer** appears at the bottom. They are useful for displaying information about the document.

Information appearing in headers and footers may include:

- The title of the document.
- The name and author of the document.
- Page numbers.
- The date and time of printing.
- The name and path of the file when it is stored on a disk drive. This makes it easier to find again on the computer!

Headers or footers can be used for automatic page numbering.

4.3.8 Templates

Setting up a **template** for a frequently used type of document can save a lot of time. Styles and layouts can be pre-set on the template and used every time a new document is first created.

Businesses use **letterheads** printed on the top of all their stationery, showing details about the business such as the name, address, email, telephone numbers and possibly a small logo. These can all be placed in position on a template, and this will mean that they do not have to be typed every time a letter is written. In order to give a more professional feel to letters, the same font and text size will be used for every letter that is written, and these can be defined in the template.

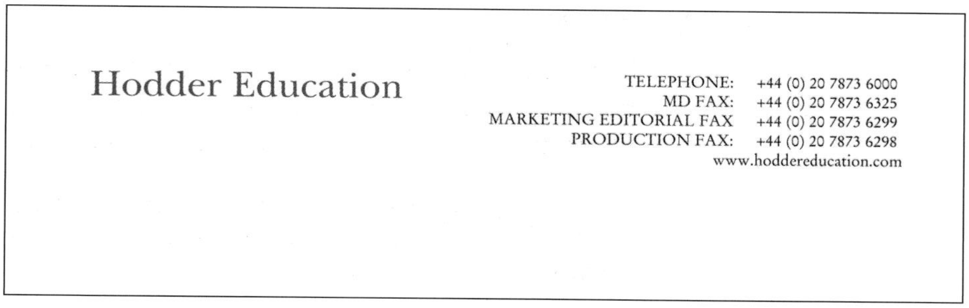

Figure 4.20 *A business letterhead.*

Hodder Education

TELEPHONE: +44 (0) 20 7873 6000
MD FAX: +44 (0) 20 7873 6325
MARKETING EDITORIAL FAX +44 (0) 20 7873 6299
PRODUCTION FAX: +44 (0) 20 7873 6298
www.hoddereducation.com

4.3.9 Macros

MACRO: A stored sequence of instructions that can be performed at any time.

A **macro** is a sequence of instructions that can be recorded, stored and labelled with a name. The macro can be run at any time, and the instructions will be executed in the given order. This can save a lot of time, and macros are usually recorded for sequences of tasks that are frequently repeated.

A **macro** can save a lot of time by recording instructions that are frequently used.

4.3.10 Spellchecker and thesaurus

A **spellchecker** checks spelling: but it does more than that! Every word that is typed is checked to see if it exists in a dictionary, and if it does not, then that word is highlighted as a possible spelling mistake. Alternative spellings are suggested, and the correct one can be selected. If the word is not in the dictionary (it may be a person or place name), then it is possible to add it so that it is not shown as a spelling error next time it is typed.

There are be some problems with spellcheckers:

Careful! Spellcheckers do not always get it right!

- A word spelled incorrectly in one meaning may be another perfectly valid in another. For example, if you type the word WHICH but spell it wrongly as WITCH, there will be no error detected.
- Words can be spelled differently in American English than in UK English. For example COLOUR in the UK is spelled COLOR in the USA.

A **grammar-checker** suggests problems with the way sentences are structured, or they can find repeated words or incorrect punctuation.

A **thesaurus** can give alternatives for words. For example, the word NICE: a thesaurus may suggest PLEASANT, KIND, LOVELY and other words with a similar meaning.

A **thesaurus** can help find words with a similar meaning.

Figure 4.21 *A thesaurus can give alternative words with a similar meaning.*

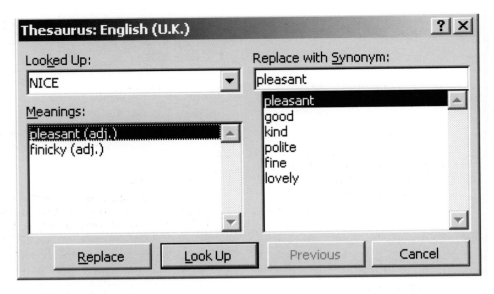

4.3.11 Mail merge

Much of the junk mail received has our personalised information on it, such as our name, address or town that we live in. Many other people have received the same letter, but with different details.

The way this is done is by using mail merge. There are three main stages to this process:

1 A form letter is created which has the main text of the letter as well as place markers to show where the data fields such as name and address are to be inserted.

Dashett Athletics Club

Dear **\<Title\>** **\<Surname\>**

This letter is to confirm that your membership of this club has been accepted and that your Membership Number is **\<MemberNum\>**. The membership starts from **\<StartDate\>**, and we hope you enjoy the facilities offered by the club.

Yours sincerely,

S.O.Swift (Club secretary)

---

2 A database of the data that is to be used in the letters is created.

Title	Surname	MemberNum	StartDate
Mr	Jones	325	12/06/05
Mrs	Hunter	326	23/06/05
Ms	Flash	327	25/06/05

3 The mail merge takes place which places the data from the database into each individual letter and prints them one for each record in the database.

Dashett Athletics Club

Dear **Mr Jones**

This letter is to confirm that your mem[...]
club has been accepted and that your Members[...]
325. The membership starts from **12/06/05**, and[...]
enjoy the facilities offered by the club.

Yours sincerely,

S.O.Swift (Club secretary)

Dashett Athletics Club

Dear **Mrs Hunter**

This letter is to confirm that your membership of this club has been accepted and that your Membership Number is **326**. The membership starts from **23/06/05**, and we hope you enjoy the facilities offered by the club.

[...]urs sincerely,

[...]ft (Club secretary)

Dashett Athletics Club

Dear **Ms Flash**

This letter is to confirm that your membership of this club has been accepted and that your Membership Number is **327**. The membership starts from **25/06/05**, and we hope you enjoy the facilities offered by the club.

Yours sincerely,

S.O.Swift (Club secretary)

A large proportion of junk mail uses mail merge.

There are many different types of document that use mail merge. Businesses send circulars to their clients, companies send bills or payment reminders to their customers, and even school pupils receive their exam results on mail-merged letters.

4.4 Desktop publishing

Desktop publishing (DTP) programs are used for designing and producing publications such as magazines, newsletters, brochures, catalogues and even books like this one. All of the facilities of a word-processing program will be included but there will be some more specialist features that we shall look at in this section.

It is common practice to prepare graphics and text documents before importing them into a publication.

Microsoft Publisher is an example of a simple DTP program.

Figure 4.22 *Microsoft Publisher is an example of a DTP program which can be used to create newsletters.*

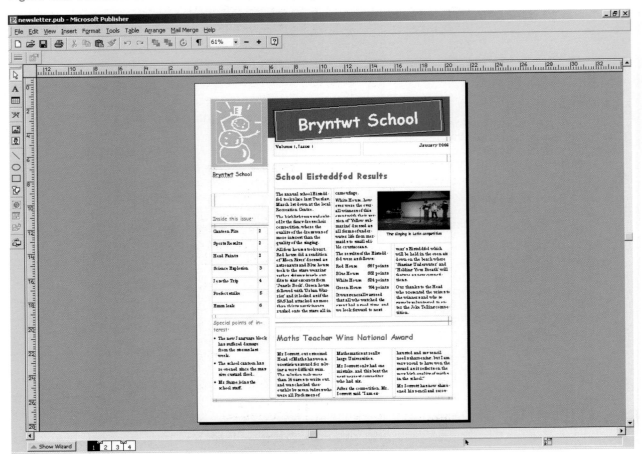

4.4.1 Templates

Figure 4.22 shows a publication based on one of a large number of **templates** which have already been designed and saved, and can be used to create a new publication.

A company will create its own templates to ensure consistency in the publications it produces, and this will give a more professional feel and look to its customers. The layout of the page is set, including the positioning of titles, columns and the company logo. Once a template is created, and it only has to be done once, then it can save a lot of time when used for publications because much of the work is already done.

Wizards make the job of creating publications much easier. Answering simple questions allows the wizard to create the publication for you.

> **Templates** and **wizards** make the creation of DTP publications much easier and therefore much faster. The template defines the layout of the page. A wizard helps you perform a task by giving you staged instructions.

4.4.2 Frames

The difference between using a DTP and a word-processing program is that text or graphics are placed in frames. Normally, the text will have been typed in and edited using a word-processing program and only after it has been finalised is it placed in a frame on the DTP page.

Frames may be linked together in an ordered sequence, so that text can flow from one frame to another. The importance of this is apparent when text is edited on the DTP page. If text needs editing and extra text is inserted, then the text at the bottom of the frame will be pushed into the top of the next frame.

Graphics that have been prepared using a graphics program are similarly placed in frames. All the frames on a page can be dragged around to reposition them if necessary, or they can be stretched to change their size.

Mr Loggett, our esteemed Head of Maths has won a prestigious award for solving a very difficult sum. The solution was checked thoroughly by seven judges who were all Professors of Mathematics at

really large Universities.

Mr Loggett only had one mistake, and this beat the next nearest competitor who had six.

Two frames that are linked on a DTP page, with text imported into them....

Mr Loggett, our esteemed Head of Maths has won a prestigious award for solving a very difficult sum. The solution took more than 14 pages to write out, and was checked thoroughly by seven judges who were all Professors

of Mathematics at really large Universities.

Mr Loggett only had one mistake, and this beat the next nearest competitor who had six.

...but more text needs to be inserted....

...the text flows out of the first frame and into the second.

Figure 4.23 *Text wrap is set to make sure the text is wrapped around the picture.*

Frames can also be **layered** so that they overlap each other. If a picture frame overlaps a text frame, the text wrap can be set so that the text does not run over the picture, as in Figure 4.23.

Mr Loggett, our esteemed Head of Maths has won a prestigious award for solving a very difficult sum. The solution was checked thoroughly by seven judges who were all Professors of Mathematics at really large Universities.

AAAClipArt.com

4.4.3 Widows and orphans

Sometimes a paragraph starts at the bottom of one frame and ends at the top of another. This makes the document less readable and should be avoided in some publications.

> Text in frames on a DTP publication can be made more readable if widows and orphans can be avoided.
>
> An orphan is a small

Orphan

> part of a paragraph left at the bottom of a frame and a widow is a paragraph ending which just overflows by one or two words onto the next

> text frame.
> DTP programs allow control over widows and orphans.

Widow

4.4.4 Transformations

The objects on a page can be rotated through any angle, clockwise or anticlockwise. This allows headlines to be placed diagonally across a page, or text to run vertically up the side.

Objects such as graphics can also be resized by stretching, or they can be cropped (i.e. have their edges trimmed).

■ Activity 4.2   Desktop publishing

The village of Bottomley are holding their annual fête. You have been asked to produce a newsletter to inform the villagers about the dates and the arrangements.

Download the text file **bottomley.txt**, and use it to produce the newsletter. There are some spelling mistakes in the text, which will need to be corrected.

Use two columns of text and incorporate a picture of the village green and its new fountain (you may need to combine and edit some pictures copied from the Internet).

4.5 Multimedia presentations

Multimedia presentations are an effective way of communicating information. They are more interesting than just listening to somebody talking.

A multimedia presentation usually involves a sequence of slides projected onto a screen or interactive whiteboard and is used to communicate information in a way that is interesting for the listeners so they can more easily understand the topic being presented. Animations, video clips or sound may further illustrate the topic.

Usually, the person who is explaining the topic also controls the slide show and the slide only moves on when the speaker is ready, however, sometimes the slides are set to move on after a given time interval.

Examples may include a teacher explaining a topic to a class in a lesson, or a salesman explaining to a panel of businessmen about their latest products.

Microsoft PowerPoint is an example of presentation software.

Figure 4.24 *Microsoft PowerPoint is an example of multimedia presentation software. Each slide of the presentation is individually designed.*

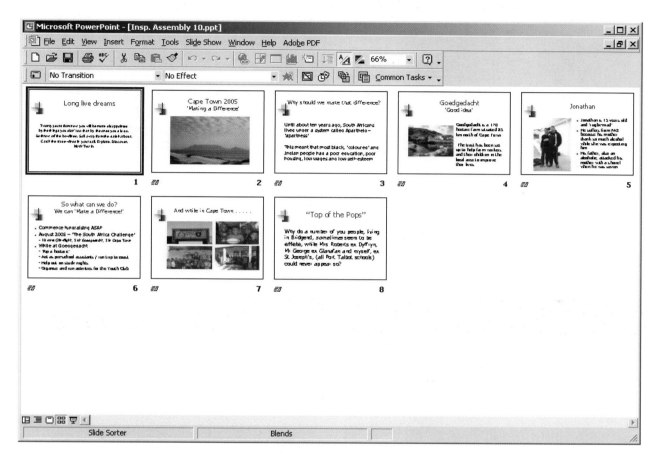

A single slide consists of a number of frames, and each frame may have some text or a graphic in it. Sound or video clips may also be placed on a slide.

4.5.1 Animation

The objects on a single slide need not all be displayed at once. Each object can be programmed to appear after a set time or at the click of a mouse or the press of a button on a remote control. The way each object appears can be selected from a number of animation effects.

Figure 4.25 *Each word in a piece of text can be made to fly in from the top, accompanied by the sound of breaking glass.*

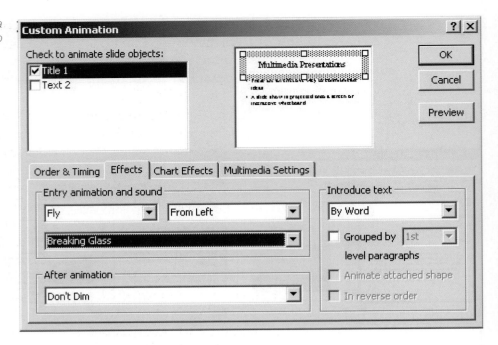

4.5.2 Slide transition

The way one slide changes into another is called the slide transition. This can be programmed as well and there are many different options to choose from.

Slide transitions and **animations** can be really irritating to viewers so do not use too many different types in the same presentation.

Figure 4.26 *Each slide can be set to 'fade through black' on the click of a mouse, accompanied by the sound of a gunshot.*

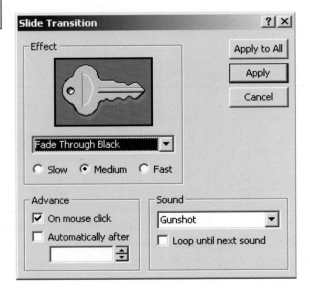

4.5.3 Action buttons and hyperlinks

The action buttons supplied within Microsoft PowerPoint can be placed on a slide to perform such tasks as moving on to the next slide, moving to the home slide, opening a document or running a movie clip.

A section of text or a graphic may be set up as a hyperlink to another slide. When the mouse button is clicked with the pointer on the hyperlink, the next slide is displayed.

4.5.4 Creation of a slide show

8.4
Careful **design** saves time. The design of a presentation must take into account the purpose and the needs of the audience.

It is most important to design carefully the content of each slide, the order in which the slides are displayed, what animation and effects are to be included and the methods of slide transition. This design is often called a **storyboard**.

The next step is to prepare the different elements that are going to be contained on the slides. Graphics need to be drawn, text prepared and sounds and video clips recorded. Then all these elements can be assembled on the slides. It is also possible to record a spoken narration for the slide show to allow people to watch it and understand it on their own.

Templates for the slides can be used to create consistency of formatting and layout.

8.5
Always **test** your slide show. It can be embarrassing in front of an audience if it does not work!

When the data has been placed on the slides it is possible to further edit it. Many of the features of a word processor are available such as text formatting and a spellchecker.

Test the slide show for timing and make sure the transitions work. Then you are ready to present your slide show.

■ Activity 4.3 Multimedia presentation

Download and run the presentation **animate.ppt** which illustrates animation effects available in Microsoft PowerPoint.

4.6 Web pages

8.6
The **design** of web pages is important. There must not be too much information on any one page, and colours need to be used carefully.

Many millions of websites now exist on the World Wide Web, and creating your own is not difficult. There are two ways of creating web pages:

● Use a special language called **Hypertext Mark-up Language** (HTML) to write a program to inform an Internet browser (such as Microsoft Internet Explorer or Netscape Navigator) how to display the page. Open any page on the Internet and view the source. You will see HTML text but you may not understand it!

● Use a special web page program (such as Microsoft FrontPage). This is much easier and you do not need to know so much about HTML.

Figure 4.27 *Programs such as Microsoft FrontPage are used to create web pages.*

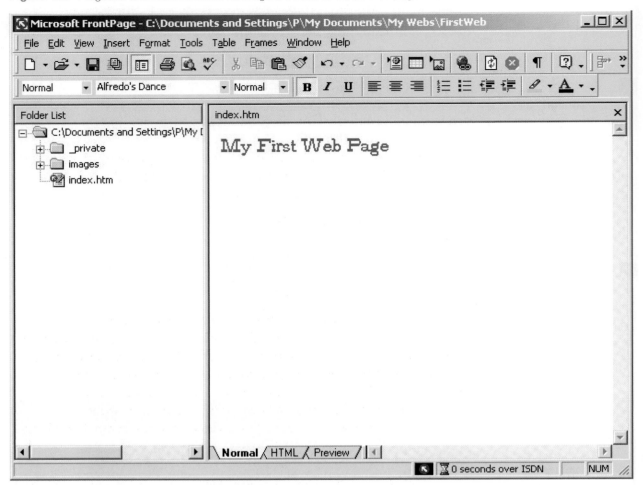

Web creation programs are very similar to word-processing programs. Text can be added to the page and formatted. Bullets, colours and text alignment can all be used and graphics included.

The layout of a page is usually managed by putting text and graphics into the cells of a table. These cells can be resized or merged together to give different spacing.

4.6.1 Webs

A web is a folder on your computer that contains all your web pages. When it is completed a web can be uploaded to an intranet or to a website on the World Wide Web.

Some web pages have counters on them that monitor how many people have visited the web page.

Web page **'hit' counters** show how popular a website is.

4.6.2 Hyperlinks

Any section of text or even a graphic can be set up as a **hyperlink** to another page. Hyperlinks are particularly useful on web pages and when a hyperlink is clicked, the new page will then be displayed in the browser. This is how you **navigate** between pages within a website or even to other websites.

A **navigation bar** should be placed on every page of a website so that you can quickly return to the home page or move quickly between different sections.

4.7 Databases

DATABASE: A database is an organised collection of related data. It is possible to add, edit, manage and retrieve data from a database. The structure of a database allows data to be found and used quickly.

A database is a collection of data that is organised to allow it to be useful.

There are many different programs that help you create and manage a database, and Microsoft Access is one of them.

What you can do with a database:

- **Add** new data, **change** or **delete** data.
- **Search** the data.
- **Sort** the data into a given order.
- Print **reports** about some aspect of the data.
- Use the data in other applications.

A database may have a number of different files (these are called **tables** in Microsoft Access) and they will all be related in some way. A database for your school may have a table with pupils' details, and another table containing data about their classes, and yet another table about the examinations they are taking. The relationship is that they all contain data about your school.

A table will have a number of **records** in it. Each record will have a number of **fields**.

Figure 4.28 *Part of a table showing four records. Each record has five fields.*

PupilID	Surname	Firstname	Form	Date of Birth
2000	Johnson	Samuel	10Y	19/04/1996
2001	Smith	Alison	10G	02/01/1996
2002	Bland	Lois	10Y	10/11/1995
2003	Thomas	Glyn	10S	29/07/1996

Each row displays the data of one record: the data about one pupil. Each column displays a different field.

4.7.1 Creating a database

As with most things in ICT, it is really important to design the database properly, as this will save time and create fewer problems later on. You will need to decide what information is stored in the database, and for each table, what fields of data are going to be stored.

The type of each field needs to be defined, for example whether it is a text field, a number, a date or currency, etc.

One of the fields of each table must be designated as a **key field**. This is the item of data that uniquely identifies each record.

A key field uniquely identifies each record. No two records will have the same data in their **key field**.

An important part of creating a database table is to set **validation rules** for some of the fields. As the data is entered it is checked to see that it obeys the rules, and any data that does not, will not be accepted. In Microsoft Access you can also set the validation text (the message that is displayed if the data is not acceptable).

Figure 4.29 *A range check is set as a validation rule for a field in a table, and the validation text is the message to be displayed when invalid data is entered.*

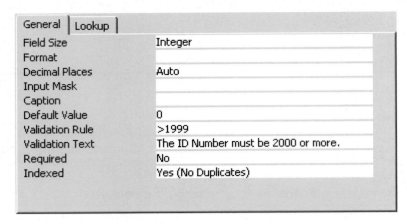

Figure 4.30 shows the error message being displayed for the validation rule shown in Figure 4.29 when invalid data is entered.

Figure 4.30 *The error message that is displayed when invalid data is entered and the validation rule shown in Figure 4.29 is set.*

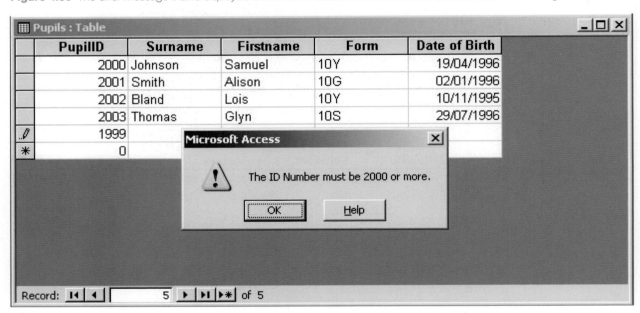

4.7.2 Searching for data

One of the main uses of a database is to allow you to find information quickly. To search for data you need to use a **query**.

A query specifies what records you are looking for and what fields out of the records you would like to display.

A **simple search** looks for data in one field only. The example shown here is a query used to find the names of all pupils who are in the form 10Y. The Pupils table must be added to the query, the fields to be displayed are selected, and the search criteria defined. The query may be written as:

(Form = "10Y").

Searching a database is often referred to as 'querying a database'.

Field names must always be given in a query's search criteria, as well as the value being searched for.

Figure 4.31 *A query for a simple search to display the names and forms of all pupils in 10Y.*

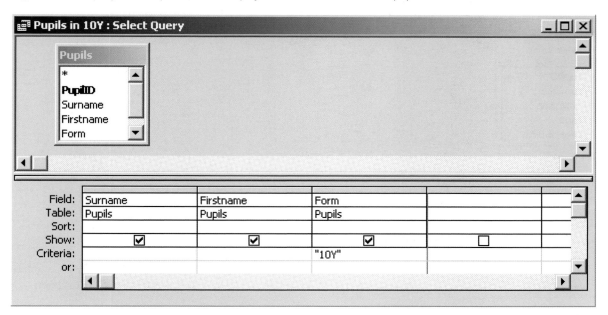

The results of this query are shown in Figure 4.32.

Figure 4.32 *The results of the query defined in Figure 4.31.*

	Surname	Firstname	Form
	Johnson	Samuel	10Y
	Bland	Lois	10Y
	Taylor	Tarnia	10Y
	Smith	Jennifer	10Y
	Tomkins	June	10Y
▶	Baker	Kevin	10Y
*			

Record: 14 ◀ 6 ▶ ▶I ▶* of 6

SIMPLE SEARCH: A search with only one search criterion.

COMPLEX SEARCH: A search that uses multiple criteria and operators such as OR and AND.

A **complex search** looks for data in two or more fields, and uses the logical operators **OR**, **AND** or **NOT**.

The next example uses a complex search to find all the pupils in form 10Y who were born before 1996. This query may be written as:

(Form = "10Y") AND (Date of Birth < 01/01/1996)

A new query is created (Figure 4.33) but this time there will be **two** entries in the search criteria row.

Figure 4.33 *A complex search for all pupils in 10Y born before 1996.*

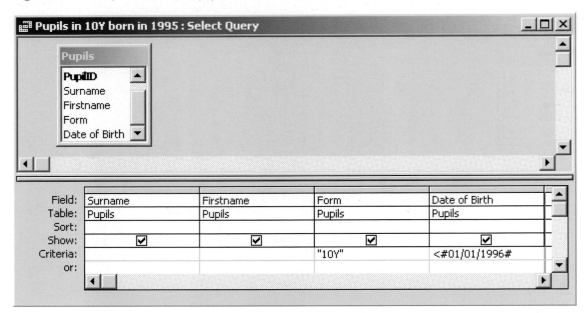

The results of this query are shown in Figure 4.34.

Figure 4.34 *The results of the query defined in Figure 4.33.*

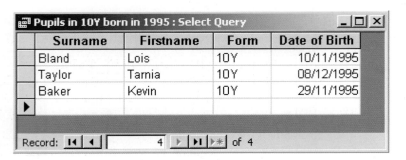

Next is another complex search which uses the logical operator **OR**.

If you want to find all the pupils who are either in form 10Y or in form 10G, the query could be written as:

(Form = "10Y") OR (Form = "10G")

In the query definition there will be two criteria lines (Figure 4.35):
The results of this query are shown in Figure 4.36.

Figure 4.35 *A complex search for pupils who are in 10Y or in 10G.*

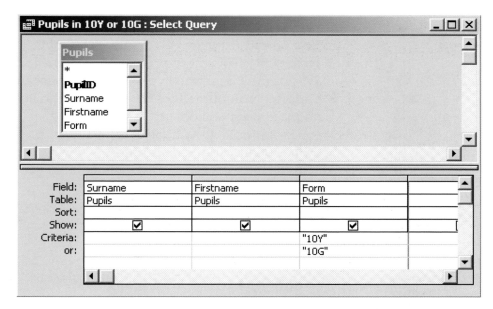

Figure 4.36 *The results of the query defined in Figure 4.35.*

Surname	Firstname	Form
Johnson	Samuel	10Y
Smith	Alison	10G
Bland	Lois	10Y
Taylor	Tarnia	10Y
Smith	Jennifer	10Y
Smithers	Mark	10G
Tomkins	June	10Y
Baker	Kevin	10Y
Layton	Linda	10G
Harris	Tom	10G

Record: 11 of 11

Wildcard characters

It is possible to use wildcard characters in searches for data that you only know part of. For example you might want a list of all the pupils born in March, or all the pupils whose surname starts with the letter 'S', or within a given range of letters.

This following table shows the wildcards that you can use in query selection criteria, and their meaning.

Wildcard	Meaning	Example	
*	Any number of characters	Like "S*"	Finds 'Smith' and 'Smithers' and 'Scott'
?	Any character	Like "Ca?"	Finds 'Cat' and 'Cab'
[]	Any character in the brackets	Like "10[YG]"	Finds '10Y' or '10G'
[-]	Any character within a range of characters	Like "10[A-M]"	Finds '10B' and '10G' but not '10T'
!	Any character not in the brackets	Like "10[!YG]"	Finds '10B' and '10T' but not '10Y' and '10G'

4.7.3 Sorting data

One powerful feature of a database is that the results of queries can be presented in sorted order, either in alphabetical or in numeric order.

Sorts may be made in ascending or descending order and can be performed on numerical or text fields. The field that is being sorted needs to be specified.

For example, the pupils in form 10Y could be listed in ascending alphabetical order of surname:

Figure 4.37 *A query to list all the pupils in form '10Y' in alphabetical order of surname.*

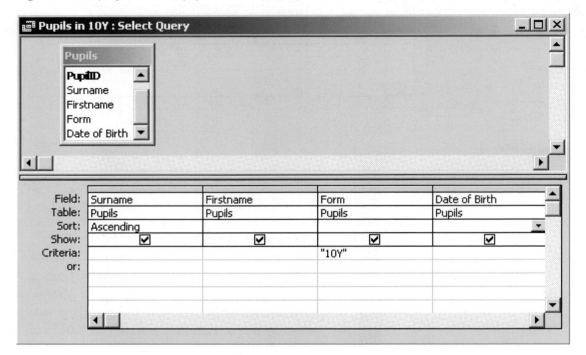

The results of this query are shown in Figure 4.38.

Figure 4.38 *The results of the query defined in Figure 4.37.*

Surname	Firstname	Form	Date of Birth
Baker	Kevin	10Y	29/11/1995
Bland	Lois	10Y	10/11/1995
Johnson	Samuel	10Y	19/04/1996
Smith	Jennifer	10Y	23/01/1996
Taylor	Tarnia	10Y	08/12/1995
Tomkins	June	10Y	15/02/1996

Record: 6 of 6

4.7.4 Forms

Forms are often used for inputting data. They can be made to look more attractive than typing into tables.

A form is a just a better way of displaying a single record. For our example, we could design a form using the form wizard so that each pupil record is displayed in a way that is more pleasing to look at.

The data in the records can be edited from this form. It is a good idea to think of the tables as the raw data, and the forms as a neat way of displaying them.

Figure 4.39 *A form displaying a pupil's record. The navigation buttons at the bottom allow movement to other records.*

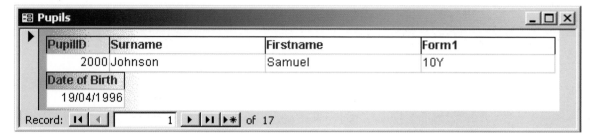

4.7.5 Reports

A **report** is a printed document that contains data from the database organised and analysed in a specific way. An example of a report that lists the pupils in each class in alphabetical order may look like that in Figure 4.40.

Figure 4.40 *A printed report of pupils organised in their forms and shown in alphabetical order of surname.*

Pupils

Form	Surname	Firstname	PupilID
10G			
	Harris	Tom	2015
	Layton	Linda	2012
	Smith	Alison	2001
	Smithers	Mark	2009
10S			
	Jones	Jonathan	2005
	King	Carla	2014
	Thomas	Glyn	2003
10T			
	Jenkins	Luke	2016

■ Activity 4.4 Database

Download the Microsoft Access database **trip.mdb** and use it for the following exercises. The database has data about pupils and teachers travelling by bus on a school trip. There are two buses.

1 How many tables are there in the database and what are they called?
2 What is the key field of the Pupils table?
3 How many records are there in the Pupils table?
4 How many fields are there in each record?
5 One pupil has been left out. Sarah Smith of 7B has been assigned to Bus 2 for the trip. Add her to the database.
6 Search and print out all the pupils in 7N.
7 Search and print out all the pupils in 7N that are assigned to travel on Bus 1.
8 When the buses returned to school, one of the teachers found a coat left on Bus 2. There was a name label in the coat but it was very faded and all that could be seen was that the surname started with the letters 'Je'. Use a query with a wildcard search to find the telephone number to ring to let the owner of the coat know.

4.8 Spreadsheets

SPREADSHEET: A means of performing calculations or of modelling real-life situations.

If there are calculations involved in your data, then a spreadsheet is needed. Spreadsheets organise data and perform calculations. Microsoft Excel is an example of a program that is used to create spreadsheets.

4.8.1 Cells

A **cell reference** always starts with a letter and ends with a number (e.g. C5). Large spreadsheets may extend to cells with double letter column references (e.g. BD23).

A spreadsheet consists of rows and columns of boxes called **cells**. The rows are labelled with numbers, and the columns with letters. Each cell is referenced by a combination of a column letter and a row number. For example, the cell B5 is highlighted in Figure 4.41.

A **range** of cells may be designated. For example (B5:B9) means all the cells in the column from B5 down to B9. A **block** of cells can be referenced in a similar way, for example (B5:D9).

The width of the columns may be changed by dragging the line of the column boundary on the column heading to the size required. Row height may be changed in a similar way.

Figure 4.41 *The width of a column can be changed.*

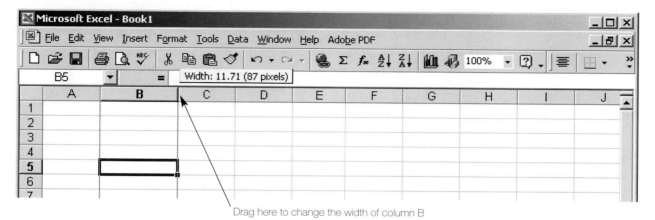

Drag here to change the width of column B

Data can be entered into any cell. This data can be of different types (text, number, currency, date, etc.) and can be formatted in the usual ways (font, size, colour, alignment). There are also ways of formatting the cells with background colours, single or double grid lines and borders.

A **macro** can be recorded that sets the font size and colour, the cell background colour and grid. This will speed up the creation and formatting of a spreadsheet.

4.8.2 Formulae

A **formula** is a mathematical calculation.

Spreadsheets do more than just display data in a neat way, and some of the cells will contain a mathematical formula. The calculation will be performed every time any of the data on the spreadsheet is edited. It is these formulae that make a spreadsheet useful.

Formulae are automatically recalculated every time the data on the spreadsheet is changed.

Cell references are used in the formulae and the symbols for the four main mathematical operations are:

+ Add
– Subtract
* Multiply
/ Divide

In Excel, a formula is differentiated from other data by placing an '=' sign at the beginning.

For example:

The data in cell D4 is to be multiplied by the data in cell D5 and entered in cell D6.

The formula entered in cell D6 is:

=D4*D5

There are some abbreviations to make a formula simpler to enter:
Instead of entering the formula:

=D5+D6+D7+D8+D9+D10

you can enter the abbreviated formula:

=SUM(D5:D10)

SUM is an example of a function. There are many functions that can be used in a spreadsheet program (including some rather baffling statistical and actuarial ones!) but there are a few that may be useful to you such as AVERAGE, COUNT or MAX.

The current time and date can be entered into a cell with the formula:

=NOW()

A spreadsheet normally displays the result of a calculation rather than the formula itself, but you can set it to display the formula in Excel by clicking Tools on the menu bar and selecting Options… . This displays the Options dialog box. Click the View tab and tick the Formulas check box.

Check this box to display the formulae.

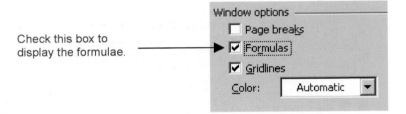

> In UK English, **formulae** is the proper plural of formula in mathematical and scientific usage. (**Formulas** is used in US English.)

4.8.3 Workbooks

In Excel a **workbook** can consist of a number of related spreadsheets. For example, one sheet might contain lists of products and their prices while another sheet works out the value of a customer's bill.

4.8.4 Filling

To speed up creation of a spreadsheet you may want to use the **Fill** options. For example, if the same data is to be entered in a range of cells in a column, it is faster to enter the data in the top cell only, and then fill down through the cells where the data is to be copied.

You can also Fill Up, Left or Right.

One useful Fill option is **Fill Series**. This can be used to enter consecutive numbers or dates into a range of cells. The first data item is entered, the cells are highlighted and Fill Series does the rest.

A similar process can be used for copying formulae into a range of cells.

If cells are not positioned next to each other, data or formulae can be copied and pasted from one cell to another.

> Using **Fill** saves time when creating spreadsheets. It copies data into a range of consecutive cells.

> If you enter the first few numbers or dates in a consecutive series in adjacent cells, you can use the fill handle to extend the series.

Figure 4.42 *A workbook consisting of two sheets. This top sheet calculates the value of an invoice by looking up the prices listed on the sheet below.*

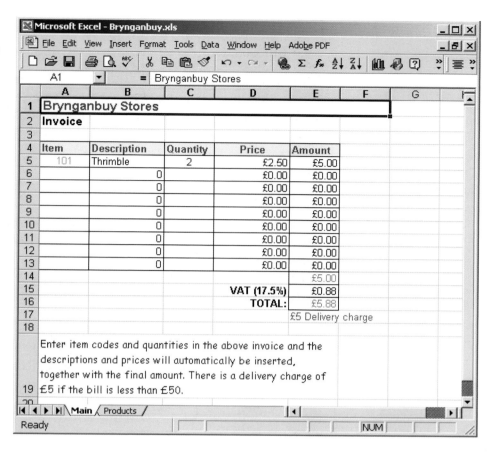

4.8.5 Relative and absolute cell references

If a formula is copied by filling down, the cell references are adjusted. This is because they are relative addresses based on their position in the sheet.

In the example in Figure 4.43, the green cell contains a Total calculated by multiplying a Price (stored in cell C5) by a Quantity (stored in cell D5).

When copying cells containing formulae, relative addresses change, but absolute addresses do not.

Figure 4.43 *Relative addressing.*

	A	B	C	D	E	F
3						
4		Item	Price	Quantity	Total	
5		Pencil	£0.10	20	£2.00 ←	=C5 * D5
6		Pen	£1.99	5	£9.95	=C6 * D6
7		Ruler	£0.50	2	£1.00	=C7 * D7
8		Ink	£1.50	1	£1.50	=C8 * D8
9						

The green cell is copied (or filled down) into the cells below, and the cell references are adjusted for each row.

In Figure 4.44 the green cell contains a formula that calculates a new price based on a percentage increase on a price stored in cell C3. The amount of the percentage increase is stored in cell F3.

Figure 4.44 *Absolute addressing.*

	A	B	C	D	E	F	G
1							
2		Item	Price	New Price		% Increase	
3		Pencil	£0.10	= C3 * (1 + $F$3/100)		15	
4		Pen	£1.99	= C4 * (1 + $F$3/100)			
5		Ruler	£0.50	= C5 * (1 + $F$3/100)			
6		Ink	£1.50	= C6 * (1 + $F$3/100)			
7							

> Absolute addresses have a $ character in front of the column letter and the row number.

The green cell has a relative address (C3) in its formula as well as an absolute address ($F$3). When the formula is copied into the cells below, the relative address changes but the absolute address does not.

4.8.6 Sorting rows of data

Rows of data on a spreadsheet can be rearranged by sorting them into numerical or alphabetical order. The column that contains the field to sort by needs to be specified.

Example: A spreadsheet containing prices of items sold in a stationery shop has data displayed in ascending numerical order of a Code number.

> Data on a spreadsheet can be **sorted** into alphabetical or numerical order. Sorting into order makes it easier to find data.

Code	Item	Price	Stock
101	Thrimble	£ 2.50	25
102	Blivet	£ 1.20	2
103	Widget	£ 0.95	12
104	Thingummy	£ 3.75	0
105	Bendle	£ 2.45	8
106	Chaintap	£ 1.99	20
107	Standpacket	£ 0.99	15
108	Grummer	£ 3.00	18
109	Flange	£ 2.00	12

To sort tables of data, the whole rows of data must be highlighted, **not** just the column of data that is the sort key.

To sort this list into alphabetical order of the Item name:

1 Highlight all the rows (not including the headings).
2 Sort the data. Select the column heading of the field to sort by.

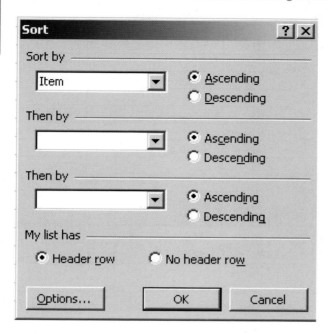

The resulting sorted spreadsheet looks like this:

Code	Item	Price	Stock
105	Bendle	£ 2.45	8
102	Blivet	£ 1.20	2
106	Chaintap	£ 1.99	20
109	Flange	£ 2.00	12
108	Grummer	£ 3.00	18
107	Standpacket	£ 0.99	15
104	Thingummy	£ 3.75	0
101	Thrimble	£ 2.50	25
103	Widget	£ 0.95	12

4.8.7 Lookups

Data can be input into a cell and **LOOKUP**s can then be used to find matching data elsewhere in the workbook.

It is possible to enter data in one area of a spreadsheet, but actually use it in another by using the **LOOKUP** function.

Example: In Figure 4.45, a Code number is entered in cell C13. The corresponding price of the item is displayed in cell C14. If the code is changed, then the price will change.

Figure 4.45 *Using Excel's LOOKUP function.*

Brynganbuy.xls

	A	B	C	D	E
1	**Code**	**Item**	**Price**	**Stock**	
2	101	Thrimble	£ 2.50	25	
3	102	Blivet	£ 1.20	2	
4	103	Widget	£ 0.95	12	
5	104	Thingummy	£ 3.75	0	
6	105	Bendle	£ 2.45	8	
7	106	Chaintap	£ 1.99	20	
8	107	Standpacket	£ 0.99	15	
9	108	Grummer	£ 3.00	18	
10	109	Flange	£ 2.00	12	
11	0		£ -	0	
12					
13		Please Enter Code:	105		
14		The Price is:	£2.45		
15					

Main | **Products**

The reason this works is that there is a function in cell C14 that looks up the code in the table. The formula in cell C14 is:

=LOOKUP(C13, A2:A10,C2:C10)

There are three parts to the LOOKUP function:

- C13 – This is the cell that contains the code being looked up.
- A2:A10 – The range of cells where the code numbers can be found.
- C2:C10 – The range of cells where the corresponding prices can be found.

Data can be looked up from different sheets of the same workbook using the LOOKUP function, but the name of the sheet where the range of cells is located must be given (e.g. Products!A2:A10).

VLOOKUP can be used to look up data from a table if the cells being looked up lie in the first column.

= **VLOOKUP(C13, Products!A2:A10,2)**

The three parts of the VLOOKUP function are:

- C13 – The cell that contains the code being looked up.
- Products!A2:A10 – The block of cells where the table can be found.
- 2 – The column of the table where the data to be returned is found.

HLOOKUP can be used if the table is arranged in rows rather than in columns.

4.8.8 The IF function

It is possible to make the data in one cell conditional on the content of another cell using the IF function.

Example: The delivery charge of an item depends on its total price. The delivery charge is 10% of the value, but is free if the item is priced over £50.

The data in some cells can be set to depend on the data in other cells using the **IF** function.

Figure 4.46 *Using Excel's IF function.*

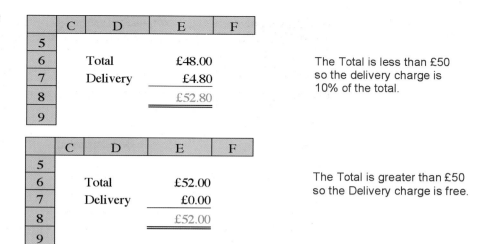

	C	D	E	F
5				
6		Total	£48.00	
7		Delivery	£4.80	
8			£52.80	
9				

The Total is less than £50 so the delivery charge is 10% of the total.

	C	D	E	F
5				
6		Total	£52.00	
7		Delivery	£0.00	
8			£52.00	
9				

The Total is greater than £50 so the Delivery charge is free.

The total cost is in cell E6. The formula that is in cell E7 is:

= IF(E6>50, 0, E6*0.1)

There are three parts to the IF function:

- E6>50 – The condition.
- 0 – The data in the cell if the condition is TRUE.
- E6*0.1 – The data in the cell if the condition is FALSE.

4.8.9 Charts and graphs

Charts make information easier to read and understand. Patterns and trends are easier to see.

Data can be selected on the spreadsheet and a chart or graph of this data can be created.

There are many different types of chart and it is important to select the one that is most appropriate. In other words, you need to choose the type of chart that best illustrates the information.

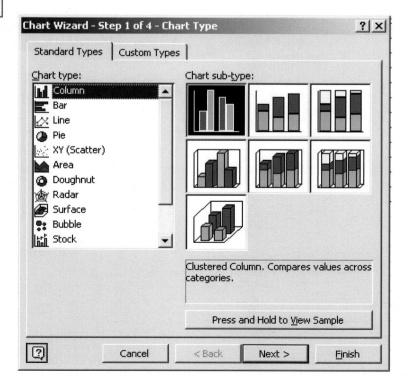

Figure 4.47 *Excel offers a wide variety of different graphical representations.*

111

- Bar graphs are used to compare different values. The bigger the bar the greater the value. (See Figure 4.48).
- Pie charts are used to show how a total is subdivided among a number of different categories. (See Figure 4.49).
- Line graphs display the trend of sequences of values by using plotted points.

Figure 4.48 *A bar graph.*

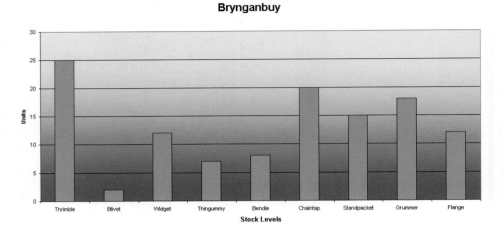

Figure 4.49 *A three-dimensional pie chart.*

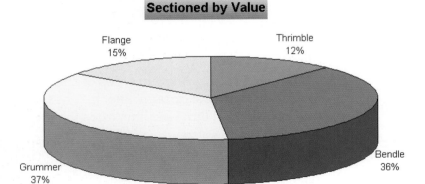

All graphs and charts should have a purpose. They should illustrate a fact or a trend, or prove a theory about the data in the spreadsheet. It must therefore be clear to the person looking at the chart, what is being shown so you need to make sure all the axes are clearly labelled.

■ Activity 4.5   Spreadsheet

1   Download the spreadsheet **brynganbuy.xls**.
Use the spreadsheet to answer the following questions:
  a)   How much would 5 Widgets, 2 Flanges and 1 Standpacket cost? Would there be a delivery charge?
  b)   Without including a delivery charge, how many widgets could you buy if you only had £20 to spend?

2   The organisers of a party use a spreadsheet to help them calculate how much to charge for each ticket so that they do not make a financial loss.
Download this spreadsheet **party.xls** and use it to answer these questions:

No of tickets	Printing Costs	Hire of Venue	Cost of Food	Total Expenses	Income	Total Profit
10	£4.80	£100.00	£45.00	£149.80	£100.00	–£49.80
20	£9.60	£100.00	£90.00	£199.60	£200.00	£0.40
30	£14.40	£100.00	£135.00	£249.40	£300.00	£50.60
40	£19.20	£100.00	£180.00	£299.20	£400.00	£100.80

Enter cost of one ticket: | £10.00 |

Tickets cost 48p each to print.
Food costs are £4.50 per person.
The Hall costs £100 to hire.

  a)   If the ticket price is set at £8.00, how many tickets need to be sold?
  b)   If 55 people are invited:
    i)   at what price should the ticket be set (using a whole number of £)?
    ii)   at what price should the ticket be set (using the nearest 10p)?

3   Create a spreadsheet that allows you to enter your exam marks, works out the average and displays a message 'Revise' after each exam mark if the mark is less than 50%.

Summary

01   Graphics may be bitmap graphics or vector graphics.
02   Bitmap graphics consist of a large number of coloured pixels.
03   Bitmap graphics lose quality when stretched but vector graphics do not.
04   Graphics tools include pencils, paintbrushes. airbrushes and fills.

05   Text may be added to graphics and formatted.

06   Textures can be used to fill shapes.

07   Clipart (graphics already drawn) saves time when creating images.

08   Effects can be used on bitmap graphics.

09   Vector graphics can be rotated and resized.

10   Layering is used to place images on top of each other.

11   Word-processing programs are used to create documents.

12   The layout of the page (size, orientation and margins) needs to be set.

13   Templates with predefined layouts can be used to save time.

14   Text can be formatted to make the document more readable.

15   A macro is a sequence of often used instructions that can be saved and run at any time.

16   Spellcheckers help avoid spelling mistakes

17   A thesaurus will suggest words with similar meanings.

18   Mail merge uses a standard letter and fields from a database to produce similar documents. This is used in a lot of junk mail.

19   Desktop publishing (DTP) is used to create complex publications.

20   DTP publications place text and graphics objects in frames.

21   Text frames can be linked together to provide flow.

22   Multimedia presentations may include text slides, graphics, video clips and sound to communicate information.

23   Another way of communicating information is displaying it on a web page.

24   A database is an organised collection of data.

25   Data is stored in tables. Each table has a key field that uniquely identifies each record.

26   Queries are used to search for data.

27   A simple query searches for data on one field, a complex query searches for data on more than one field and uses logical operators (OR, AND or NOT).

28   Wildcard characters can be used to search for similar data.

29   Data can be sorted into alphabetical or numerical order.

30   Forms are a good way of displaying data in a more readable way.

31   Reports are used for printed data analysis.

32   Spreadsheets display data in a neat way but also perform calculations.

33   Each cell is referenced by a column letter and a row number.

34   Data in a cell may be text, numbers or even graphics.

35   A formula can be placed in a cell to perform a calculation.

36   Each time data is changed, the calculations are carried out.

37   Several sheets can be used in a workbook and these sheets can interact with each other.

38   Rows of data can be sorted into alphabetical or numerical order.

39   In a formula, cell references can use relative addresses (e.g. B3) or absolute addresses (e.g. $B$3).

40   When a formula is copied, relative addresses change but absolute addresses do not.

Practice questions 4

1 A drama club keeps details of its members in a database. Part of this database is shown here:

Membership No.	Surname	First Name	Sex	Tel. No.	Date Joined	Preference
0132	Thomas	Kelly	F	635227	01/05/05	Acting
0139	Davies	Tom	M	668940	03/03/02	Acting
0142	Williams	Shelley	F	630200	01/05/04	Lighting
0143	Jenkins	Billy	M	625331	01/04/03	Sound
0148	Newman	Paul	M	673221	01/02/05	Acting

    a) How many records are shown here? [1]

    b) How many fields are shown? [1]

    c) The producer of a show wants to contact all those who prefer working with the Lighting. Describe how this could be done. [1]

    d) The producer wants to contact all male actors. Describe how this could be done. [3]

2 The drama club uses a spreadsheet to budget the cost of putting on a show.

	A	B	C	D
1	**Expenditure**	**Estimate**	**Actual Cost**	**Difference**
2	**Costumes**	£350.00	£300.00	£50.00
3	**Printing**	£250.00	£250.00	£0.00
4	**Publicity**	£200.00	£180.00	£20.00
5	**Props**	£100.00	£110.00	–£10.00
6	**Lighting**	£300.00	£250.00	£50.00
7	**Sound**	£300.00	£300.00	£0.00
8	**TOTAL**	**£1500.00**	**£1390.00**	**£110.00**

    a) Which of these formulae could be used to give the Difference in cell D4?
    i) B4+C4, **ii)** B4–C4, **iii)** D2–D3. [1]

    b) Which of these formulae could be used to give the Total Estimated Cost in cell B8?
    i) B8–C8, **ii)** SUM(B2:B7), **iii)** D8–C8, **iv)** B2+B3+B4+B5+B6+B7. [1]

    c) The Actual Printing cost in cell C3 is changed. What three other cells will change? [3]

SECTION

2

Information technology: Applications

5 Applications of ICT

5.1 Process control in industry

10.4
Computer systems are often used to control a manufacturing process.

The number of factories producing goods in this country has declined in recent years, but there have been many changes in the way that industrial processes work. These processes have had to adapt to using ICT in many different ways.

The types of work that people do have changed from the dangerous and monotonous jobs to those requiring ICT skills such as programming or robot and machinery maintenance.

Figure 5.1 *Many industrial processes are controlled by computer systems.*

One major change has occurred in the way a manufacturing process is controlled. You are less likely to see people standing around watching a process and taking measurements such as temperature and weight with portable instruments, or timing with a clock, pushing buttons and pulling levers. Instead, you are more likely to see computerised control processes where the actions are carried out automatically by computer systems that are controlling all the operations.

Input data comes from **sensors**. These sensors measure quantities such as temperature, light, sound, weight or stress. Some sensors will detect when an object moves in front of them, and accurate clocks will measure defined time intervals.

10.5
Measurements from sensors provide the input for a control process.

SENSOR: A device used to provide input to automatic control systems.

The measurements from all sensors are taken at regular intervals and input to the controlling computer, which then analyses the data to decide if any actions need to be taken.

For many measurements, there will be a range of values defined within which the reading from the sensor should always lie. If the measured value lies outside that range then the controlling program will decide that some action needs to be taken.

If action is needed, the computer will **output** a **control signal** to devices that operate the system. An actuator is a device that controls a motor, a switch or a tap. It will receive a signal from the controlling

CONTROL PROGRAM: A program that analyses the data input to it and may output control signals to devices operating machines.

computer either through a cable or possibly by means of a wireless signal and activate a device.

An output signal may be in the form of a bit pattern, that is a number of binary digits (0s or 1s). Each bit may control a separate device.

0 = 'Switch Off'
1 = 'Switch On'

Example: A four-bit output signal is used to activate a heater, a fan, a ventilator and a sprinkler.

Heater	Fan	Ventilator	Sprinkler
0	1	1	0

FEEDBACK SYSTEM: A control system where the output actions affect the input data which affect the output actions, which affect the input data, which…, etc.

The output signal, 0110, will switch the fan on and open the ventilator, but turn the heater and the sprinkler off.

Feedback is used in many control systems to maintain a stable environment for a process. Sensors input data, and actions are taken which may influence subsequent readings from the sensors, which are input to the computer, and so on. This is sometimes called a closed-loop system.

Figure 5.2 *Feedback is used to control an environment.*

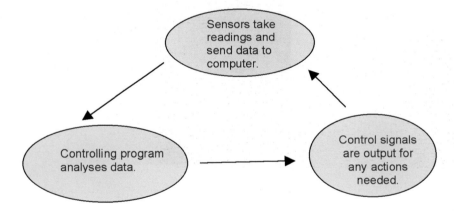

Process control is an example of a **real-time system**. Data received by the controlling computer is immediately analysed by the stored program, and this allows the system to respond immediately to any variations in the processing.

The advantages of process control:
- **Little human interaction needed:** This has implications about the number of people that need to be employed in a factory, and workforces have been reduced as more control processes are used.
- **24/7**: The process can continue 24 hours a day, every day, resulting in greater output for manufacturing industries.
- **Automatic and immediate response to problems**: This means that safety has been improved.
- People can be kept away from and so are **protected from dangerous environments** such as radiation or an atmosphere heavy in spray paint fumes.

Disadvantages of process control:

- **Expensive** equipment and computer hardware need to be purchased and installed.
- There has been some **unemployment** as fewer employees are needed to run the process.
- Some problems may arise which may need human decisions.

■ Case Study   Glass manufacturing

When glass is manufactured, the raw ingredients of sand, soda ash, limestone and recycled glass are heated in a furnace up to 1500°C. It is important that the molten glass is allowed to cool at the proper rate. If it cools too slow or too fast, the glass will be of poor quality with visible defects, or it may lack the proper strength.

Figure 5.3 *Process control is used in the manufacture of glass.*

'Annealing' of glass is the controlled cooling process and is normally done in a special oven. The glass is allowed to cool down to a certain point and then kept at that temperature for a while to allow stresses in the glass to relax, before the final cooling.

Process control oversees this annealing process, as it is able to control the cooling rate.

Sensors carefully monitor the temperature in the oven. If the glass is cooling too quickly in the annealing oven the computer will send a signal to increase the heat. If the glass is cooling too slowly, the computer will send a signal to activate a cooling fan.

The controlling program stored in the computer system receives the input data from the temperature sensors and compares the readings with maximum and minimum values stored on the computer. If the data lies outside the acceptable range, action is taken.

The annealing process needs no human intervention and should result in perfect glass every time.

Figure 5.4 *A system flowchart showing how an annealing control system works.*

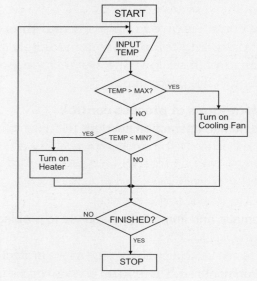

Summary

- [01] Process control in industry has replaced humans in many repetitive or dangerous jobs.
- [02] Input is from sensors, and output is in the form of control signals to operate machines.
- [03] Feedback provides a stable environment for a process.
- [04] Process control provides uninterrupted processing with consistent results.
- [05] Process control is an example of a real-time system.

5.2 Payroll

All companies need to make sure that the people who work for them get paid. Some people get paid a salary (this is normally a fixed amount each month). Some people get paid an hourly rate and the number of hours they have worked is recorded.

Some companies pay their employees at the end of every week, some at the end of every month. Whichever system is used, at the end of the pay period a payroll system is run on the computer, which calculates how much each employee should be paid.

The hardware needed to run a payroll system depends on the size of the company and the number of employees needing to be paid. It is possible to run some payroll programs on PCs for small companies with only a few staff.

Input

The sources of data used as input for the payroll program may include:

- A **database** of the employees' details such as employee identity number, name, pay rate or salary, National Insurance number and tax code. This will be the Employee master file.
- **Timesheets** provide data about the number of hours an employee has worked during the time period, and whether any overtime has been done. Timesheets used to be recorded on paper but it is more likely to be done on a computer now. Special timesheet software is available which is similar to a spreadsheet.

There will need to be some validation of input data. For example a range check on the number of hours worked by an employee should make sure that no number too large could be input.

> A payroll database will need tight security measures such as passwords to prevent unauthorised access.

Processing

The Employee master file will be sorted in order of its key field. Before the timesheet file can be processed it needs to be sorted into the same order as the Employee master file. This speeds up the processing.

The computer will need to calculate:

- The **gross amount** that each employee has earned. This will either be a fixed monthly rate, or it may be calculated by multiplying the number of hours worked by the hourly pay rate.
- Any **bonuses** or **overtime** earned.
- **Deductions** such as National Insurance, tax or pension scheme payments.
- The **net amount** that each employee needs to be paid. This is calculated as the gross payment and bonuses, with all the deductions taken away.

Output

There will be some printed outputs from the payroll process, but also some of the fields in the employee database will need to be updated with new values.

- **Printed payslips** include a summary of the employee's pay and deductions for that period and will be given to the employee to advise how the pay has been calculated. These will normally be printed on special pre-printed stationery.
- **Updated fields** such as the 'total amount of payments this year' or 'total tax paid this year' need to be stored in the records of the employee database.
- Data will need to be sent to the **BACS** system so that money can be transferred to the bank accounts of the employees.
- **Reports** will be output summarising the company's pay for the period and the accountants in the financial department will use the data to update their accounting system.

BANKERS AUTOMATED CLEARING SYSTEM (BACS): A system used to transfer money directly into employees' bank accounts.

Figure 5.5 *An example of a payslip.*

My Company Ltd						Weekly Payslip

Emp.No.	Employee Name		Nat. Ins. No.	Tax Code	NI Code
13	A.N.Other		AB001299×Z	BR	B

Additions				Deductions			
Description	Rate	Factor	Amount	Description	Rate	Factor	Amount
Basic Pay	£12.00	37.5	£450.00				
Overtime Rate 1	£15.50	17.5	£271.25				
Fuel Expenses			£12.50				

Total Gross Pay	£733.75	Deductions (excl. Tax & NI)	£0.00

	Period	To Date		Period	To Date
Taxable Pay	£721.25	£1,241.00	Income Tax	£158.67	£273.01
Nat. Ins. Pay	£721.25	£1,241.00	Nat. Ins. Contribution 'EE	£19.10	£35.68
			Nat. Ins. Contribution 'ER	£74.61	£125.43

Tax Period: 29	Net Pay	£555.98

A payroll system is an example of a **batch processing** system. All the timesheets and files are prepared and collected and the payroll system is run at an off-peak time such as at night or at the weekend. There is no human intervention required once the payroll program has been started and the payslips are prepared and printed automatically.

A **system flowchart** is a visual way of illustrating how a system works. Different shaped boxes have different meanings and are labelled. Arrowed lines show the flow of data through the system. It is often easier to understand how a system works from a diagram than from a text description

A system flowchart makes it easy to understand how a system works.

Figure 5.6 *A system flowchart showing how a payroll system works.*

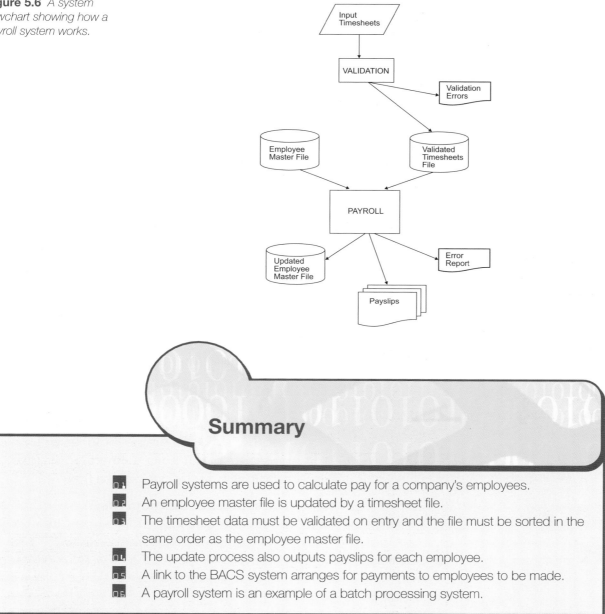

Summary

- **01** Payroll systems are used to calculate pay for a company's employees.
- **02** An employee master file is updated by a timesheet file.
- **03** The timesheet data must be validated on entry and the file must be sorted in the same order as the employee master file.
- **04** The update process also outputs payslips for each employee.
- **05** A link to the BACS system arranges for payments to employees to be made.
- **06** A payroll system is an example of a batch processing system.

5.3 Weather forecasting

Some of the world's most powerful computers are used to forecast the weather. Accuracy of forecasts is improving all the time and many people rely on these forecasts: TV companies, shipping, farmers, the military, etc.

108

Many people rely on accurate weather forecasting and large computers are used to monitor and predict weather patterns.

109

Input data is received from sensors measuring weather data. Many **sensors** are online to computer systems and collect data automatically at regular intervals.

Computer systems are also used for hurricane and tornado tracking: not really needed in the UK! If weather disasters can be predicted then people can be warned before they happen and take precautions. Whole areas may be evacuated before a hurricane strikes, saving many lives.

Large computers are also used to monitor global warming: the increase in the average temperature of the Earth's surface. They also monitor the ocean temperatures and currents. El Niño is a warming of the eastern Pacific ocean that affects global weather patterns every few years.

Data collection

Many millions of items of data are collected daily from all round the world. The data may consist of readings of temperature, humidity, atmospheric pressure, rainfall, visibility, or even radar data or infrared levels.

The most commonly used sensors used for measuring the weather are:

- **Thermometer**: Measures the air or sea temperature.
- **Barometer**: Measures the atmospheric pressure. Changing pressures are the main influence on weather.
- **Rain gauge**: Measures the amount of precipitation (rain, hail, sleet or snow).
- **Hygrometer**: Measures the amount of water vapour in the air.
- **Psychrometer**: Consists of two thermometers (a wet one and a dry one) and measures relative humidity.
- **Anemometer**: Measures wind speed.

Figure 5.7 *An anemometer is used to measure wind speed.*

Many weather sensors are connected to a computer and readings are taken automatically at regular intervals. Some weather stations in remote places will have to be manned and have meteorologists take the readings visually and record them.

The sources of this data are:

- **Weather stations** are sited all round the world, even in some of the remotest regions.
- **Satellites** are constantly transmitting weather readings to weather centres on earth. Visual and infrared images of weather systems can be built up from the received data.
- **Weather balloons** are released and rise up through the atmosphere taking weather readings.
- **Aircraft** can collect data as they fly through the upper atmosphere.
- **Radar stations** can detect any rainfall.
- **Weather ships** out at sea send data back to shore.
- **Weather buoys** permanently anchored out at sea can collect important data from places difficult to get to.

110

Weather centres collect data from all over the world and even outer space.

Figure 5.8 *Satellites orbiting the Earth transmit visual and infrared data so that pictures of weather patterns can be viewed from space.*

Only the largest most powerful computers can manage complex weather forecasting programs.

In the UK, the computer system at the Meteorological Office at Exeter collects the weather data from all these sources, validates the data and uses it as input for its weather program. It has two supercomputers to process the data.

Processing

Processing millions of items of data is often called **number-crunching** and can take some time, so high-powered computers are needed with fast processors and large memory and disk storage capacities.

Producing weather forecasts is a very complex process involving solving large numbers of mathematical equations. Only the most powerful computers can do this effectively.

The modelling software used to make weather and climate predictions is called the **Unified Model** and was programmed using a language called Fortran. It is very complex, constantly being upgraded and we do not need to learn about it here (thank goodness!).

■ Activity 5.1   Internet investigation

Use the Internet to investigate the computers that are used at the Meteorological Office in Exeter to process all the weather data.

Try to find:

● the name of the computer;
● how many processors it has;
● the size of its memory;
● how many calculations per second it can perform.

Output

The data is processed to produce the following outputs:

● **Charts**: For example, maps of atmospheric pressure, wind maps, rainfall charts. A succession of these charts will show how the weather is changing.

125

- **Forecasts**: Previous weather patterns are used to predict future weather.
- **Weather warnings**: If there are any predicted weather problems such as flooding or difficult driving conditions then these are issued.
- **Archives**: All the data is stored in archives. The more information that is known about previous weather behaviour, the better the predictions of future weather will be.

The Meteorological (Met.) Office makes use of a network of weather stations around the country and around the world. Many airfields have weather stations and can transmit their readings automatically across the network.

The Internet has made weather data and forecasts more widely accessible and the Met. Office's website, www.metoffice.com, provides up-to-date and reliable weather information. For example the radar rainfall chart, www.metoffice.com/weather/europe/uk/radar/, shows where it has recently been raining in the country.

Summary

01 Many millions of data readings are collected from sensors all over the world.
02 Sensors measure temperature, air pressure, humidity, wind speed, rainfall.
03 A large mainframe computer is needed to process the data.
04 Complex modelling calculations are performed to output weather forecasts.
05 Output consists of weather charts.
06 Weather warnings can be given in plenty of time.

5.4 Libraries

Librarians depend on computer systems to manage the facilities provided by the library such as book lending.

Most towns and cities have a library where people can go and read books. To borrow a book from a library you have to become a member. When you apply to become a member of the library, your

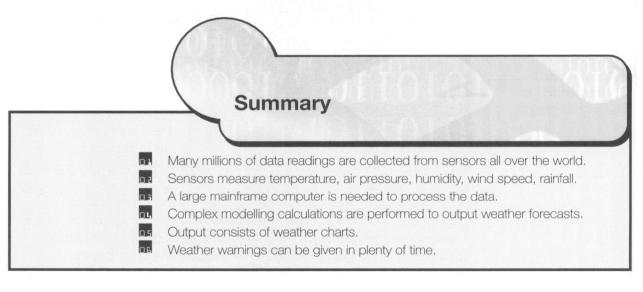

Figure 5.9 *A library membership card will have an individual barcode assigned to it.*

Figure 5.10 *Every book in a library will have a barcode assigned to it.*

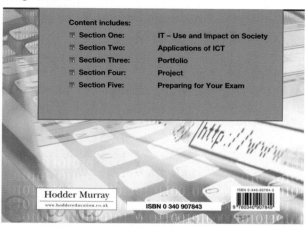

details are recorded and you will be issued with a library card that has your membership number and a barcode printed on it.

Once you have become a member you will be entitled to use all the facilities of the library that may include using their online computer databases and Internet as well as borrowing books and magazines.

Also, every book in the library will have a barcode either stuck on it, or on a card inserted into a sleeve inside the cover of the book.

The library computer system will store a database and one of its files will be a file of all its members' details. One record of this file may look similar to this:

> A key field uniquely identifies each record. No two records will have the same data in their **key field**.

Field	Field Value
Member ID (key field)	324795
Name	Mary Thompson
Address	19, Oak Tree Avenue,
Date of Birth	12/05/88
Date of Joining	19/02/06

The library database would also have a book **catalogue:** a file that stores the details of all the books kept in the library. One record from the Books file may look similar to this:

Field	Field Value
Book ID (key field)	0 340 883081
Title	ICT Really is Fun
Author	I. M. A. Robot
Shelf	D27
Date Last Borrowed	16/12/05
Available	YES

The Shelf field is used to locate a book in the library. Every shelf in every bookcase will have its own unique label.

The Date Last Borrowed field is important for the librarians to know whether the book is popular or not. Books that are not borrowed may be removed from the shelves and replaced by more popular books.

The Available field lets the librarian know whether the book is currently on loan. A member may come into the library and ask about a book. A search of the database will quickly determine if the book is available or not.

Every book has a unique number. This is the International Standard Book Number (ISBN), and this 10-digit number may be used as the key field for the Books file as no two titles in the world will have the same ISBN. (There will soon be an update to 13-digit ISBNs.)

Books may also have a Dewey classification number. This is a three-digit number that depends on the subject matter of the book. Books are often arranged on the shelves in a library according to their Dewey classification.

Borrowing a book

When a member of the library wants to borrow some books, he or she must take them to the desk. The barcode on the member's card is input using a barcode reader (usually a hand-held wand), as well as the barcodes from all the books to be borrowed.

The date on which the books are borrowed is also recorded and the date when the books need to be returned is calculated and stamped on a card inside the book to inform the borrower.

When the data is input, it will need to be validated to make sure the data is sensible and that it has been read correctly. **Range** checks and **length** checks can be carried out on ID numbers.

One of the digits in an ISBN number is a **check digit** and is used as a validation check. The computer recalculates the check digit on input to determine if an error has been made.

These details are all recorded in the library database in a **Transactions** file. One record from the Transactions file may look similar to this:

Field	Field Value
Transaction ID (key field)	34112
Member ID	324795
Book ID	0 340 883081
Date Borrowed	23/11/06
Date of Return	

The table shows the record of the borrowed book in the main library database books file.

Returning a book

When a book is returned to the library, the barcode in the book is read again and the computer will determine whether a fine needs to be paid if the book has been returned late.

The transaction record is located and updated with the date of return of the book.

The book record in the database needs to be updated to show the book has become available again.

> **Validation** of data is important to make sure that no errors are input.

The library system

A library computer system is used to perform the following tasks:

- **Maintenance of database**, including adding, editing or deleting records of members or books.
- Recording of book **borrowing transactions**.
- Recording of book **requests**. Members may request a particular book that is on loan, and be notified when the book is returned and becomes available.
- **Information retrieval**. A member may ask for a particular book. The database can be searched to find out if the book is available. It is important that this information can be found quickly.
- Daily **reports** such as:
  - overdue books;
  - books that are unpopular and need to be replaced;
  - unpaid fines.

Many branches of libraries have networked their library systems. This allows them to share information or make requests to transfer books. A library member may ask for a book that is currently on loan to another member. The librarian can use the network system to find out if the book is available at another nearby branch, and, if it is, they could ask for it to be transferred.

A library system is an example of a **real-time transaction system**. As books are borrowed or returned the records in the database are immediately updated. If a search is made of the database, then up-to-date information is always returned.

> **115**
> A real-time system always has up-to-date information.

Summary

01 Members of a library have membership cards with barcodes.

02 Every book in the library has a barcode.

03 When a book is borrowed the barcodes of the member's card and the book are input and stored.

04 Large databases store details of the books and publications, and these can be searched for book availability.

05 A library system is an example of a real-time transaction system.

5.5 Robotic and embedded control

A **robot** is a machine that can be programmed to perform a sequence of actions. Many robots are now used in industry, particularly in manufacturing where jobs are repetitive and boring for humans. Many conveyor belt jobs are now performed by robot arms that have a number of 'joints' (like elbows and wrists) which allow the arm to move in any direction. The arm may also have some sort of grip, which allows it to pick up an object or use a tool such as a drill (see Figure 3.1).

There are also robots that move around. A guidance system makes sure that the robot does not crash into solid objects.

The types of jobs that industrial robots do:

- **Repetitive**, boring jobs that require the same sequence of movements over and over again. For example, a robot arm may place electronic components into a circuit board.
- **Dangerous** jobs. Humans may be at risk from handling toxic materials or unhealthy levels of toxic materials in the atmosphere. There may be radiation or extremes of heat and cold.
- **Difficult** jobs. A robot would find it easy to perform a job needing precision whereas a human hand might shake a bit!
- **Heavy** jobs. Humans would get tired of lifting and carrying heavy objects repeatedly. Robots would not.

A computer program is an ordered sequence of instructions that a computer can execute. A robot needs a program to define and sequence its actions. This program will run continuously whenever the machine is switched on.

Robots can be programmed in two ways:

- Instructions can be written using a special computer **programming language**.
- **Guiding** the robot through the actions manually. The robot will 'remember' the movements and be able to repeat them.

A robot may have sensors built into it, which are used to detect when an object passes in front of it. A moving robot would need sensors to detect the proximity of solid objects so that it does not crash into them. The data from these sensors acts as input for the controlling program.

Robots that grip objects or turn them may have a sensor that measures the strength of the grip, or the torque.

Output from the program consists of control signals that cause the machine to perform a number of actions.

Among many other things, industrial robots can:

- assemble parts
- weld or rivet
- spray paint
- lift and carry parts (robots can follow tracks on the floor and fetch parts from a warehouse)
- handle machine tools such as drills or grinders
- turn objects such as tightening bolts to a specified torque.

116
Robots are used in hostile places like the surfaces of other planets where the temperatures are too extreme for humans.

Figure 5.11 *A robot can assemble complex electronic circuit boards accurately.*

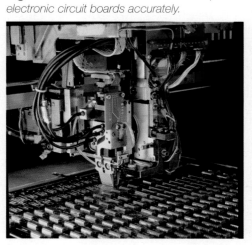

117
Humans use programs to give instructions to robots. Not the other way around like you sometimes see in films!

118
Data from sensors provides input for the controlling program.

119
Torque is rotational force.

There are even robots that can harvest fields of crops, detect and defuse bombs, explore the bottom of the ocean, or mow a lawn.

Advantages of using robots:

- Ensures **consistency** of quality in a job. A human performs a job less well if tired or distracted. A robot performs the job equally well all the time.
- **Breaks** or holidays are not required. A robot can repeat their programmed actions all day and every day.
- Robots **do not need to be paid** an hourly or weekly wage.
- Creation of **new jobs** such as robot maintenance and programming.
- Robots carry out **boring or dangerous jobs** that humans would not like to do.

Disadvantages of using robots:

- Initial installation and programming **costs** are high.
- Robots do not respond well to **new situations**. Some do not have the capacity to analyse a new situation and be able to respond with the appropriate action. This could be a major problem if something goes wrong!
- Some **unemployment** has resulted in the manufacturing industry as humans have been replaced by robots.

Embedded systems

An embedded system is a device that contains a ROM chip. Stored on this chip is a program that controls the functions of the device, which will be dedicated to a particular job and it will not normally be possible to program it to do another one.

You can find many examples of embedded systems in the home: washing machines, microwaves, televisions, cookers, etc. All of these have chips embedded in them which control their actions.

> **EMBEDDED SYSTEM:** A built-in programmed microprocessor for controlling devices. The microprocessor is 'dedicated' to a particular task (unlike most computers which can be programmed at different times to perform many different tasks).

■ Case Study Car manufacture

The manufacturing of cars is based on a moving assembly line. The process starts with the basic chassis to which parts are added, or a sequence of operations is performed on it as it moves along a conveyor belt. Some of the jobs are done by people, but many of the jobs are done by robotic machines.

Figure 5.12 *The assembly line in a car manufacturing plant. Some jobs are done by people but many are done by robots.*

Some of the jobs that robots may be doing:

- **Fetching and carrying parts** from an automated warehouse. The robots can lift heavy objects and carry them along tracks embedded or painted in the floor. Sensors will detect when the robot leaves the track and will correct the direction of movement.
- **Welding** parts together. A robot arm can perform precision spot-welding.
- **Applying** adhesives or sealants.
- **Spray-painting** the body parts. Robots can achieve a more even coating than humans (and they will do it perfectly every time!). Robots will not be worried about the amount of paint fumes in the air.
- **Testing** engines (sensors take measurements of timing and engine emissions).

Figure 5.13 *Robots spray-painting bodies of cars.*

The introduction of robots on the car assembly line has resulted in increased production (an assembly line produces cars 24 hours a day every day). The quality of the finished cars is consistently good, which should impress customers who buy the cars, and satisfied customers are more likely to return!

Summary

01 Robots have replaced humans in doing repetitive or dangerous jobs.
02 Robots are programmed to repeatedly perform a sequence of tasks.
03 Industrial robots can assemble, lift and carry, weld, spray paint, or handle tools such as drills or grinders.
04 Robots allow uninterrupted production to a consistent standard.
04 Embedded systems have programmed chips which carry out tasks.

5.6 Stock control and order processing

Most large shops now have automatic stock control systems to make sure none of the items they sell either runs out or is over-ordered. Customers will not be happy if the item they want to buy has run out and they will probably take their custom elsewhere. There is also a problem for the shop if they stock too many of an item. Unsold goods are a source of waste and unnecessary expense, as they may have to be removed from the shelves to be replaced by more desirable items. Supermarkets will have a problem with perishable goods if they are not sold before their 'sell-by date'.

It is not just shops that have stock control systems. Factories need to keep stock of the raw materials they use, offices need to keep stock of their stationery and warehouses must keep control over the stock levels of their finished goods.

An effective stock control system will maximise the profitability of a business, minimise unnecessary expenditure and avoid wastage or supply problems.

The **stock level** of an item is the number of that item remaining. Computers keep an up-to-date record of the stock level of every item. **Stock control** is the administration of stock levels.

> 1.20
>
> Businesses must always try to keep their customers happy!

Figure 5.14 *Stock control in a warehouse is important.*

Stock control system

A good stock control system will:

- Keep track of the stock levels of all goods.
- Order more goods from the suppliers if the stock level falls below the reorder level.
- Analyse which items are selling well and which are not. Reorder levels may be adjusted on the basis of this information.
- Analyse sales patterns. There may be a need for seasonal adjustment for some items. For example, there may be more need for shops to stock umbrellas in the winter, or sunglasses in the summer.

In a supermarket or large shop, input data is collected from a POS terminal, where barcodes or sales tags are read on each item sold. Large stores or supermarkets may have a real-time transaction stock control system where every sale is processed immediately the data is input and stock levels adjusted. Orders for new goods are automatically sent to the suppliers without human intervention and delivered the next day or as soon as possible.

Other shops may operate a **batch processing system** where there is a **stock master file** holding details of all the goods the business

> STOCK MASTER FILE: A permanent file with details of all items sold or bought by the business, including the stock level (i.e. how many of the items are currently stored).

either sells or buys. One record of the master stock file may look similar to this:

Field	Field Value
Stock ID	B67820
Description	T-Shirt (Blue) Large
Selling Price	£4.99
Stock Level	17
Reorder Level	10
Supplier	Casual Wear Ltd

This is a very simplified record and many more fields would be stored such as the date of the last sale of the item, and the amount usually ordered from the supplier.

If the stock level falls below the **reorder level**, then an order for more of that stock needs to be sent to the supplier.

Whenever an item is bought or sold, a record is created and stored in a transaction file. One record of a **transaction file** may look similar to this:

Field	Field Value
Order Number	32554
Customer ID	ThompsonJD
Transaction Type	Sale
Stock ID	B67820
Quantity	2
Date/Time	12/01/2006 11.32

Mrs Thompson bought two Large Blue T-shirts costing £4.99 each at 11.32 a.m. on 12 January 2006. After this transaction has been processed, the stock level for this item will be reduced from 17 to 15.

For factories or warehouses, anything that causes a change in the stock level of an item is recorded as a transaction. This may be anything from using 50 kg of onions to make pickle, or receiving a new consignment of 20 cm iron bolts.

At the end of each day the transaction file is used to update the stock master file. The transaction file is first sorted into the same order as the stock master file, and each record of the stock master file is input, adjusted if necessary and then stored on a new stock master file.

Sales reports can be produced giving total sales figures or a list of the best selling items. Most importantly, a report of all items that need re-ordering will be output. Some companies may order new items over the Internet using e-commerce websites.

Data **validation** is used to check that data is sensible before it is processed. Typical validation checks are range checks, presence checks, format checks and the use of check digits.

TRANSACTION FILE: A **temporary** file of recent sales or purchases. The transaction file is used to update the master file.

Figure 5.15 *A system flowchart showing the process of updating a stock master file.*

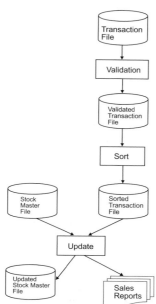

ORDER PROCESSING: The administration of customer orders including arranging for the goods to be delivered, preparing and sending invoices, receipt of payments, and updating of stock files.

Order processing

Some retail companies do not have shops, but instead they receive orders from customers either by telephone, by mail or more frequently these days over the Internet. All the orders received are **validated** and placed on an **orders file**. The orders file is processed at regular intervals, and will involve the following stages for each order:

● The order is checked carefully. Stock levels of items are checked to make sure there is enough of each item available to fulfil the order.
● The customer account is checked to make sure there are no problems such as lack of credit or unpaid invoices.
● The warehouse or stores department are informed of the items on the order and prepare the goods ready to be sent.
● The **stock levels** of each item need to be adjusted.
● An invoice is prepared. Prices are looked up from the stock master file. VAT and any extra charges such as delivery charges are added.
● The goods are dispatched and the invoice is sent to the customer.

A computerised order processing system will ensure that orders are processed quickly. Customers do not want to have to wait a long time for their orders to arrive.

Summary

01	Stock control is the administration of stock levels.
02	Stock control makes sure there is no wastage and that nothing runs out.
03	Some stock control systems operate as real-time transaction systems.
04	A stock master file is updated using a file of recent transactions.
05	The transaction file must be validated and sorted in the same order as the stock master file.
06	Order processing is the administration of customer orders.

5.7 Expert systems in medicine

EXPERT SYSTEM: A system that takes the place of a human expert. A large database of knowledge can be searched and deductions made on the basis of the search results.

Imagine discussing your medical problems with a computer instead of a doctor. The computer might then suggest a diagnosis of your disorder and recommend a course of treatment, and then print you a prescription for medicines. Is this a glimpse of the future? No, it is happening now: and not just in medicine! Computers are taking the place of experts in a variety of different fields. However, it is the intention that expert systems will help doctors rather than replace them. Computers have their limitations!

An expert system simulates the knowledge and skill of an expert.

- It has a large **database** of knowledge.
- It allows the database of knowledge to be **interrogated**. Search tools can quickly find information.
- It has an **inference engine**. This is a clever piece of software that allows the computer to make deductions based on the facts that have been input and the data in the knowledge database.

Figure 5.16 *Some web-based medical diagnosis expert systems are available.*

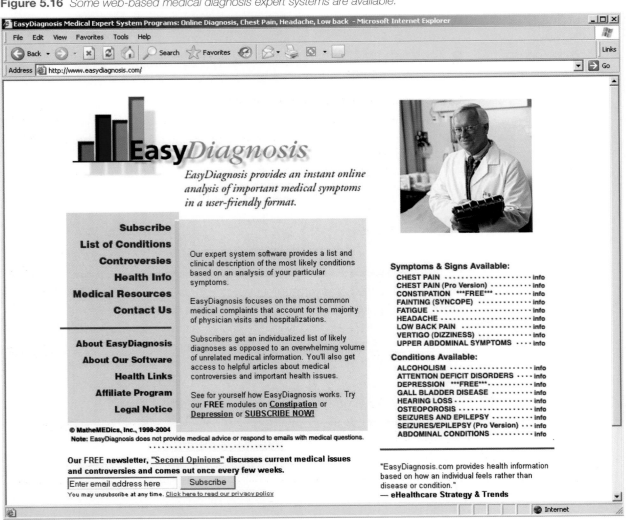

In medicine, there are expert systems that are being used to diagnose illnesses. A large database of diseases and their symptoms is stored in a database. A patient will answer a sequence of simple questions by typing in the answers at a keyboard or possibly using a touch-screen device to select one of a number of options.

The responses are analysed by the expert system, and the inference engine uses a set of rules to make deductions about the probable illness. It may assign probabilities to each diagnosis and may also output recommendations about treatments or medicines.

The program that runs the expert system will have been written using an artificial intelligence language such as Prolog.

1.2.2

Expert systems are not replacing doctors but are being used to help them. There are ethical and legal reasons for this: if a computerised diagnosis is wrong, who do you sue?

1.2.3

An expert system can store far more information than a human, and can remember all of it perfectly.

Advantages of an expert system:

● The knowledge in the database can be far more than a human is capable of remembering. New data can be added at any time as new medical research is undertaken. This is an advantage for the doctor as there is no need to learn as much information.

● The expert system should never get facts wrong. This is an advantage to the patient as humans make mistakes and may not be able to remember important facts correctly.

● Human experts retire when they get old. The expert system lives for ever, with no loss of knowledge, and may evolve into bigger and better hardware and software.

● Some people would prefer to enter personal data into a computer than discuss them with a doctor.

Disadvantages of an expert system:

● Some people may prefer the personal touch of discussing medical matters with a doctor. They may feel the doctor is more likely to understand their personal feelings and be more sympathetic.

● Expert systems are not cheap and considerable expenditure is needed to install one.

Summary

01 An expert system takes the place of a human expert.
02 A large database of knowledge can be interrogated.
03 An inference engine can make deductions.
04 An expert system can store more knowledge than a human and can remember all of it perfectly.
05 Expert systems are programmed using artificial intelligence languages.

5.8 Booking systems

Booking systems do more than record bookings. They also respond to customer searches for availability.

Whether booking a holiday in a Spanish villa, a flight to Paris, or a seat in a theatre, the chances are that a computerised booking system will be used to make the reservation.

■ Case Study   Theatre booking system

Theatregoers can reserve seats for performances of shows either by telephoning the theatre or by using an online website. They can check whether seats are available on a particular day and where in the theatre they can sit. If suitable seats are available then they can be booked. Payment is normally made by credit or debit card.

The person booking the seats needs to input data about:

- the number of seats they want to reserve;
- the time and date of the performance;
- their details (e.g. name, address, telephone number, etc.);
- their card details for payment.

Tickets for the show can be mailed to the customer.

The system will also need to cater for people who turn up on the day of the performance and buy tickets at the door.

Theatres may offer a service where customers can input their email addresses and have information sent to them about shows being performed in the future.

A large database needs to be stored on the theatre's computer, which has details about every seat in the theatre for every performance of every show that takes place.

BOOKING SYSTEM: A large database which stores bookings. Searches can be made to find out if seats are available.

A typical record in this database may look similar to this:

Field	Field Value
SeatID	R32
Date	16/08/06
Time	19:30
Price	£12.00
Available	NO
CustomerID	JenkinsJD

This record shows that Mr Jenkins has booked seat number R32 for a 7.30 p.m. performance on 16/08/06.

When a customer contacts the theatre and wants to make a booking, the database is searched to find seats that are available for the requested performance. If the booking is confirmed, then the customer's details are entered into the record and those seats are shown as being no longer available, and the record is saved.

▶

This needs to be done immediately in case somebody else wants to book the same seat for the same performance. The database must be updated as soon as the booking is made so that users of the system are always looking at up-to-date information about seat availability.

The system is therefore a **real-time** system.

Advantages of a booking system:

● There should be no **double-booking** of seats, where two people book the same seat at the same performance on the same date.
● Fast response to queries about seat availability from customers.

Disadvantages of a booking system:

● Initial costs of buying and installing the system will be high.

Online booking systems

Many booking systems are web-based and bookings can be made through the Internet. A theatre may have information about its performances on a website where you can check if seats are available and what their prices are.

Some websites can look for seats in a number of different theatres, so if you cannot find what you want in one theatre, it may be available in another.

1.2.5
A booking system is an example of a real-time transaction system. Bookings are immediately updated to avoid double bookings.

1.2.6
Some booking systems operate on the Internet.

Figure 5.17 *Many ticket agencies have websites where available seats can be searched for and bookings can be made.*

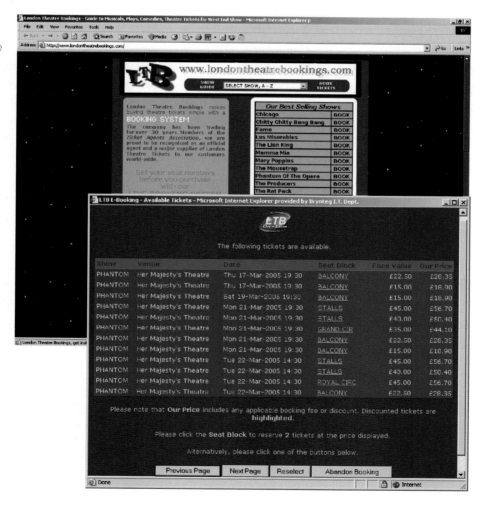

Multi-user systems

Some booking systems are operated as a **multi-access system**. For example, each branch of a travel agency may have workstations connected to a central computer. The agency branches may be all over the country and the main computer may be in London. Each branch computer has a network link directly to the main computer, which has a database storing the booking database.

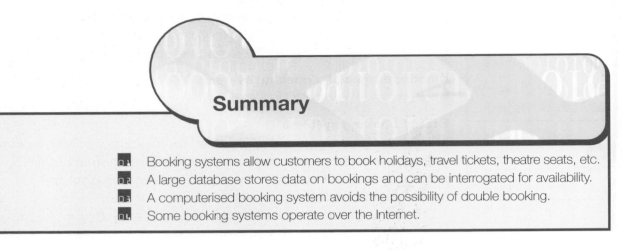

Summary

- 01 Booking systems allow customers to book holidays, travel tickets, theatre seats, etc.
- 02 A large database stores data on bookings and can be interrogated for availability.
- 03 A computerised booking system avoids the possibility of double booking.
- 04 Some booking systems operate over the Internet.

5.9 Computer control in hospitals

> 127
> Computers are used to control life-support equipment in hospitals because they are more dependable than humans.

Computer systems are used for many different reasons in hospitals, but one of them is to control equipment. Important examples of this are controlling life-support systems in intensive care units or in premature baby units. Doctors and nurses are very busy people and computer-controlled systems will remove some of their workload, and allow them to carry out duties other than constantly monitoring a patient's condition.

Sensors attached to the patient measure:

- pulse rate
- temperature
- blood pressure
- blood gases (such as oxygen)
- breathing rate.

> 128
> The inputs are from sensors. The outputs are signals to alarms or large monitors.

The readings are taken at regular intervals (fractions of a second) and are used as inputs to the computer system.

If any of the readings falls outside an acceptable range of levels, an alarm is sounded so that treatment can be immediately given.

The readings are **output** in the form of a graph displayed on a large monitor easily visible to nurses and doctors in attendance. Any changes are apparent and the state of the patient can be quickly assessed. Control signals may also be output to sound an alarm.

Figure 5.18 *Output from the intensive care monitoring system is displayed on large monitors for easy viewing.*

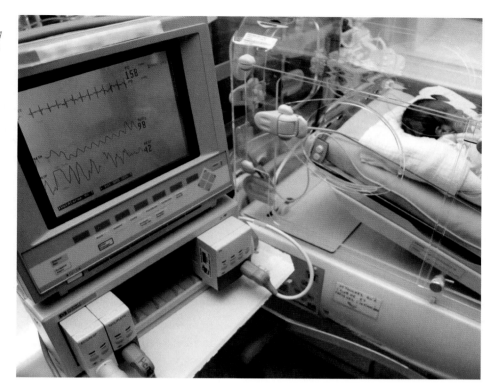

Advantages of medical control systems:

● Monitoring of patients is continuous.
● Automatic alarm systems.
● Reduced chance of human errors due to tiredness.
● Frees nursing staff to perform other duties.

Disadvantages of medical control systems:

● The initial costs of buying and installing the systems are expensive.

The control system is an example of a **real-time** system. The computer processes the data as soon as it is received because it must check immediately whether an alarm needs to be sounded.

The computers running a control system will be **dedicated** computers. They constantly run the control program and cannot be used for anything else.

Power cuts are a serious problem to hospitals and could result in patient death, so back-up generators are used to make sure there is an uninterrupted power supply. Additionally, in case of breakdown, hospital administrators make sure there are always spares readily available.

> **129**
> Medical control systems are run by **dedicated** computers as they must not be affected by other applications.

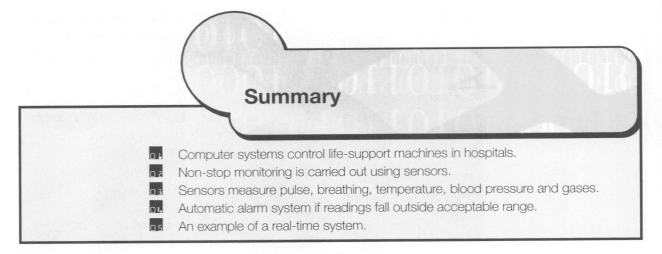

Summary

0.1   Computer systems control life-support machines in hospitals.

0.2   Non-stop monitoring is carried out using sensors.

0.3   Sensors measure pulse, breathing, temperature, blood pressure and gases.

0.4   Automatic alarm system if readings fall outside acceptable range.

0.5   An example of a real-time system.

5.10   Billing systems

> 130
>
> Bills to customers must be accurate and on time if a business is not going to lose customers.

From the smallest one-person business to the largest global companies, an accurate and reliable billing system is the lifeblood of a business. The survival of a business depends on the customers paying their bills for goods or services, so they must be presented on time, and they must be accurate. If customers are irritated by bills that are incorrect, they will take their business elsewhere.

A billing system will produce bills for customers at regular intervals; possibly every month, or every quarter (three months). We do not get a bill for electricity every time we turn a light on in the house. Instead, the usage is measured and we receive a bill at the end of the quarter. Similarly, regular customers of a retail business may receive a bill for all the goods they have bought in the given time period.

A **billing system** must perform the following main tasks:

- Keep records of all **goods** or **services** purchased by customers.
- Keep accurate records of **customer details**.
- Produce accurate **bills** for customers at regular intervals.
- Print customer **statements** of all business transactions.
- Process **payments** received.
- Keep the company **accounts** updated.

Data

At the heart of a billing system there will be a database (master file), and this will consist of a number of different related files. The main files in this database may be:

- **Customer accounts file**: This would have all the details about the customers such as their customer account number, name, address, telephone number, amount of money billed this year, the total amount of money paid.
- **Transactions file**: This contains records of all the purchases or services requiring billing.

TURNAROUND DOCUMENT: A document produced by a computer and then used as an input document using an OCR or OMR reader.

Figure 5.19 *System flowchart for the billing process.*

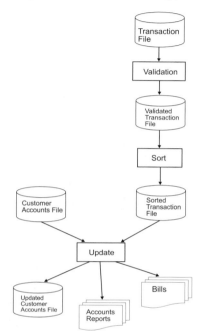

BILLING SYSTEMS: An example of a **batch processing system**. There is no immediacy for processing, and no human intervention is required once the processing has started.

Validation checks will be made on the data as it is entered to make sure that it is sensible data. It is important that customers do not receive extremely large bills because incorrect data has been input, or the complaints line will be very busy!

Data capture

The methods of data capture will depend on the type of business that a company carries out. A retail business may receive orders online through emails or from a website. Public utilities such as telephone, water or electricity companies will have meters monitoring usage of their services.

A **turnaround document**, such as an electricity meter reading form with the customer's name and address printed on it, is created by a computer to record a new meter reading. The form is fed into an OCR reader to input the data.

Other systems may be used, but whatever method is used, the data is recorded in a **transaction** file, which will be needed at the end of the time period to produce the bills.

Processing

The first part of the update process is to sort the transaction file into the same order as the master (Customer Accounts) file. The master file is updated using the transactions file at the end of the period. Bills will be printed and sent out to all the customers.

Reports will also be printed to help the accounts department keep track of the company's finances. These will include data on total payments made and how much is still owing from customers who have not made payments yet.

The billing system is an example of a **batch processing** system.

Summary

- Billing systems administer the sending of bills to customers and receipt of payments.
- A customer accounts file is updated using a file of recent transactions.
- Validation checks must be carried out to make sure bills are not too large.
- A billing system is an example of a batch processing system.

5.11 CAD/CAM

COMPUTER-AIDED DESIGN (CAD): A software drawing tool utilising computers to assist designers create graphic designs of objects. CAD can be used to design cars, houses, kitchen layouts, aircraft, bridges, electronic circuit boards, etc.

Every object that is manufactured, from the smallest bottle top to the largest aircraft wing, must have been designed by somebody. The size, shape, colour and material must have been thought about and decided upon. It is easy to forget this when we are surrounded by so many material objects, but it is not only objects which have to be designed, there are designs needed for kitchen layouts, for motorway signs, for housing estate plans and for many other uses.

There are software packages that help designers in their work. **CAD** stands for **computer-aided design**, and CAD packages use computers to make the process of design simple and quick. CAD packages use **vector graphics** to create designs.

Designs are displayed on a monitor and can be edited using either a mouse or a **graphics tablet**. Finished designs can be saved or printed out using a printer or, for larger designs, using a graph **plotter**. Some CAD packages use touch-screen monitors.

Figure 5.20 *Complex designs are easier to draw using CAD software.*

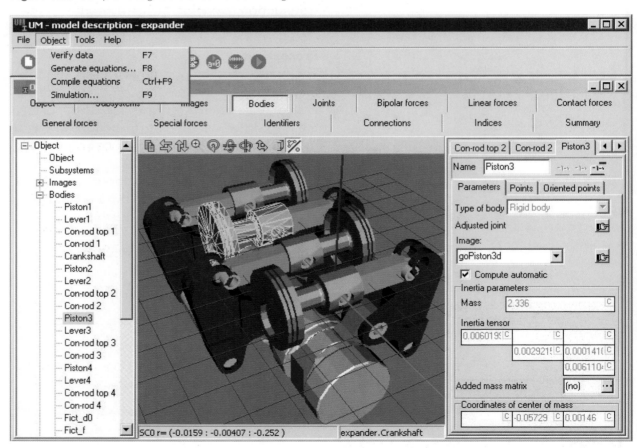

What you can do using a CAD package:

- Draw and edit shapes and lines.
- Work in two (2-D) or three (3-D) dimensions (and convert between them).

- Render colours and textures onto shapes.
- Add pre-drawn shapes, components such as cogs, or clipart.
- Perform transformations such as stretch and rotation.
- Zoom in to edit small details.
- View 3-D models from different angles.

Some CAD packages allow calculations. For example you might design a building and be able to test the amount of stress at various key points. The model may then be coloured to show the high stress areas.

Areas and volumes of shapes are easily calculated so the amount of material needed to make the model can be found. Some CAD software produces bills of materials so that production of the model can be costed.

CAD packages for designing electronic circuits may allow you to test the circuits in advance of building the real thing.

Advantages of using CAD software:

- Much **faster development** of designs. Pre-drawn components speed up creation of designs, as they do not have to be drawn from scratch.
- **Three-dimensional views** of models cannot easily be drawn on paper. The angle of view can also be changed so you can see the model from all sides.
- Designs can be **easily edited**. This allows for some experimentation with the design as features can be tried out, and then edited if they are not appropriate.
- Designs or parts of designs can be saved and **re-used** in other projects.
- Fast and automatic **calculation** of quantities such as stress in a building.

Once a design is finished it can be saved, and then:

- Printed on a printer, but more usually it would be output to a graph plotter which can draw on large pieces of paper.
- Output to a computer-aided manufacturing (CAM) process.

Computer-aided manufacturing

Output from a CAD design can be converted into a sequence of instructions for special types of CNC machine, which will then manufacture the item.

CNC machines may be:

- lathes for turning metal or wood;
- milling machines for cutting metal shapes;
- drills for making circular holes;
- welding machines for welding metal parts together;
- soldering machines for creating electronic circuit boards;
- knitting and sewing machines for manufacturing garments;
- robots.

CAD/CAM is the term used for the whole process of using a computer to design an

> Computer Numerical Control (CNC) machines receive instructions as a sequence of numbers and can be used for CAM.

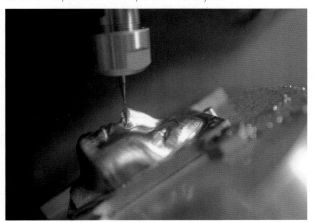

Figure 5.21 *A milling machine may be used as part of the CAD/CAM process to shape a metal object.*

CAD/CAM greatly speeds up the process of designing and manufacturing.

object and then outputting the finished design to a CNC machine, which manufactures it.

Computer-controlled machinery will produce accurate results and will minimise wastage. More importantly, it will do so consistently. The manufacturing process can be continuous and changes in design can be made with little interruption to the manufacturing process.

Summary

- **01** CAD/CAM is the process of using computers to design and then manufacture objects.
- **02** CAD (computer-aided design) is used to draw and edit a design in three dimensions using a vector graphics program.
- **03** Completed designs are sent to CNC (computer numerical control) machines such as milling machines or lathes which manufacture the item.
- **04** CNC machines use numerical input as instructions for the machine to manufacture an object.
- **05** The whole process of design and manufacture is fast.

5.12 CAL and computers in school administration

COMPUTER-ASSISTED LEARNING (CAL): A way to learn a skill using a computer and interactive software on CD or DVD, or by using the Internet. Using CAL programs can be a more enjoyable way to learn than traditional methods.

Computers are being used in schools to make the learning process easier and more enjoyable, and if learning is fun then pupils are going to be better motivated. CAL stands for computer-assisted learning and describes educational software that is run on computers to help people learn about a particular subject.

CAL programs are usually interactive. This means that the pupil participates when the program is running, either by selecting options or entering data. An example of this may be a multiple-choice test on a topic just covered. The test is marked automatically and feedback is given to the pupils about how well they did, and what they should do to revise their weak points.

A CAL program may use:

- **Text**: To describe and explain the subject matter.
- **Graphics**: Pictures are often a better way to illustrate a topic than lots of text.
- **Videos**: Short movies.
- **Animation**: Moving graphics.

Figure 5.22 *A CAL program can use self-assessment tests.*

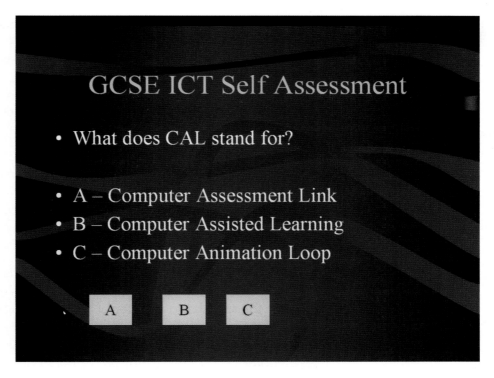

- **Sound**: A commentary may be recorded, or sound effects. A piece of music can add atmosphere when played in the background.
- **Hyperlinks**: Click on a hyperlink and the display will change to another screen.
- **Self-assessment**: Tests to see how well you are learning.

Many CAL programs are developed using multimedia software applications such as Microsoft PowerPoint, but some are now web-based and can be found on the Internet.

An example of a CAL site which will help you learn about GCSE ICT is http://www.theteacher.org.uk.

Advantages of CAL:

- Pupils can learn on their own and at their own speed.
- Pupils can repeatedly go over topics that they have found difficult to understand.
- There is immediate feedback from assessments so the pupil knows how well they are doing.
- More interesting ways of learning result in better motivation.

Disadvantages of CAL:

- The teacher may not be aware of a pupil who has some difficulties.
- CAL programs have to be bought.
- It takes time for teachers to develop their own CAL software.

Learning does not stop when you leave school. CAL programs can help study at home: they do not have to be used only in lessons, and they are a great help when revising for exams!

CAL programs can be used in colleges or even in adult evening classes for people who want to learn new skills such as learning a foreign language or composing music.

133

Pupils generally learn better when they study on their own and can learn at their own pace.

147

134

Computer databases in schools allow important information to be found quickly.

School administration

Computers in schools are not only found in the classrooms. The school office probably has several, and they are used for a wide range of administrative tasks.

There will be a database of all pupil details stored on the school computer system. The details stored on this database will be:

- Pupil personal details (name, date of birth, nationality, religion, etc.).
- Home details (address, telephone number, etc.).
- Contact (name and telephone number of person to contact in case of emergency).
- School details (date of joining school, form, form tutor, etc.).
- Other fields may include details about how the pupil travels to school, school dinners, and any medical problems the pupil may have.

This database can be searched to produce class lists or to quickly find the contact details for any specific pupil.

Every school takes a register of pupils, usually twice a day, and the attendance record is stored on the computer system. It should make it easier to determine whether any pupil is absent from school and whether there are abnormal patterns of absence that need to be investigated.

Some schools use a swipe card system of registration or an OMR reader to input attendance register information from sheets marked by the teachers.

135

Many schools have computerised systems of registration.

Figure 5.23 *A school register uses OMR to input attendance data.*

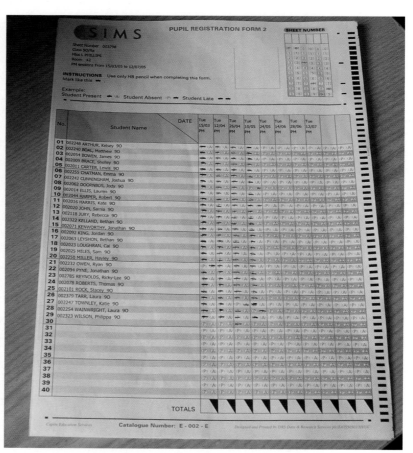

Storing the results of assessments and exams in each subject will monitor pupil progress. In this way, pupils who are failing to make progress can be identified and the reasons investigated.

Computers are also now widely used by school administrators for creating the timetable, the schedule of lessons, and which teachers and rooms are assigned to them. Creating a school timetable is a complex exercise and a computer is programmed to identify when problems occur (e.g. a teacher assigned to take two classes at the same time).

Here is a list of a number of school administration tasks that could be done on the school computer system:

● Spreadsheets could be used to plan the school **budget**. Allocations of money could be made, keeping the total expenditure within fixed limits.

● Word-processing programs could be used to prepare **circulars** or **letters** to parents.

● **Orders** and **invoices** can be tracked by recording them on a computer database.

● In secondary schools the process of administering pupil entries for **exams** is complex, but is made simpler by using a computer database.

● In many schools the **library** is administered using computers. A database of all titles kept in the school library helps pupils to find books quickly, and the computer system will also record book loans. See Section 5.4 for more on computers in libraries.

● An **inventory** of all items the school has bought can be kept up-to-date using a database. This may be important for insurance purposes.

● A school **intranet** may have a number of useful web pages for pupils.

The benefit of using computers in school administration is mainly that jobs can be completed faster and in an organised manner, and the results can be stored in such a way as to be useful later on.

<table>
<tr><td colspan="2">Using a computer to create the school timetable means it will be done quicker and there will be fewer mistakes.</td></tr>
</table>

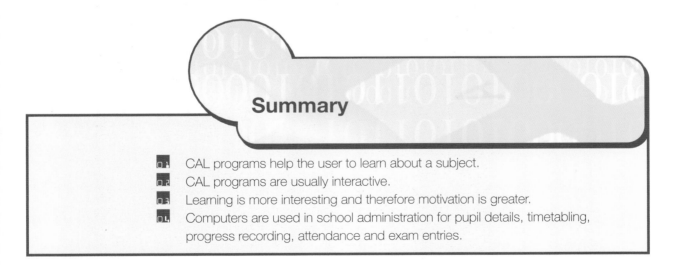

Summary

01 CAL programs help the user to learn about a subject.
02 CAL programs are usually interactive.
03 Learning is more interesting and therefore motivation is greater.
04 Computers are used in school administration for pupil details, timetabling, progress recording, attendance and exam entries.

Practice questions 5

1 Computer systems are used to process many millions of weather data readings to produce weather forecasts.

   a) State three different types of sensor used to take weather readings. [3]

   b) Give two situations where accurate weather forecasts are needed. [2]

   c) What sort of computers are used to produce weather forecasts? [1]

2 Robots are often used in the car manufacturing process to perform a number of different tasks when making cars.

   a) Describe three different jobs that robots can do. [3]

   b) Give three advantages of using robots. [3]

   c) Give two disadvantages of using robots. [2]

3 Life-support systems are used to monitor patients in hospitals.

   a) State three sensors used in a life-support system. [3]

   b) Give three advantages of using a computer-controlled life-support system. [3]

Can you remember…?

1 What does CAD stand for? What does CAM stand for?

2 What is an expert system?

3 What are the benefits of using a computerised expert system instead of a human expert?

4 Are the following real-time, batch-processing, or online real-time transaction systems?

- Theatre booking system.
- Billing system.
- Process control in car manufacturing.
- Payroll.

5 What input method is mainly used in libraries?

6 What does CAL stand for? What are the benefits of CAL?

Stages of information processing

Computers process data to produce information.

The data processing that computers do can really be thought of in three separate stages:

- **Input:** Data is entered into the computer in digital format.
- **Processing:** The data is processed in some way.
- **Output:** The results are displayed for humans to read, or are sent in digital format to another computer or digital device.

When computer programmers write software, they normally deal with these sections in turn. A simple program would have an input section, a processing section and an output section.

Example: A computer program can be used to calculate the average of a number of exam marks.

Input: The exam marks need to be input (perhaps typed in at a keyboard).

Processing: The marks are added up, and divided by the number of marks that were input.

Output: The average mark is output (printed or displayed on a monitor).

Practice questions 6

Each of these are **non-computer** systems. Identify the input, processing and output sections.

1 A DIY enthusiast builds a chest of drawers after reading the instructions that came in the kit. He then shows it off to his wife.
2 John played a tune very loudly on his trumpet. He pressed the stops on the trumpet to alter the notes which he read from a sheet of music.

For each of the following **computer** processes, can you say what is involved in each of the three data processing stages.

● What data is input?
● What processing is done?
● What is output?

3 Using a computer to print out the fixture list for a football club. The fixture list must be printed in the order the games are played.

4 A computerised burglar alarm system.

7

Controls on data

7.1 Data collection

The first part of any computer processing system involves collecting the data before it can be input. All data must come from somewhere, and the methods of collecting it are many and varied.

7.1.1 Questionnaires

Many research projects involve obtaining data from people, and one way of doing this is by printing sets of questions on paper, and asking people to write their answers on the same sheet.

The design of questionnaires is important, and clear instructions must be given to make sure the respondent fills in the answers properly. The questions must generate answers that are useful as input data, and not vague and indecisive responses, which cannot be used.

Here is an example of a bad question:

What did you think of your 'Cherrybobbins' chocolate bar?

There are a large number of different responses to a question like this. That makes it difficult to enter as data, and the computer may not be able to analyse them enough to be able to give a measure of the popularity of the chocolate bar.

Here is an example of a better question:

How did you find your 'Cherrybobbins' chocolate bar? (Tick only one box.)

| **Disgusting** ☐ | **Unimpressed** ☐ | **Average** ☐ |
| **Fairly tasty** ☐ | **Delicious** ☐ | |

When the questionnaires are returned by the people who have filled them in, the answers are usually entered into a database, which will then analyse them and output reports on the research.

Advantages of questionnaires:

- Many questionnaires can be issued at one time.
- Questions can be set whose answers match the fields in a database. This will make the responses easier to transfer to the computer ready for analysis.

> **137**
> Questionnaires are a good way of collecting data from people, but they must be easy to understand and easy to fill in.

> **138**
> Questions with options to select are more useful than 'open' questions.

Disadvantages of questionnaires:

● People do not always like filling questionnaires in, so there may be a poor response with very few completed ones returned.

■ **Activity 7.1** **Spreadsheet**

Design a questionnaire to enable you to collect data about how much pocket money pupils are given each week. Print out a number of copies and distribute them among other pupils who you know.

When you get the forms back, enter the details on a spreadsheet which you have designed for this purpose, and use it to calculate the average amount of pocket money they receive.

How do your results compare with those from other pupils?

7.1.2 Data capture forms

DATA CAPTURE: Another name for collecting data and getting it into the computer.

Another method of collecting data on paper is to use a data capture form. This is a specially prepared form that is filled in and returned to the computer, where the data is entered.

We all have to fill in forms at some time, whether we are applying for a driving licence or a bank account, joining a club or ordering some items from a mail order firm.

Boxes are frequently used for entering data, where one character only is entered in each box. This forces the person entering the data to write clearly, and avoids errors arising from a data entry clerk not being able to read the data.

Boxes also mean that data will be in the correct format, for example where a postcode is to be entered:

Postcode:

As with questionnaires, each item of data that is filled in on the form should correspond with a field in a database. The data on the form should be arranged in the order in which it is to be entered on the computer, and it would be helpful for those entering the data if the layout of the form on the computer screen is very similar to the layout of the form on paper.

Copying data from forms and typing them into a computer is called **transcribing** the data, and this process is the source of many errors in data. This is hardly surprising as it must be very tedious to type data from forms all day long!

When data capture forms are created much thought is put into their design. It is most important that the data returned is accurate, legible and not missed out!

Design features of data capture forms include:

The data from data capture forms is transcribed into a computer (usually into a database).

● **Instructions** should be given on how to fill in the data. They must be unambiguous (in other words their meaning should be clear).

● **Boxes** are used for each letter or digit. To improve legibility, the form may ask for capital letters only to be used.
● **Examples** may be given. Some fields may be entered in a variety of different ways. For example a date may be given as '05/11/06', 'November 5th 2006', etc.

Here is a badly designed data capture form:

Smoking survey

Name: _____

Age:_____Year:_____

Do you smoke?_____

If you smoke, how many do you smoke per day?_____

Do your parents smoke?_____

Here is a well-designed data capture form:

Smoking Survey
Please complete all sections and return this form to your form tutor.

SECTION 1 : Personal Details

First Name ☐☐☐☐☐☐☐☐☐☐☐☐

Surname ☐☐☐☐☐☐☐☐☐☐☐☐

Form (E.g. 8B) ☐☐   Date of Birth ☐☐/☐☐/☐☐
E.g. 03/05/88

SECTION 2 : Smoking habits

[1] Do you smoke cigarettes?
Tick one box
☐ No
☐ Less than 10 per day
☐ 10–20 per day
☐ More than 20 per day

[2] Do your parents smoke cigarettes?
Mother Father
☐ ☐ No
☐ ☐ Less than 10 per day
☐ ☐ 10–20 per day
☐ ☐ More than 20 per day

7.1.3 Datalogging

DATALOGGING: An automatic way of collecting data from sensors. Readings are measured at regular intervals and sent to the computer.

Computers can only process **digital** data.

Datalogging is useful for taking regular measurements over a fixed time period. It is particularly useful in places where humans do not want to go.

Collecting data using questionnaires or data capture forms often involves gathering many sheets of paper, and then keying in the data from the responses written on them. There are automatic methods that do not require any human involvement.

Readings from sensors are taken at regular intervals and used as input to a computer. The frequency at which the readings are measured depends on the application. A system measuring a patient's pulse in a hospital, will take measurements more often than a sensor measuring the temperature of the air for a weather station.

Examples of measurements taken by sensors may include temperature, light, sound, pressure, humidity or levels of infrared radiation. Readings from sensors are normally analogue readings and so they need to be sent to an analogue-to-digital converter (ADC) to change them into digital signals so the computer can process them.

In datalogging systems, the data is stored and analysed later. The data may be input to a spreadsheet, where it could be used to produce graphs or statistical information, or it may be stored in a database and used to produce printed reports.

Datalogging systems do not need humans to intervene so they are often used in remote places, or places where it is dangerous such as places with high levels of radiation.

Examples of datalogging systems:

● A science experiment in school has sensors measuring the temperature of a hot liquid as it cools in different types of container. The readings are taken every 30 seconds and input into a spreadsheet. A chart of the cooling rate can then be displayed.

● A weather station has sensors measuring the air pressure and temperature every 5 minutes. The readings are stored in a database so that patterns of weather can be studied, to help with future weather forecasting.

Figure 7.1 *Datalogging can be used to record data from science experiments.*

7.1.4 Optical mark recognition

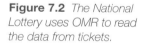
Pre-printed sheets of paper have boxes on them where lines or marks may be drawn. These sheets are then put into an Optical Mark Reader that detects where the marks have been drawn by measuring light reflected from the paper: dark lines reflect less light than white paper.

Schools often use optical mark recognition (OMR) for recording attendance. Registration sheets are marked in one of two columns to indicate whether a pupil is present or absent. The sheets for each class are collected together and fed into an optical mark reader, which automatically inputs the attendance data into the computer system.

Another use for OMR in schools is marking multiple choice exam papers. Each question has a number of possible answers and the pupil has to select the correct one and mark their choice on an OMR sheet. The sheets are fed into the reader and automatically marked. The computer processes the data and outputs the results for each pupil. See also Section 2.1.6.

Advantages of OMR:
- It is much faster to feed sheets into an optical mark reader than type in the data. The results are processed and output very quickly.
- Writing marks on a sheet of paper is easier than typing in the data.
- Scanning is accurate.
- Eliminates transcription errors.

Disadvantages of OMR:
- Sheets may not be readable if they are soiled or crumpled.
- Useful only for situations with a limited number of possible responses.

Figure 7.2 *The National Lottery uses OMR to read the data from tickets.*

7.1.5 Optical character recognition

Optical character recognition (OCR) is a method of inputting text that uses light to identify characters printed on a sheet of paper. The page of text is first scanned to create an image, then patterns of light and dark are sensed and compared with stored patterns to find the

7.1.5

Pages of text can be scanned and OCR software interprets the text which can then be edited in a word-processing document.

OPTICAL CHARACTER RECOGNITION (OCR): A means of reading text directly from paper using a scanner and placing it into a word-processing document. This can save a lot of time, as there is no need to type the text.

nearest matching character, which is then stored in a file. In this way pages of text can be converted into editable files. This is clearly much faster than typing the whole document again. See also Section 2.1.6.

Some advanced OCR software can also reproduce lines, shapes and tables, as well as scan pictures, so that complex pages can be input directly into a DTP publication.

The Post Office uses OCR to input postcode data from letters so that an automatic machine can sort them.

Advantages of OCR:
● A much faster method of text input than typing.

Disadvantages of OCR:
● Only a limited number of fonts will scan accurately. Obscure fonts such as script fonts will result in a large number of errors.
● Text will still need to be proofread. Spellcheckers may help here, but they may not find all errors.

7.1.6 Magnetic ink character recognition

MAGNETIC INK CHARACTER RECOGNITION (MICR): This is a method of input used by banks to read data from bank cheques. It is a fast method of processing cheques but the equipment is expensive to set up.

Banks use magnetic ink character recognition (MICR) to read data from bank cheques. See also Section 2.2.3.

The numbers and characters printed at the bottom of a cheque (cheque number, sort code and account number) are printed in magnetic ink, which is magnetised when fed into an MICR reader. The reader senses the magnetic patterns formed and the data is input automatically to the computer.

The standard MICR font used on bank cheques has only 14 characters:

0 1 2 3 4 5 6 7 8 9 ⑆ ⑈ ⑉ ⑇

Advantages of MICR:
● A fully automatic input method. No human intervention is needed apart from feeding the cheques into the reader.
● High-speed input.
● Soiled or crumpled cheques can still be read.
● High security. The font and ink are difficult to forge.
● Eliminates human errors (transcription errors).

Disadvantages of MICR:
● MICR equipment is expensive.
● The system can only use a few characters.

Small MICR readers are used in retail stores and supermarkets for reading data from cheques. The amount of the cheque still needs to be keyed by hand as it is not encoded in magnetic ink characters at the bottom of the cheque. Some MICR readers also read magnetic stripes off plastic cards.

Figure 7.3 *Small MICR readers can read data from one cheque at a time.*

7.1.7 Barcodes

A bar code is a set of parallel lines of differing thickness, which is used to identify a particular item. The lines represent a numerical code. See also Section 2.1.5.

Country Code   Manufacturer Code   Product Code   Check digit

Figure 7.4 *A 13-digit bar code (using the EAN-13 system).*

Most items have a 13-digit barcode (a system called EAN-13). There are some deviations from this pattern on some items. For example some smaller countries have 3-digit country codes, and books usually start with a 3-digit code (978) to show the remaining digits are the ISBN number.

Note that the price of the item is not coded as part of the barcode. This is because different shops may sell the same item at different prices, or a shop may want to offer the item at a reduced sale price. Barcodes are usually printed on to the item and cannot be changed.

Barcodes are read using a barcode reader. This can be a hand-held wand that is passed over the barcode, or it may be a barcode scanner built into a checkout over which the barcode is passed. A correct reading of the barcode is indicated by a beep. If no beep sounds, there is a reading error and the digits of the code will need to be keyed in manually.

A low-power laser beam passes over the barcode and the pattern of reflected light is sensed (dark lines reflect less light than white). The code pattern is converted into numerical data and input to the computer.

Barcodes are used:

- On most goods now sold in retail stores and supermarkets. The items being bought are scanned by a barcode reader at the checkout (POS terminal) (see Section 2.1.1);
- In libraries for recording the loan of books. Each book has a unique barcode and each member of the library has a membership card with a barcode printed on it (see Section 5.4).

■ Activity 7.2 Internet investigation

Use the Internet to find the countries that manufactured goods with these barcodes:

1 5060043493424;
2 4893022036142.

7.1.8 Magnetic strips

> Many credit or debit cards have magnetic strips with data recorded on them. The cards are read by swiping them through a card reader.

A magnetic strip (or stripe) is a short length of recordable magnetic tape sealed onto the surface or embedded into a card or ticket. The strip will have data recorded on it that identifies the card or its owner. This may be the account number of the cardholder.
To **swipe** a card with a magnetic strip means to pass the card through a **card reader** so the data on the strip can be read. See also Section 2.2.4.

Examples of magnetic strips:

Figure 7.5 *A magnetic strip is often found on the back of plastic cards.*

- **Credit cards** and **debit cards**: Recorded onto the strip is enough information about the bank and the owner's account for the card to be used to complete a financial transaction.
- **Credit card**: You borrow money from the credit card company, and have to pay it back later.
- **Debit card**: money is transferred directly out of your account.
- **ID card**: An identification card will have details about the owner of the card.
- **Phone card**: The strip stores the number of units left on the card.
- **Tickets**: Some travel tickets such as train tickets carry a magnetic strip.

Magnetic strips are easy to copy and card fraud has become an increasing problem. To guard against fraud, new methods of storing data on cards have been developed.

7.1.9 Laser cards

> Laser cards and smart cards are less easy to forge than magnetic strip cards.

Data is stored on the card using optical laser CD technology. Much more data can be held on a laser card than on a magnetic strip card: about 2 MB of data on current laser cards.

7.1.10 Smart cards

A very thin **memory chip** is embedded in the card. Personal information or account information is stored on the chip, but because they can store more data than a magnetic strip, they are being used for other applications such as storing a person's medical information.

Smart cards are more secure than magnetic strip cards and are less likely to be stolen and used in card fraud.

Many credit cards store a PIN, a secret personal number, and when you pay for an item, the card is swiped through a card reader and you are asked to enter the PIN on a keypad. This is for user authentication, checking that you are the rightful owner of the credit card. See also Section 2.2.4.

Figure 7.6 *Chip and PIN system. The credit card is swiped and the PIN needs to be entered before payment is allowed.*

7.2 Validation

1.50
Data **validation** is used to check that data is sensible before it is processed. Typical validation checks are range checks, presence checks, format checks and the use of check digits.

It is often very important to make sure that no 'freak' readings are entered into a data processing system. Data validation is the process of making sure the data meets these requirements. In other words, validation makes sure that the data is sensible data.

It is important for businesses to check data carefully. Incorrect data can cause customer dissatisfaction if incorrect bills are sent out, or if incorrect amounts of money are deducted from people's bank accounts. Businesses spend a great deal of time and money in making sure that there are no mistakes in their input data. (See also Section 1.3.1.)

7.2.1 Range check

1.51
Data is rejected if it is outside the specified limits of a **range check**. This is a check for data that has been recorded or transcribed incorrectly.

A range check makes sure that an item of data lies within a specified range of numbers. A 'smallest' allowable value is set as well as a 'largest', and every time a numerical item of data is entered a check is made to see whether it falls within this range of values. If it does not, the data is not accepted for processing.

Examples:

● The month part of a date must lie between 1 and 12.
● A pupil's percentage exam mark must lie between 0 and 100.

● Appointment times for a doctor. The hour part must lie between 0 and 24.

Ranges are normally set for numerical data, but ranges may be defined for other types of data. For example, an exam grade may be restricted to a set of characters 'A' to 'G'.

7.2.2 Check digits

Another type of validation check involves an extra digit that has been added onto the end of numerical data. This **check digit** is calculated from the other digits using a predefined formula.

When the data is entered, the calculation is performed by the computer to make sure the check digit is correct. If it is not, then it means the data has not been read correctly and will not be accepted for processing.

Check digits are used on data that is input using reading devices such as barcode readers or card readers.

Examples of check digits:

● **Barcodes**: In 13-digit barcodes, the 13th digit is the check digit calculated using the first 12. When a barcode is read by a barcode reader, the computer calculates the check digit to make sure it is correct. If it is not, the barcode is rejected.
● **ISBN**: Most books have an ISBN (International Standard Book Number). The final digit of this is a check digit.
● **Credit/debit cards**: Some credit card numbers are quite long (16 digits) and the last digit is a check digit.

Using a **check digit** makes sure that data automatically input has been read correctly.

■ Activity 7.3 Spreadsheet

Making a check digit calculator

1 Find an item with a 13-digit barcode on it (e.g. 5016442001876).
2 Make a note of the first 12 digits. The 13th digit is the check digit and this is how to make a barcode calculator to check it.
3 Put the first 12 digits into the first column of a spreadsheet starting from cell B3 as shown in Figure 7.7. Draw headings and boxes.

	A	B	C	D
1				
2		Bar code	Calculations	
3		5	5	
4		0	0	
5		1	1	
6		6	18	
7		4	4	
8		4	12	
9		2	2	
10		0	0	
11		0	0	
12		1	3	
13		8	8	
14		7	21	
15			74	
16		Check Digit is:	6	
17				

The calculations in column C are as follows. (Make sure you enter a formula in each cell from C3 to C14.)

The digits in cells B4, B6, B8, …, (every other digit) are multiplied by 3.

The other digits in cells B3, B5, B7, …, remain as they are.

The results are added up in cell C15.

The final calculation in cell C16:

The check digit is the number that needs to be added to the total in cell C15 to make the result an exact multiple of 10.

The formula in cell C16 is this: =10 – MOD(C15,10).

4   Now try it out on other 13-digit bar codes you can find on items from your kitchen.

7.2.3   Presence check

The computer makes sure that a field is not null. A null field is one where data has not been entered when it should have been. A presence check is a check for missing data: data that may have been missed when transcribing, or maybe somebody forgot to enter it.

Example: When supplying details on an on-screen form, users have to enter items such as their name, address, postcode, telephone number, etc. This form may be part of a database system, or it may be a web page application such as a member registration form. Some of the fields may be marked as essential and the data will not be accepted if any of these fields are left blank.

Figure 7.8 *In Microsoft Access, users can designate fields as essential by setting the Required property to 'Yes'.*

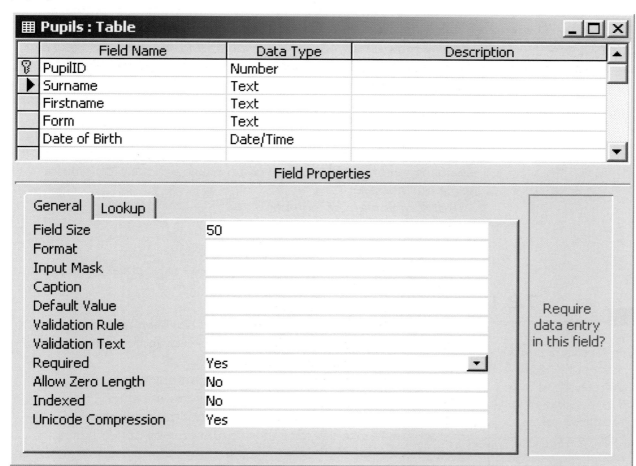

Pupils : Table			
Field Name	**Data Type**	**Description**	
PupilID	Number		
Surname	Text		
Firstname	Text		
Form	Text		
Date of Birth	Date/Time		

Field Properties

General	Lookup

Field Size	50
Format	
Input Mask	
Caption	
Default Value	
Validation Rule	
Validation Text	
Required	Yes
Allow Zero Length	No
Indexed	No
Unicode Compression	Yes

Require data entry in this field?

7.2.4 Batch total

If a number of records of data are collected together and entered at the same time, there may be a batch total included.

This is a total that is calculated using the data from all the records. When the data is entered, the batch total is also entered and the computer will check that the batch total is correct. If it is not, then it usually means that some item of data has been missed out, or one of the numbers has been incorrectly entered.

Sometimes when keying in numbers it is easy to transpose some of the digits. For example the number 12345 may be entered as 12435. The batch total will not then agree, and the computer will indicate that an error has occurred.

Example: A list of 20 items and their prices are to be entered into a database. The prices are added together to provide a batch total. When the data is keyed in, the batch total is also entered. The computer checks whether the total is correct, and will not accept the data if it is not.

Hash total

A hash total is really the same as a batch total but the resulting number has no meaning. For example, it may be the sum of people's telephone numbers or the sum of account numbers.

7.3 Verification

If data is copied from one medium to another, for example when data on paper is keyed into a computer and saved on the hard disk, it is called **transcribing** the data.

Data may also have been sent (transmitted) from one computer medium to another, and verification checks are needed to make sure the data received is the same as the data that was sent.

Verification checks whether data has been transcribed correctly.

The problem with humans is that they get tired and make mistakes, and mistakes in data could cause serious problems for some businesses.

Transcription errors may be:

- **Omission**: Leaving data out.
- **Transposition**: For example, typing 1324 instead of 1234.
- **Spelling mistakes**: For example, typing Davies instead of Davis.

7.3.1 Visual check

One of the simplest ways to verify data that has been typed into a computer is to compare visually the source data and the transcribed data.

If the data that has been typed is a document, this is called proofreading. There are many errors that are not found by a spellchecker such as misspelled words that are perfectly valid words themselves, and these could only be noticed using a visual check.

Visually checking large amounts of data can become very tiring and it is easy to miss errors, so this method of verification is not guaranteed to find all the transcription errors.

7.3.2 Double keying

A more reliable method of verification is double keying. The data is entered twice, usually by two different data entry clerks and the two versions of the data are compared. If they are identical, the computer will accept them for processing, but if there are any differences, this means that one or other of the clerks has made a mistake, and the data will be checked or entered again.

It is extremely unlikely that two different people will make the same typing mistake, and although double keying of data takes much longer and is double the amount of work, it is a very effective way of making sure no errors are made when transcribing data.

7.3.3 Parity

Parity is a method of verifying that transmitted data has not been corrupted. If data is transmitted through telephone lines or over a network there are many possible sources of 'noise' where the data may be accidentally changed.

Parity methods will not be able to correct the error, they will only be able to detect whether an error has occurred. If there is an error, the data will need to be transmitted again.

All data in computer systems, whether it is text, graphics, sounds or video clips, is represented as numbers. These numbers are usually thought of as binary numbers that only involve 0s and 1s so an item of data may look like:

01001011

Parity checks involve adding an extra bit (binary digit) onto the end of a binary item of data. An even parity system makes sure that the total number of 1s in each number is an even number; an odd parity system uses an odd total number of 1s.

Example: Assume an even parity system is being used.

All characters can be represented by 7-bit ASCII codes. An extra 8th bit is added onto each number before it is transmitted.

Even parity means that when all the bits in a number are added together the total is an even number (i.e. the number of 1s is an even number).

0110100 has a total of three 1s, so a parity bit of 1 must be added to make it 01101001.

0101110 has a total of four 1s, so a parity bit of 0 must be added to make it 01011100.

When the transmitted data is received, each number is checked to make sure that the total of all binary digits in each number is even.

154

Double keying data is an effective method of verification even though it takes much longer than normal data entry.

PARITY CHECK: A means of checking for data transmission errors. An extra bit is added to the end of each binary number.

ASCII: The American Standard Code for Information Interchange. A system of binary digits representing letters, numbers and other characters. It is the most widely used system of allocating a numerical code to each character.

155

In an even parity system the total number of 1s in an item of data is an even number. Odd parity systems may also be used, in which case the total number of 1s in an item of data is an odd number.

■ Activity 7.4 Parity exercise

A computer using even parity receives the following data. Each 8-bit number consists of a 7-bit ASCII code and a parity bit.

1 Which number has been corrupted?
2 Find a table of ASCII codes on the Internet, and use it to translate the message into text.

> **10010000**
> **10001011**
> **10011000**
> **10100000**
> **01000001**
> **10011010**
> **10001011**

Summary

- 01 Questionnaires are a good way of collecting data from people, but they must be designed properly.
- 02 Responses on data capture forms correspond to fields in a database.
- 03 Responses from questionnaires and data capture forms have to be transcribed into a computer.
- 04 Datalogging uses sensors to automatically capture data.
- 05 OMR senses where marks are written on a pre-printed sheet.
- 06 OCR uses a scanner to input text from a printed document into a word processor so it can be edited.
- 07 MICR uses a special reader that magnetises characters printed on bank cheques.
- 08 Barcodes are a fast method of capturing data which identifies items such as goods in a supermarket or books in a library.
- 09 Card readers are used to read account data from magnetic strips embedded into the back of cards or tickets.
- 10 Smart cards have memory chips with authentication data stored on them.
- 11 Validation is a method of checking whether data is sensible.
- 12 Range checks make sure that data lies within predetermined limits.
- 13 Check digits are extra digits added onto numerical data.
- 14 Computers check that the check digits are correct when data is input.
- 15 Presence checks make sure that no essential data is missing.
- 16 Batch totals are totals of similar numerical data items. The batch total is also input so the computer can check it is correct.
- 17 Verification checks for transcription errors or transmission errors.

18 Proofreading a document is an example of a visual check.

19 Double keying involves entering data twice. The computer only accepts the data if the two copies are identical.

20 Parity bits are extra bits added to data to check for transmission errors.

Practice questions 7

1 Which input method (OMR, OCR, MICR or barcodes) is most likely to be used for each of the following?

   a) Reading data from bank cheques.

   b) Reading data from lottery tickets.

   c) Scanning text into a word processor.

   d) Recording details of book lending in a library.   [4]

2 Describe a suitable validation check for each of the following types of input data:

   a) The month part of a date given in numerical format (e.g. 12/04/05).

   b) A set of exam marks.

   c) The number of a credit card account.   [3]

3 John Smith was born on 12/09/85. When his data was entered into a computer database, the data appeared as John Ssmith and 12/99/85. Which of these two errors would most likely to have been picked up by a validation check and which one by a verification check?   [2]

Can you remember…?

1 What validation method is used with barcodes?

2 What are the two main methods of data verification?

3 What does a presence check do?

4 What does OMR stand for?

5 What does OCR stand for?

6 What does MICR stand for?

7 Why is parity used? What does it mean if a system uses even parity?

8 When collecting data, what advantage do questionnaires have over interviews?

8 Storing information

8.1 Data types

Computers appear to be able to process a wide variety of different types of data. The table below lists the main types of data:

Data Type	Example	Description
Text String (Alphanumeric)	John Smith	Text consisting of letters, numbers or other characters such as punctuation marks.
Integer	43	Any whole number (positive or negative but no fractions).
Decimal (Real)	432.5	Any number including whole numbers and fractions.
Currency	£12.50	Money (even in foreign currencies such as $ or €).
Date/Time	04/10/06	Any time or date. The way the time or date is displayed depends on how it is formatted.
Calculated field	An average of exam marks	Data that is calculated from other items of data.
Picture		A graphic (bitmap or vector).
Sound	A beep from a bar code reader	
Video	A video introduction to a computer game	

ASCII: The American Standard Code for Information Interchange. A system of binary digits representing letters, numbers and other characters. It is the most widely used system of allocating a numerical code to each character.

The last two data types demonstrate the disadvantage of paper as these two types of data cannot be shown on the printed page, whereas computers can produce sounds and display video clips or animated graphics.

In fact, computers can only process numbers, so data of all these types must be represented as numbers before they can be processed. For example, every character in a piece of text has a numerical code associated with it, and each pixel of a bitmap graphic can be coded by its colour.

8.2 Files, records, fields

FIELD: A single data item.

A **field** is a single data item. When data is stored in a field, the type of the data has to be specified and no data of other types can be stored in it.

Examples of fields and their types:

- Surname – string
- Date of birth – date
- Selling price – currency.

RECORD: A collection of related fields.

A **record** consists of a collection of related fields. For example, a pupil's record in a school database will have fields only related to that pupil (surname, forename, date of birth, form, etc.) and not any of another pupil's data.

FILE: A collection of related records.

A **file** is a collection of related records. An example of a file is the file of records of all pupils in the school.

DATA STRUCTURE TABLE: A list of a file's fields and their types.

Example: A school would like to create a simple file of pupil names and their dates of birth. The file of pupil's data has the **data structure table**:

Field Name	Field Type
Pupil ID	Integer
Surname	String
Forename	String
Date of Birth	Date

The file itself is displayed in the next table:

Pupil ID	Surname	Forename	Date of Birth
4001	Jenkins	Jennifer	16/05/1992
4002	Smith	Sally	04/09/1991
4003	Thomas	Talfryn	12/05/1992
4004	Williams	Iestyn	16/04/1993
4005	Williams	Walter	03/06/1991

This **file** consists of **five records**. (The highlighted yellow row is one record).

Each **record** in this file has **four fields**. (Each column represents a field.)

One of the fields is used to **uniquely identify each record**. This is called the **key field**.

The key field in this example is the **Pupil ID** field: no two pupils would have the same Pupil ID number (but, for example, they may have the same name or date of birth).

A file may be **sorted** in order of its key field.

Sometimes there is more than one field used as a key and they are then referred to as the primary key field, the secondary key field, and so on.

> **156**
> A key field uniquely identifies each record. No two records will have the same data in their **key field**.

8.3 Fixed and variable length fields

There are two types of field:

- **Fixed length field:** The length of the field (the number of characters in it) is predetermined, and is the same in every record of the file.
- **Variable length field:** The length of the field may be different in each record.

8.3.1 Fixed length fields

The data in a fixed length field always has the same length.

When numerical fields such as integers are stored they are usually saved in memory or on disk as a fixed number of bytes. The number of bytes is already set and depends on the software. The same applies for decimal, currency or date fields.

If fixed length fields are used for strings (text) then 'space' characters may need to be added to pad out the data until it is the specified length.

If all the fields in a record are fixed length fields, then the file has fixed length records: each record is the same size. This will speed up processing of the file, because the computer will know how large each record is, and will be able to calculate where each record begins in the file.

It will also be able to calculate where in a record a field value will begin, as it can count the number of characters.

Direct methods of data access may then be used, which will speed up the retrieval of information.

> **BYTE:** A defined number of bits (1s or 0s). **1 byte = 8 bits**. Typically represents one character.

> **157**
> Fixed length fields allow the computer to calculate where data can be found, so data access is faster.

Pupil ID	Surname	Forename	Date of Birth
4001	Jenkins	Jennifer	16/05/1992

Integer (Fixed size = 4 bytes)   25 characters (= 25 bytes)   30 characters (= 30 bytes)   Date (Fixed size = 4 bytes)

In this example of fixed length fields in a record, the record length is 63 bytes. Every record in the file will be exactly 63 bytes long.

8.3.2 Variable length fields

158

Variable length fields do not need extra characters added to data to pad out fields to specified lengths, so the fields will only be as long as they need to be for the data values. For example, the field whose value is 'Tom' will be smaller than the field whose value is 'Jonathan'. Record sizes will therefore be smaller than for fixed length records.

The computer will need to know where one field ends and the next begins, so special characters called separators are used between each field and between each record. To find a specific item of data the computer will need to go through the file counting the number of separators.

> Variable length fields do not have extra (sometimes 'padding') characters, so file sizes are smaller.

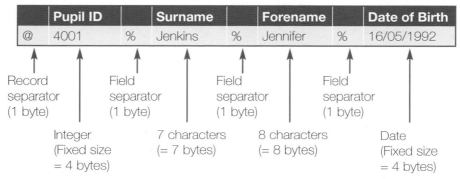

In this example of variable length fields, the total record length is 27 bytes, but every record will be a different length depending on the data values.

Fixed length records or variable length records?

- Fixed length: Processing the data will be faster, but the file sizes will be larger so more storage space will be needed when the file is saved in memory or on disk.
- Variable length: Smaller file sizes, but the computer cannot use direct access methods so processing the records will be slower.

8.4 Uses of files

There are many applications where whole files are used for processing, and all the records are used, but there are times where only one record at a time is needed. Some files are permanent and need to be kept up-to-date but some are temporary and can be destroyed once they have been used.

8.4.1 Master file

A master file is a permanent file. It is often the main file of data used by a business, and may contain a large number of records with many fields. The data stored will be important data that the business

MASTER FILE: The main file that a business uses, and must be regularly updated.

needs to use frequently, such as customer details, stock control data or sales information.

It is vital for a business to safeguard against the loss of a master file, as the successful running of the business probably depends very much on it. Security measures must be in place to avoid all risk of the master file being damaged or accessed by hackers.

Master files are usually sorted into order of their primary key field.

Example fields in a stock master file:
- **Stock ID:** The key field that uniquely identifies each item of stock.
- **Description:** What the item is.
- **Selling price:** The amount the item is sold for.
- **Stock level:** How many of the item are currently held in stock.
- **Reorder level:** When the stock level gets to this, more of the item needs to be ordered.
- **Supplier ID:** The code of the supplier of the item.
- **Sales this month:** How many of the item have been sold this month.
- **Sales this year:** How many of the item have been sold this year.

There will be many more fields including details of how many items have been ordered this year, the date when an item was last sold, category codes, reorder quantities, buying prices, barcode, etc.

8.4.2 Transaction file

TRANSACTION FILE: Temporary file used to update the master file each period.

Transaction files are temporary files that are used to update the data in the master file.

A business will decide on a **period of processing**. This will be the amount of time between updates of the master file. It may be a day, a week, a month or even a year.

Once the update has been completed, the transaction file can be deleted. In practice, however, for security reasons, it will be kept for a while in case there are any problems with the master file, in which case the transaction update run can be done again.

A retail business may put its sales for each period on a transaction file. There is no need for all the fields on the master file to be recorded, so the transaction file will be a smaller file than the master file. There would then be an update of the master file each period.

Example fields on a simple sales transaction file:
- **Transaction ID:** The key field that uniquely identifies the transaction.
- **Type:** Sale or purchase.
- **Date:** The date of the transaction.
- **Stock ID:** The item that has been sold.
- **Quantity:** How many of the item were sold or bought.

Other fields may include the identity of the sales person or the customer identity (if it was a mail order sale), but it is also important to identify the fields that are not stored on the transaction file. For example, there is no need to have the selling price or the item description as part of the transaction, because that information is already stored on the master file and does not change for each transaction.

8.4.3 Archive file

ARCHIVE FILE: Files kept in long-term storage for legal reasons and are rarely accessed.

An archive file is a file put aside for long-term storage. It may never be used again, but just occasionally, a situation may arise where an auditor or the police may need to access an item of information from it.

An archive file will contain records that are no longer in current use, but may need to be accessed occasionally.

There are sometimes legal reasons for storing archive files. A business may be legally bound to store details of its business transactions for several years.

Archive files are often stored off-site. It is not a good idea to fill a computer system's storage space with archive files that are rarely needed.

There are also archive files that are kept for historical reasons. Libraries may store scanned copies of documents or newspapers for future reference.

8.5 Databases

DATABASE: A database is an organised collection of related data. It is possible to add, edit, manage and retrieve data from a database. The structure of a database allows data to be found and used quickly.

A database is an organised collection of related files.

The important thing about a database is that it is organised in such a way as to make access of information fast and simple.

Example: A school may keep a database which has:

- a file of pupil details;
- a file of staff details;
- a file of the current timetable.

It needs to be easy for a teacher to find out exactly where a pupil can be found at any time (the room, the teacher and the lesson being taught).

When you create a database (which you will need to do for your coursework), the first task is to decide on the files (Microsoft Access calls them Tables) that are going to be stored and the relationships between them: some of the files may be linked through common fields. For example, a Timetable file may have a field 'Staff ID' which also appears in a Staff file.

A database allows you to:

It is important to decide on the files in a database and the **relationships** between them. A **properly structured** database does not store the same data twice.

- define and edit the **data structure** (the field names and types);
- **enter** and **edit** the data;
- **import** data from other databases or applications;
- **search** for data;
- **sort** data into alphabetic or numeric order;
- **validate** the data when it is entered;
- create **forms** that display the data in an attractive way;
- output **reports**;

- set **security levels** to restrict access to some data;
- access the data on other computers if the database is on a **network**.

See also Section 4.7.

8.6 File storage

FILENAME: A means of identifying a file.

FILE EXTENSION: A means of identifying the type of a file.

BACKING STORAGE: Storage used to store data and programs that are not currently being used. It is non-volatile storage: data is permanently saved.

Files may have a structure other than a collection of related data records. There are graphics files and sound files that have different structures.

When a file is saved onto backing storage, it is given a name and an extension. For example a word-processed document may be saved as **project.doc** on the hard disk of a computer.

The name can be any text that enables the user to easily identify the file, but the extension is an indication of the type of the file and is defined by the software that created the file. Some common file extensions are given in the following table.

File extension	File type
.doc	Microsoft Word document
.mdb	Microsoft Access database
.xls	Microsoft Excel spreadsheet
.ppt	Microsoft PowerPoint presentation
.txt	Text file
.bmp	Bitmap graphic
.jpg	Compressed bitmap graphic
.htm or .html	Web page
.exe	Application (executable file)

It is possible, but not advisable, to change the extension of a file as the standard conventions enable the computer operating system to identify the type of data a file contains, and automatically load the appropriate software to process it.

All backing storage devices have limited capacity, and large files will fill up the available storage space quickly, so a general rule when creating files is to keep them as small as possible. Large files will also load up slower than small ones, and will take longer to find and access the data in some cases.

If data is transmitted across a network, smaller files will be sent faster than large ones.

One way of keeping database files small is to use coded data. For example, a field in a pupil file may show whether the pupil is 'Male' or 'Female'. It is better to enter the single codes 'M' or 'F' in this field.

Reasons for coding data:
- File sizes will be **smaller**. This means faster access to data, less space used to store the file, and faster speeds when sending the file across a network.

- It is **less likely mistakes will be made** when entering the data.
- A simple **validation** rule will check the data when it is entered.

8.7 Data compression

Data compression is another way of making file sizes smaller. A variety of techniques can be used to 'pack' the data of a file so it takes up less storage space when it is saved or transmitted over a network.

Before the data file can be processed, it will need to be de-compressed.

Advantages of data compression:
- **Smaller file sizes**. Files will take up less storage space when saved on hard disk or other storage media.
- **Faster transmission** when sent over a network, or downloaded from the Internet.

Text files can be used to replace common combinations of characters with single characters.

Example: The following sentence has 88 characters (including spaces).

> **There are several methods of compressing files so they are smaller when they are stored.**

If the combination of characters 're' is replaced by the character '@', as follows:

> **The@ a@ several methods of comp@ssing files so they a@ smaller when they a@ sto@d.**

The paragraph now only has 82 characters.

By replacing more of the common character combinations by single characters, the file size can be made to be much smaller.

Graphics files have different methods of compression. Bitmap graphics can be very large, but can be considerably reduced in size by converting them into different formats (such as **JPEG** or **GIF**). Some detail may be lost, but usually this is not noticeable to the human eye.

If you create a website, the space you are allocated may be limited, so it is important that bitmap graphics are compressed into formats with smaller sizes.

Video files can be compressed by converting them into files that compare one frame to the next, and only sending data about the changes between them. (The standard format for compressed video files is **MPEG**.)

Sound files are usually compressed into **MP3** format. The bit rate at which the sound is recorded can be chosen. The higher the bit rate, the better the quality of the recording, but the larger the file. Small files with low bit rates will have poor sound quality.

160

Files can be **compressed** to make them smaller when stored, and faster to transmit over a network, but they will need to be **de-compressed** before they can be used.

161

Bitmap graphic files are large but can be compressed into other formats such as **JPEG** (.jpg) or **GIF** (.gif), for example for use on web pages, with little loss of quality.

162

Compressed .mp3 sound files with low bit rates will be how files but will be poor in quality.

Small files allow people to download music files from the Internet: even the ones they are not supposed to! There is also a certain amount of controversy because it allows musicians to sell their music directly over the Internet and by-pass the large music recording companies.

There are also general purpose compression programs which will compress any file to a smaller size. This is commonly referred to as **zipping** a file and the file extension of the resulting smaller file is **.ZIP**. The process of decompressing the file is referred to as **unzipping** the file.

Often, when files are archived, they are saved in compressed format, and many files can be compressed into a single archive file.

> **163**
> Groups of files can be **zipped** into a single compressed file, but it will need to be **unzipped** before the files can be used.

■ Activity 8.1　**Graphics and compression formats**

1 Find a bitmap graphic and save it as a .BMP file. This is uncompressed, and the colour of every pixel of the image is stored.
2 Make a note of the size of the file.
3 Now, save the same picture in different formats (.JPG, .GIF, .TIF, .PNG, etc.), and compare their file sizes.
4 Create a spreadsheet and record the sizes of the files, and calculate the percentage of the original size.
5 Try this for different graphics. Choose some photographs and some graphics with large areas of the same colour (such as a cartoon).

8.8　Securing data

> **164**
> Loss of important data is really bad news for businesses.

Security is a major issue with most businesses and organisations. The problems that arise with the loss of important data could have serious consequences for a business and may result in:

● Loss of customers. Unhappy customers will go elsewhere.
● Payments for goods may not be received.
● Bad publicity. A business relies on its good reputation.
● Cash flow problems as the accounting system breaks down.
● Management unable to make decisions due to lack of information.

Data is often stored on the hard drives of computers, so it is important that the computers themselves are safe. There are a number of physical methods of making sure that data on computers is secure, and there are also some software methods.

If data is secure then:

● It cannot be destroyed.
● It cannot be accidentally or maliciously altered.
● It cannot fall into the hands of unauthorised people.

8.8.1 Physical methods

Computers need to be protected from natural disasters such as fire and flood, as well as from deliberate damage or theft. If a computer is damaged or stolen then so is the data stored on it.

Locks

Computer rooms should be locked and only authorised people with keys allowed to access them. Computer rooms should not be on the ground floor where people can see the equipment by looking through windows. It is also important to make sure that windows are locked.

Some computers have cases with locks which prevent them being switched on.

Computers may also be bolted or attached by a strong steel cable (with a lock) to a desk so they cannot be stolen.

Alarms

Burglar alarm systems should be in place for computer rooms or rooms where important or valuable equipment is stored. Sensors should detect any attempt to enter the room and respond by sounding an alarm.

Fire protection systems should sense if a fire starts and attempt to control it by using non-water methods (possibly filling the room with a gas such as carbon dioxide).

Identification

A computer system sometimes needs to be able to identify the person trying to get access to the room or the computers.

To gain access to a room a user may have to swipe an identity card through a card reader. The card reader is connected to the computer system, which checks that the user is authorised to enter, before opening the door.

Biometric systems use physical characteristics such as voice recognition to identify a user. The person speaks into a microphone and the computer analyses the voice pattern to see if it belongs to an authorised user.

Other systems use fingerprint scans, retina scans of the eye, even facial feature recognition. These systems, although not yet foolproof, offer high levels of security but are expensive to buy and install.

165
> Locking computer rooms and strong cabling will make it difficult to steal computers.

Figure 8.1 *Computers can be attached by strong steel cables and locked to prevent theft.*

Figure 8.2 *An identity card may need to be swiped through a card reader to gain access to a room.*

BIOMETRIC SYSTEM: A security system that uses physical characteristics such as fingerprints, voice, facial features and eye scans to identify people.

Figure 8.3 *Retinal scans project a low power infrared beam onto the pattern of blood vessels at the back of the eye.*

8.8.2 Software methods

Authentication means identifying a person and verifying that they are who they claim to be.

Password system

Another way of identifying a user is a **password** system. Every authorised user of a computer system is given a user name, which can be recognised by the system. Each user also has a password that must be entered every time they log in. The computer will only allow access to a user that it recognises, and who also enters their correct password.

Single files can be password-protected. The user has to enter a password before being allowed to use the file.

Back-ups

Important data should be backed-up regularly. This means making a second copy of the data. If a problem arises with the data file, then the back-up copy can be used instead.

Back-up copies of data files can be made locally (the back-up is saved on the same computer hard drive as the original) but there is no point keeping the back-up on the same computer if that computer is stolen!

Back-up copies can be made on removable media such as CD, DVD or tape cartridge. The back-up copy of the data should be kept in a secure place such as a locked room or a fireproof safe and preferably in a different location to the original.

Many organisations back-up their data every working day. Computers can be scheduled to make back-ups at regular time intervals (possibly every night when the computers are less busy).

PERSONAL IDENTITY NUMBER (PIN): A security system where only the rightful owner of a credit card knows the PIN which is stored on it. PINs are also used on locks to allow access only to authorised personnel.

BACK-UP: A duplicate copy of a file kept in case the original is lost or corrupted.

Encryption

Data can be changed into secret codes so that it is not readable by anyone who does not have authorisation. This is called **encryption** and it is a good way of making sure that sensitive or personal data that may be accessed or intercepted on a network cannot be used. The intended user of the data would have a way of decoding the data. For example, credit card account numbers would be encrypted when sent over the Internet. If the data was intercepted by a hacker, the data would be meaningless.

File attributes

There are some characteristics of a file, called the file attributes, which the user can set. One of them is a 'read-only' attribute. If this is set then the file can be viewed but cannot be changed. Many data problems are caused by users accidentally changing or deleting files and the setting of the read-only attribute will prevent this happening.

Figure 8.4 *Setting a file's read-only attribute will prevent it from being accidentally changed or deleted.*

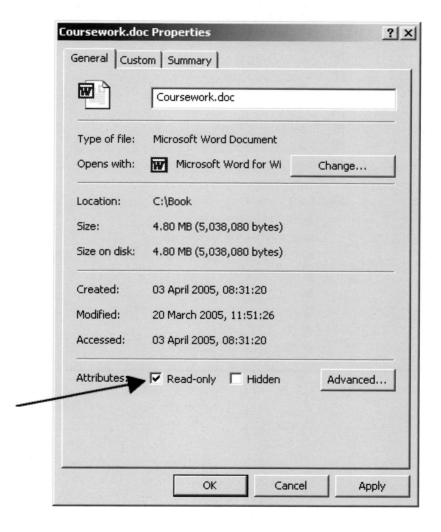

Summary

01 There are many data types, but all data is represented as numbers so the computer can process it.

02 A file is a collection of related records.

03 A record is a collection of related fields.

04 A field is a single data item.

05 A data structure table gives a list of fields in a record and their types.

06 A key field uniquely identifies each record.

07 Fixed length fields always have the same number of characters.

08 Variable length fields are stored with separator characters between them.

09 Fixed length fields are processed faster.

10 Variable length fields need less storage space.

11 A master file is a large file of permanent data.

12 A transaction file is a temporary file used to update the master file.

13 An archive file is a file in long-term storage.

14 A database is an organised collection of related files.

15 Filenames are used to identify files when they are stored.

16 File extensions indicate the types of files.

17 Data compression makes a file smaller (it will need less storage space and be faster to download or send over a network).

18 Data can be made safe and secure by:
- locking rooms and computers;
- using burglar and fire alarms;
- using identity cards to limit access to rooms and computers;
- using biometric systems to limit access to rooms and computers;
- using passwords;
- taking regular back-ups and storing them safely;
- encrypting data;
- setting file attributes.

Practice questions 8

1 A shop selling music CDs holds information about them on a database. Part of this database is shown here.

Code	Title	Artist	Type	Cost(£)	Stock
7203	Gnashing Teeth	Gnashing Snarlers	Rock	£9.99	5
7204	Blue Fudge	John Lou Hacker	Blues	£5.99	2
7205	Wild Days	The Cramps	Rock	£7.99	3
7206	Smooth Living	Dave Miles	Jazz	£7.99	1

a) What data type are the following fields: Artist; Stock; Cost(£)? [3]

b) Which field is the key field? [1]

c) Name two other fields which may be used in this database. [2]

d) Give one reason why the owner of the shop would add a new record. [1]

e) Give one reason why the owner of the shop would delete a record. [1]

f) Give one reason why the owner of the shop might edit a record. [1]

Sometimes data is stored as fixed length fields and sometimes as variable length fields.

g) Give one advantage of using fixed length fields. [1]

h) Give one advantage of using variable length fields. [1]

2 It is important that a business keeps its data files secure.

a) Describe two physical methods of keeping data secure. [2]

b) Describe two software methods of keeping data secure. [2]

Can you remember…?

1 What is a field? What is a record? What is a file?

2 A transaction file is often used to update a master file. What are the differences between a master file and a transaction file?

3 What is an archive file?

9 Manipulating information

9.1 Organising and updating files

Files of data rarely remain the same for very long and often need to be changed. Businesses change all the time. They may expand, taking on new staff or moving to new premises, they may grow smaller, or the goods they sell may vary. There is no point in having data that is incorrect or out-of-date, so the data files need to be constantly updated.

The order that the data is stored may need to be changed. Imagine a telephone directory where the names are stored in numerical order of the phone numbers. It would be easy to find the person whose phone number is 639247 but very difficult to find the telephone number of a particular person! The data needs to be sorted in alphabetical order of the person's name before it becomes easy to find the phone number for, for example, Thompson P.J.

The data itself may need to be edited. The following table gives the four main reasons for updating files and uses a library application to illustrate each one.

File update	Reason
Sorting the data	**To speed up searching the data.** A request for a book may lead to the data file being searched to find if the book is in the library.
Editing the data	**The data may need changing or correcting.** A female member of the library may marry and her name would need to be changed on the members file.
Adding new data	**A new record may need to be added to the file.** A newly published book is added to the library's stock, so the data needs to be added to the stock file.
Deleting old data	**A record may need to be removed from the file.** An old book may be permanently lost or too damaged to lend, so it would be removed from the library's stock file.

9.2 Searching for information

People frequently need information, for example to write a business report, complete a homework assignment, solve a problem or create a presentation for a children's party, etc. There are many sources of information these days, and when information is needed, the first step is to decide where to look.

Here are some places where information can be found. Not all of them may be suitable for a particular search.

> Finding relevant and up-to-date information can take some time and you need to know where to look.

9.2.1 Databases

> **SIMPLE SEARCH:** A search with only one search criterion.

A business may have a large database with useful information that is needed by its employees, or your school may have a database that allows staff to quickly find information such as the home address of a pupil.

Searching a database is done by creating a Query, which specifies the data you are searching for and the fields that you would like displayed in the result.

> **COMPLEX SEARCH:** A search that uses multiple criteria and operators such as OR and AND.

The items of data that you are searching for make up the search criteria. If the search criteria involve only one field, then it is called a simple search. If the search involves more than one field, it is called a complex search. (See also Section 4.7.2.)

9.2.2 Internet

> Don't be led astray by old websites that are not up-to-date and may provide incorrect information.

The Internet is a valuable source of information but you must be careful! It is better to find more than one source of information and go to reputable websites.

To find information on the Internet use one of the many search engines. You need to be precise with searches or you may get overwhelmed with the number of responses! (See also Section 2.3.4.)

9.2.3 CD-ROMs and DVDs

CD-ROMs and DVDs are available which have searchable databases on them. Some have whole encyclopaedias including text, sound and video clips and some are available for specialist topics.

Figure 9.1 Encyclopaedias such as Encarta can be bought on DVD. Search facilities will be provided to help you find information.

183

9.2.4 Files saved on disks

Files such as documents may be saved on a disk and used again or edited later, but it is sometimes difficult to remember the location where you saved them. It is important to do some proper 'house-keeping' of your disks:

- Make sure each file is given a **meaningful name** when it is saved.
- A **proper directory (folder) structure** should be created with sensible names. This should be arranged in a hierarchical structure, that is a main folder with subfolders. Each of these subfolders may themselves have subfolders, and so on.
- If you use **floppy disks** they should be clearly labelled.

Computers have search facilities to find files saved on disk. You can search for a file with a particular name, or use wildcards for partial names. You can also search for text files that have particular words or phrases contained in them, or files that were saved at given times.

Figure 9.2 *Windows allows you to search for files which have the word 'Homework' in them.*

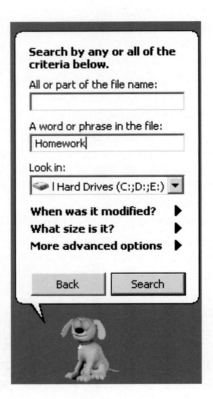

9.3 Developing information

When you have found the information you need, what next? Well that depends on what type of project you are doing. If it is research, a homework task or a piece of coursework, you will need to get all the text, statistics or graphics together in one place. The easiest way of doing this is to create a new project (a blank document, DTP publication, spreadsheet or database) and use 'copy and paste' techniques.

Files that are saved on disk, CD or DVD can be imported into your project. Text files can be imported into a document or publication, data files can be imported into a database or into a spreadsheet. Graphic images can be imported into almost any application.

Once the data is in your project, you can start to develop the information.

Once you have your data, you need to develop it.

File type	Development
Documents and publications	The layout of the **text** and **images** can be manipulated to make sure the finished project looks good. The text may need to be adjusted to fit into the space allocated with no widows or orphans. The size of the font can be changed for headings, and final formatting of the text will make words or phrases catch the eye.
	The size of images may need to be adjusted to fit better, but bitmap images lose their quality if enlarged too much.
Presentations	The contents of each slide of a presentation can be animated – the way they appear or disappear. They can be set to fly in from any direction or just appear suddenly, or fade slowly away.
	Slide transitions – the way one slide changes to another – can be defined in various ways.
	Sounds or **music** may be added to enhance the presentation and make it more interesting to view.
	Some of the slides may have **hyperlinks** to other slides.
Websites	**Hyperlinks** need to be defined on each page so that the viewer can navigate between the pages of the site. Some of the links may be to other websites, and some of them may be defined to send an email or download a file.
Spreadsheets	Once the data has been entered and the formulae defined in the cells of a spreadsheet, it can then be used to carry out investigations. Many spreadsheets simulate events in the real world, and the definitions of the **formulae** are designed to imitate behaviour in the real situation. Models of situations that are difficult or dangerous to reproduce can be simulated using spreadsheets – you could not conduct an experiment on nuclear fusion in the classroom, but you could use a spreadsheet to simulate it.
	Simulations can be explored by examining the effects of changing the information in a spreadsheet, and predictions can be tested.
	Charts and **graphs** can be drawn from the data to illustrate results of an investigation.
Databases	There may be a number of files (tables) in a database and **relationships** between some of the data fields can be defined. This is normally done by having common fields in each of the related files, but these should only be key fields.
	The data may be **sorted** into alphabetic or numeric order to make it easier and faster to find information.
	Searches can be defined by creating queries, organising the data to be displayed and the search criteria to be used.
	Preparing **reports** to be printed will involve deciding which fields are to be included, how they are to be searched and how the results are to be sorted and grouped. **Calculations** such as totals or averages may also be included.

9.4 Presenting information

> The way of presenting information must take into account the needs of the audience and it must suit the specified purpose.

In practice, a project will probably consist of a combination of the methods described in the previous section and the results will need to be presented in a variety of different ways. An example may be a researcher using a database to carry out searches of data, entering the results in a spreadsheet, drawing graphs of the results and presenting the final conclusions on a website.

There are a number of different ways of presenting information, and it is important that the most appropriate method is chosen. The method selected and the style must take into account the **target audience** (i.e. it meets the needs of those who are going to view it) and it must suit the specified **purpose** of the project.

The style of writing is also important. It is no good using difficult words if your audience is a group of children, and don't write slang if the viewer is your boss!

Presentation medium	Style
Printed document or publication	These may be formal documents such as legal letters or offers of job interviews, or they may be informal, such as party invitations.
	The choice of style must be appropriate. The style is defined by the layout, fonts used and graphics selected.
	For example a letter of resignation to your boss would need a different style to an invitation to a children's birthday party. The first would need a formal document with professional layout and font, but the second can be more informal and use plenty of colour, graphics and weird fonts.
	Some publications such as advertisements or magazines need to be eye-catching to attract viewers, so plenty of bold and colourful lettering and graphics may be needed.
	Large publications also need consistency of layout and style. It is a good idea to use a template for each page of a large publication.
	Reports created in databases are usually printed.
Screen display	Output may be displayed on a monitor screen. Layouts should be simple, but interesting with only necessary information displayed. It is difficult to look at a cluttered disorganised screen of information.
	The advantage of screen displays is that sounds and video clips can be included – you cannot do this on a printed document!
Multimedia presentation	Multimedia presentations are more appropriate for situations where a speaker will give out information to an audience. Slides are displayed on a screen, and may include text, graphics, sound or video clips. There may be a few bullet points displayed on a slide and a speaker explains each of them.
	They can also be used for single user presentations where the slides are presented on a monitor and a user interactively works through the display, with a soundtrack recorded to explain the information.
Website	Pages of text can be displayed on websites with hyperlinks between them.
	This method of presentation attracts a worldwide audience, but must be made to look attractive if it is an advertisement designed to attract customers to a business.
	Web pages are interactive and allow the viewer to select the pages they wish to see.

Sound	Information can be presented as a recorded soundtrack – it may even be a piece of music.
Video	A video clip can combine moving pictures and a soundtrack.
	Videos can be included in web pages or multimedia presentations.

However the information is to be presented, it must be accurate and it must be clear. Spellcheckers can be used on documents to make sure text is correctly spelled and data used in a project should be validated to ensure that all the data used is sensible data.

Information can then be stored for future use, but make sure it is saved with recognisable names in an appropriate folder, so that it can easily be found when it is needed again.

Summary

01 Data files frequently need updating. They may need:
- sorting into order;
- data edited;
- new data added;
- old data deleted.

02 Data may come from documents, databases, the Internet, CD-ROMs, DVDs or other files saved on disk.

03 Files saved on disk must be given meaningful names and placed in an organised collection of folders.

04 Information can be brought together using copy and paste or by importing.

05 Information can be arranged on documents and publications to form an appropriate layout and style.

06 Information must be checked carefully for accuracy.

07 Presentations can be animated and used to give out information.

08 Websites reach a worldwide audience.

09 Spreadsheets can be used to model real-life situations.

10 The effects of changing information on spreadsheets can be studied.

11 Charts and graphs of results on spreadsheets can be created.

12 Printed reports can be created using data from databases. They select the fields to display and organise them in a defined way, and may even include calculations such as totals.

13 Information must be presented in a way that is appropriate to the needs of the audience and must suit the specified purpose.

14 Information may be presented as:
- a printed document or publication;
- a screen display;
- a multimedia presentation;
- a website;
- sound or video.

Practice questions 9

1 A person receives two documents in the post:

a) A letter from a solicitor.

b) An invitation to the office Christmas party.

Describe three ways in which the style of these two documents might differ. [3]

2 A business wants to create an advertisement for a new product.

Describe three different ways that this advertisement could be presented by its sales department, and give an advantage of each. [3]

10 Hardware

Hardware is the equipment that makes up a computer system.

10.1 Types of computer

A **computer** is an automatic, programmable, digital data processor.

● Automatic: it operates without human intervention when necessary.
● Programmable: stored instructions (programs) control its actions.
● Digital: it uses distinct numbers for everything.
● Data processor: this is what a computer does – it processes data.

10.1.1 Mainframe

MAINFRAME: The largest and most powerful type of computer.

Mainframe computers are very large and very expensive. They can support many hundreds of users at the same time and have very powerful processors that can process vast quantities of data very quickly.

The actual mainframe may not be much larger than a small filing cabinet, but a whole room may be filled with many peripherals connected to it. There are a large number of disk drives, printers, and other devices under its control. The floors and ceilings of the computer room probably hide many miles of cabling.

Figure 10.1 *A mainframe computer.*

Mainframes have very large memories and can run very complex software. Some will use a single processor but most large mainframes will have many processors working together (parallel processing).

The room in which the mainframe sits is air-conditioned to dissipate the heat generated, and may have dust filtering systems to keep the air clean.

A back-up generator will be available in case there is a power failure.

You will find mainframes only in large institutions such as banks, universities, the police, the Meteorological Office or global business companies.

The most powerful mainframes are often called **supercomputers**.

10.1.2 Microcomputer

MICROCOMPUTER: A computer based on a single **microprocessor**. Microprocessors are often called chips.

173
Microcomputers are used for interactive, personal computing.

Figure 10.2 *A typical microcomputer configuration.*

Microcomputers are computers based on a single microprocessor and they come in several sizes.

Desktop computers are often called PCs (personal computers) and are designed to be used by a single person at a time. Typically, they cost a few hundred pounds.

A typical configuration consists of a keyboard and mouse for input, a monitor and printer for output, and the microcomputer in a case that also houses memory and disk drives for data storage.

They are used in small businesses, in schools and even at home for personal computing or for playing games. In practice, networks of microcomputers are replacing some of the larger computers in businesses because they have recently become more powerful.

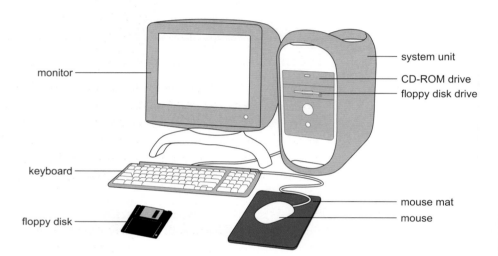

174
Laptops are portable and can be used anywhere because they are powered by a battery.

Figure 10.3 *A typical laptop computer.*

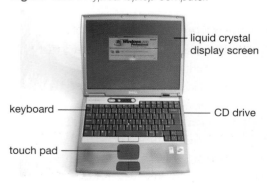

Laptop computers are physically smaller microcomputers where all the devices are built into a single case similar to a briefcase. The laptop opens to reveal a keyboard and a pointing device such as a touchpad, with a monitor screen in the lid. Along the side of the case are the disk drives (floppy, CD or DVD), and connections for other devices such as printers.

Laptop computers are designed to be small enough to carry around and are powered by a battery so they can be used while travelling or at business meetings.

As the development of chips and devices allows smaller components to be manufactured, the laptop sizes have also become smaller. Portable Digital Assistants (PDAs, sometimes called palmtop computers) can easily be carried around in one hand or tucked into a pocket. Software is usually included

Figure 10.4 *Palmtop computer.*

with a PDA to allow files to be transferred to a PC. PDAs are typically used for simple office tasks or for Internet access. A PDA can be used as a personal organiser, typically with software for a clock, diary, address book, task organiser and a calculator. There is no keyboard and input is sometimes done by writing with a stylus (pen) on a pad or by pressing a flexible button.

10.1.3 Embedded computers

A microprocessor/microcontroller can be embedded in a device to control its operation. There may be a small circuit board with several components including the microprocessor and a memory chip on which the controlling program is stored. Some sensors may provide input.

There can be no human access to the microprocessor and the program stored on it cannot be changed. The embedded computer will only perform a predefined task and cannot be used for other applications.

Some embedded computers are part of larger systems. For example an anti-locking brake system on a car may use an embedded computer.

Embedded computers can be found in washing machines, microwaves, clocks, cameras, televisions, and many other situations. (See also Section 2.5.12.)

10.2 Computer memory

MEMORY is used for temporary storage of data and programs.

All computers, from mainframes to palmtops, will have some memory. It is a place where data and programs can be temporarily stored while the central processor needs to use them.

175
Moving data in memory is about 1000 times **faster** than moving data in backing storage.

176
Memory is also known as **Immediate Access Store** (IAS).

Figure 10.5 *A SIMM that is slotted into the motherboard of a PC to increase the memory size.*

SIMM: Single in-line memory module.

Data can be read from or saved to memory very quickly, much faster than from a backing storage medium such as a hard disk, so data that is currently being used by the central processor is stored in the memory to speed up the operation of the computer. Generally a computer with more memory will run programs faster than one with less memory. Memory size is limited, so data that is not being used will be stored in backing storage. Think of memory as the workspace of the computer.

The complexity of computer systems and networks, combined with the ever-increasing demands of users has led to modern software needing more and more memory. You cannot run modern software on old computers with small amounts of slow memory: the program would run too slowly, if it runs at all!

10.2.1 RAM and ROM

177
Data stored on **RAM is temporary**. Data stored in **ROM is permanent**.

The main types of memory are:

- **Random Access Memory (RAM)**: Data can be read from it and saved to it. In other words, data stored on RAM can be changed.
- **Read Only Memory (ROM)**: Data can be read but no data can be saved. The data stored on ROM cannot be changed.

Data stored in **RAM is volatile**. This means that the data is lost when the power is turned off, but data stored in **ROM is permanent**.

10.2.2 Disk cache

ACCESS TIME: The average time it takes a storage medium to respond to a request for data.

178
Using a disk cache speeds up processing.

Accessing data from a disk is much slower than accessing data from memory.

Sometimes a program frequently requires reading large amounts of data from a disk. This can dramatically slow a program down, so to speed up processing, a part of memory is set aside to be used as a disk cache, and any data recently read from the disk is stored in it.

When the central processor needs an item of data, it first checks the disk cache to see if it is there, and only accesses the disk if it is not.

10.2.3 Bits and bytes

A powerful microscope would show that computer memory consists of many thousands of small electronic circuits that can be in one of two 'states'. We will refer to these as state 0 and state 1. Think of them as light switches if you like, which can be switched off (state 0) or switched on (state 1). This is how the binary number 10011010 would be stored using light switches:

The system of numbers that uses only digits 0 and 1 is called the **binary number system**, and binary numbers do not have any digits other than 0s and 1s in them.

A single **binary digit** is called a **bit**, so the number 1001 is a 4-bit binary number, the number 101101 is a 6-bit binary number and so on.

In computers, all data is stored as binary numbers, whether it is text, graphics, sound, videos or even a computer program. The size of a computer's memory is measured by the amount of numbers that can be stored in it. The unit of measurement is a byte, which is eight bits and is enough memory to store one text character such as the letter 'A'.

Example: The word 'FROG' would need four bytes of memory (or 32 bits) to store it.

When talking of memory sizes, the numbers of bytes is large so we generally refer to memory size in terms of kilobytes, megabytes or gigabytes.

> 1 kB (kilobyte) = 1024 bytes
> 1 MB (megabyte) = 1024 kB (approx 1 million bytes)
> 1 GB (gigabyte) = 1024 MB (approx 1 billion bytes)
> 1 TB (terabyte) = 1024 GB (approx 1 trillion bytes)

A **word** is defined to be the amount of data that a processor can process at one time. Large mainframes would have larger word sizes than smaller microcomputers, enabling them to process data much faster.

You can think of data stored in memory (or on disk) as looking like a string of 1s and 0s, for example:
1011001011001010
0110100100010111
1110101110110100
1101101000100010
0001001010010010
1001011011101010
…

BYTE: A defined number of bits (1s or 0s). **1 byte = 8 bits**. Typically represents one character.

STORAGE CAPACITY: The amount of data that can be stored.

WORD: The amount of data that a processor can process at one time.

▇ Activity 10.1 Internet investigation

● Find out the size of the memory in your computer. In Microsoft Windows, you can do this by right-clicking on the 'My Computer' icon, and then selecting Properties.

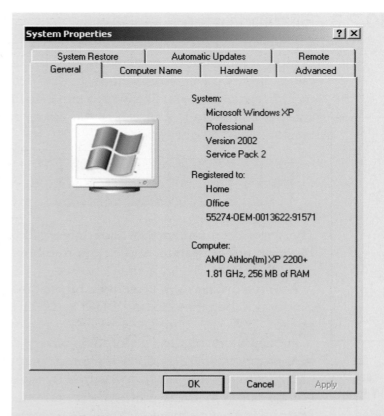

- Use the Internet to find websites of computer retail companies, and study the specifications of the computers they sell. What is the size of memory in them?
- How do memory sizes of laptops compare with desktop PCs?
- What about PDA memory?
- What is the largest mainframe memory size you can find?

10.3 Storage devices

The disadvantages of storing data in memory are:

- The storage capacity of memory is small.
- Memory is volatile. The data is lost when the power is turned off.

BACKING STORAGE:
Storage used to store data and programs that are not currently being used. It is non-volatile storage: data is permanently saved.

It is for these reasons that it is necessary to have a large permanent backing store on a computer that will store the data when power is turned off, and where, for example, large databases can be stored.

The disadvantage of backing store is that reading and writing the data is slower than from memory.

Do not be confused between the terms:

- Backing storage **device** (e.g. a floppy disk drive).
- Backing storage **medium** (e.g. a floppy disk).

Medium is the singular of media.

Loading data means transferring data from backing store to memory.

Saving data means transferring data from memory to backing store.

There are many devices that can be used for backing storage. We will study some of these in the next few sections.

10.3.1 Hard disk

An example of a backing storage medium is a **hard disk**, and the device that uses it is a hard disk drive (often abbreviated to **hard drive**). This is the most common type of backing store and all microcomputers are sold with a hard drive in them. Storage capacities are high and increasing every year.

A hard disk is a magnetic medium. Circular plates of metal or glass are coated with a magnetic material. Data is saved by magnetising particles on the disk surface.

The hard drive is a sealed unit containing the disk, which rotates at high speed. A moving arm has the read/write head at the end of it.

10.1

All magnetic disks must be **formatted** before they can be used. This marks out the tracks and sectors ready for use (a bit like painting the lines on a sports running track).

Figure 10.6 *A hard disk drive showing the disk and the read/write arm*

10.2

The **read/write head** floats so close to the disk that a small speck of dust will ruin the disk. This is why the drives are sealed.

Some hard drives have two or more disks to increase the storage capacity.

Advantages of a hard disk:
● High storage capacity: large amounts of data can be saved (far more than on a floppy disk).
● Fast access compared to other devices such as a floppy disk drive.
● The sealed unit protects the disks from dirt and dust and means greater reliability.

Disadvantage of a hard disk:
● The disk is (generally) not portable. You cannot easily transfer it from one computer to another.

10.3.2 Floppy disk

FLOPPY DISK: A portable magnetic backing store. It has small capacity and is not very reliable. Better portable backing store devices are replacing floppy drives.

A floppy disk is a 3.5 inch diameter circle of soft magnetic material protected by a hard square plastic cover. A sliding metal shutter opens when the disk is inserted into the floppy disk drive (floppy drive), which allows the drive's read/write head to access the disk.

A write-protect tab is provided which, when opened, prevents data from being written on to the floppy disk.

Figure 10.7 *A floppy disk.*

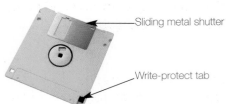

Sliding metal shutter

Write-protect tab

l83

Do not:
- leave floppy disks in heat (e.g. the sun) or damp;
- open the sliding metal shutter: it lets in dust!
- touch the brown disk inside.

Advantages of floppy disks:
- A floppy disk is portable. Data can be transferred from one computer to another.
- The write-protect tab provides some security from accidental deletion or corruption of data.

Disadvantages of floppy disks:
- Reading and writing data is slow compared to other media such as hard disks.
- A floppy disk can hold 1.44 MB. This may have seemed a lot 20 years ago but is considered too small today.
- A floppy disk is not reliable enough as dirt can easily get into it.

The days of the floppy disk are numbered. There are now other portable backing store devices with higher capacity and greater reliability.

10.3.3 CDs and DVDs

Figure 10.8 *A CD writer with a CD–R.*

CD stands for **compact disk**. CDs are optical storage media and the data they hold is read by lasers. Many multimedia applications use them because of their large storage capacity.

CDs have been used for music for many years now, but they are also used for backing storage on microcomputers. Most CD drives in computers will also play audio CDs.

There are three main types of CD:

- CD-ROMs are read-only disks. These are normally bought with data already stored on them, which can be read but cannot be altered.
- CD-Rs are blank CDs that can be written onto only once by a CD-writer.
- CD-RWs can be written onto and the data can then be deleted, and the disk rewritten.

Advantages of CDs:
- Large storage capacities, about 650 MB.
- Portable. They can be used in any computer with a CD drive.
- Cheap to produce. For this reason CDs are normally used for distributing software.

Disadvantages of CDs:
- Slower access times than hard drives.
- A CD-writer is needed if data is to be written onto CD-Rs or CD-RWs.

A DVD (Digital Versatile Disk) can store a lot more data than a CD. A single DVD can store up to 17 GB of data and so they can be used for full-length feature films. A DVD drive looks very similar to a CD drive and can usually read CDs as well.

DVD-ROM disks can only be read (the data stored on them cannot be changed). A DVD writer is needed to record data onto a DVD-R or onto a DVD-RW. You cannot read DVDs using a CD drive.

10.3.4 Magnetic tape

Magnetic tape devices are still widely used for backing up large amounts of important data. For example an organisation may make a back-up of the entire contents of a hard disk every night as a security measure.

Mainframes often use large spools of tape because of the volume of data they need to copy, but these are being replaced by tape cartridges that are inserted into a device called a tape drive or a tape streamer.

A magnetic tape cartridge is a little smaller than an audio cassette tape, but can hold large amounts of data.

> **184**
> Magnetic tape is a cheap and effective way of backing up large amounts of data.

Figure 10.9 *An external tape drive and a tape cartridge.*

Advantages of magnetic tape:
● Drives and cartridges are comparatively cheap.
● Large storage capacity.

Disadvantages of magnetic tape:
● Reading or writing data is slow.
● They do not act like a disk drive: you cannot quickly access a file from the middle of the tape.

10.3.5 Removable media

Magnetic tapes and floppy disks are examples of removable media. They can be removed from their drives and used in drives on other computers. There are other examples of removable media:

● **Zip drives** use high capacity Zip disks. They look similar to floppy disks but hold a lot more data (as much as 250 MB is common).
● **Rev drives** use disks with even greater storage capacity. A Rev disk can hold 35 GB of data.

> **185**
> Removable media allow easy transfer of data from one computer to another.

Figure 10.10 *A Zip drive.*

> **186**
> USB memory sticks allow you to work on your coursework in school and at home, but make sure your software is compatible for both systems!

● USB memory sticks – often called pen drives – are small and can be inserted into the USB port of any computer and used as backing store.

Figure 10.11 *USB memory sticks are a useful portable small backing store.*

Large capacity hard drives that sit on your desk and are connected to your computer through the USB port are also available.

10.4 Input devices

> **PERIPHERAL:** Any hardware device that can be connected to a computer.

To **input** data means to get data into a computer. Some input methods are automatic but some need an **input device**. This section looks at a number of peripherals that are used as input devices.

10.4.1 Keyboard

> **DIRECT DATA ENTRY (DDE):** The input of data using a keyboard, where the data is saved on a disk, and used later as input to a batch processing system.

The most common method of input uses a QWERTY keyboard (the name comes from the start of the top row of letters on the keyboard). Pressing a key makes a connection, which sends a signal to the computer.

There are keys for alphabetic and numeric characters, as well as for punctuation marks. Some keys have two characters and require the Shift key to be pressed if the top character is to be entered.

Figure 10.12 *Standard layout for a QWERTY keyboard.*

>
> **Braille keyboards** have Braille characters embossed on the keys to help visually impaired people.

> **188**
> The **Print Screen** key can be useful for taking screenshots when doing coursework.

Some of the keys, called **function keys** and labelled F1, F2, ..., F12, are programmable when using some software.

Most keyboards have a **numeric keypad** on the right, designed to speed up the entering of numbers.

Control keys include arrow keys for moving the screen cursor, and keys such as Insert, Page Up, and Home.

Figure 10.13 *Some keyboards are ergonomically designed to cause less strain for people who spend a lot of time typing.*

Concept keyboards have overlays that are placed on them before data is entered. These are often seen on tills in shops or restaurants, and are also used to help teach small children who may find large keyboards difficult to use.

10.4.2 Mouse

MOUSE: A common input device. Movement of the mouse controls the movement of a screen pointer. Clicking its buttons allows the user to interact with the computer according to the selection made by the screen pointer.

A mouse is an input device that should be very familiar. Moving the mouse across a flat surface controls the screen pointer because there is a ball in the mouse and small sensors measure the amount of the rotation. In an optical mouse there is no ball and the movement is measured using light sensors, and a laser mouse uses a laser beam.

Figure 10.14 *Cordless mice use wireless technology to transmit their signals to the computer. The one in this picture also has a scrolling wheel.*

Two (sometimes three) buttons on the mouse are used to send a signal to the computer to perform an action such as opening an application, selecting a menu option or printing a document.

The main actions you can perform with a mouse are:

- **Click:** press a button once.
- **Double click:** press a button twice quickly.
- **Drag:** hold a button down while moving the mouse.

Some mice have a wheel for scrolling through a list or a long document and this wheel may act as a third button if it is clicked.

The plural of a computer's mouse can be mouses or mice.

10.4.3 Tracker ball

A tracker ball is a bit like an upside-down mouse. The ball is on the top and is rotated by hand. The movement of the ball controls the movement of a screen pointer. Tracker balls may be found built into some laptop computers.

10.4.4 Touchpad

Drag a finger across the surface of a touchpad and it acts like a mouse. A pointer moves across the screen in the same way as the motion of the finger.

Touchpads are often built into laptop computers. If the pad is tapped it acts like the click of a mouse, but there may also be buttons to click.

190

Touchpads are useful on laptops if they are being used where there is no flat surface to use a mouse.

Figure 10.15 *A touchpad is a common input device on a laptop.*

10.4.5 Joystick

A joystick is used mainly for playing games or for simulation programs such as a flight simulator, or they may be used to control the movement of robotic devices.

Figure 10.16 *A joystick is mainly used for playing games or for controlling machinery.*

Movement of the stick can be in any direction and there are some buttons on the joystick base.

10.4.6 Graphics tablet

A **graphics tablet** is a board covered by a touch-sensitive membrane that can detect the position of a pointing device on its surface. It can be used to hold a drawing while the user traces it, or to hold a sheet of menus, icons and shapes, which the user can select.

A **stylus** is a pointing device for a graphics tablet.

A **puck** is a mouse-like input device for a graphics tablet that is moved over the surface of the tablet. It has cross-hairs to position it accurately and a number of buttons for different actions.

> A graphics tablet is sometimes called a **graphics pad** or a **graphics digitiser**.

Figure 10.17 *Drawing with a graphics tablet is easier than drawing with a mouse.*

10.4.7 Light pen

A light pen resembles a normal pen but it is connected to the computer and is used to write on the monitor. The light pen software can calculate where on the screen the pen is being held and selections on menus can be made or simple graphics such as lines can be drawn.

10.4.8 Scanner

DIGITISE: To convert into digits (in other words, numbers). A computer can then process the data.

A scanner can be used to digitise graphics that are printed or drawn on paper. With a flat-bed scanner, the paper (or photo) is placed face down on a glass screen under a closed lid. Light is systematically beamed onto the image from a moving scan bar and the reflection patterns analysed, and converted into numbers before being input to the computer.

Different scanners have different resolutions. This is measured in dots per inch (dpi) and high-resolution scans will result in better quality images.

Figure 10.18 *A flat-bed scanner.*

DIGITAL CAMERA: A camera that does not use film. The images are stored on a memory chip. These chips are removable and blank chips can be inserted to store more images.

Most scanners are flat-bed scanners like the one in the picture, but other types exist such as hand-held scanners which are passed manually over an image, and sheet-feed scanners where paper sheets are automatically fed into the device in a similar way that a fax machine takes in paper.

Optical character recognition (OCR) software can also be used to digitise text. The text on the paper is scanned as an image and the OCR software analyses the shapes of the characters and converts them into text ready for input to a program such as a word processor. (See also Sections 2.1.7 and 7.1.5.)

10.4.9 Digital camera

Another device for inputting an image is a digital camera. When photos are taken they are stored as digital files, so they can be downloaded directly into a computer and saved on backing store such as hard disk or CD-R.

Digital cameras have different maximum image resolutions. The more expensive cameras have higher resolutions.

The resolution of the images can be set. More photos can be stored in the camera if a low resolution is selected, but the quality will not be as good as with a high resolution setting.

You can view the photo you have taken much faster using a digital camera than with an old-style film camera.

10.4.10 Digital video camera

Similar to a digital camera, a digital video camera stores video clips as digital files in the camera, which can later be downloaded directly to a computer. Many video cameras also take still photos.

A **webcam** is a digital video camera connected directly to a computer and set up in a fixed position. The webcam can be used to feed a stream of video or still pictures at regular intervals to a website. There are now many thousands of web pages with webcam images on them and it is possible to view real-time images of places all over the world.

WEBCAM: A camera often used to feed pictures at regular intervals to web pages.

Figure 10.19 *A webcam can be used to feed pictures to a website.*

Webcams are often set up to monitor conditions such as the weather, the skiing conditions on mountains or the traffic on congested roads.

Webcams are also used in teleconferencing to allow two computer users in different places to communicate through video and audio links.

10.4.11 Touch-sensitive screen

Touch-sensitive screens are special monitors that allow users to make selections by touching points on the screen. They work best for menus or multiple-choice inputs.

They can be found in places such as information centres and museums, or in entertainment centres for quiz games.

The big advantage of touch-sensitive screens is that there are no loose devices that can be damaged or stolen by users.

> **INTERACTIVE WHITEBOARD (IWB):** Touch-sensitive screen used in classrooms. A special stylus is used to touch the screen.

10.4.12 Microphone

The process of converting an analogue signal to digital data is called sampling. Sound is an analogue signal. At evenly spaced intervals, the sound is measured and converted into numbers. The more frequently the sampling is done, the better the sound quality but more storage is required.

A microphone can be used as an input device but the sound needs to be sampled by a **sound card** inside the computer to convert it into a digital file before the computer can process it.

Microphones are used for teleconferencing or in speech recognition systems where the user can speak commands to the computer. This is useful for people whose hands are occupied (surgeons, people driving vehicles or flying aircraft).

Microphones can also be used in offices for dictation systems: for inputting spoken words into a word processor.

> **MICROPHONE:** An input device for sound, but a **sound card** must be installed to sample the sound and digitise it (convert it to numbers).

10.4.13 Musical instruments

Musical instruments can communicate with a computer using a defined standard called MIDI (Musical Instrument Digital Interface).

MIDI instruments are musical instruments that can be connected to a computer. As the instrument is played, digital signals are input and these can then be stored as a data file and later processed, edited or played back through the instrument (in this last sense the instrument is an output device, see Section 10.5).

For example, keyboards are common MIDI instruments, and the musician can play a piece of music that is directly input to the computer and stored digitally. The piece can easily be edited with special software by changing the notes, tempo, dynamics and even the sound of the instrument before playing it back through the keyboard.

Other common MIDI instruments are guitars, drums and synthesizers which produce artificially produced sounds.

> Any device with a MIDI-OUT port can control any device with a MIDI-IN port. This is because MIDI is a defined standard.

10.4.14 Sensors

Many control systems use sensors for input. Environmental measurements are taken and input to a computer, which analyses the data and takes action if necessary by sending output signals to other devices.

Analogue measurements such as sound, light or temperature must be converted to digital data so the computer can analyse and process the data.

Here is a list of commonly used sensors:

Sensor	Example of use
Temperature sensor	Automatic weather readings, manufacturing processes
Sound sensor	Burglar alarm systems, monitor noise pollution
Light sensor	Street lighting (automatically turns on the light when light levels fall too low)
Humidity sensor	Automatic greenhouse
Pressure sensor	Robotic hands (so they can pick up delicate objects)
Proximity sensor	To make sure moving robots do not crash into objects
Infrared sensor	Photocells may be used to detect a break in a beam in a burglar alarm system

Sensors are used in datalogging systems where measurements are taken at regular intervals over a predefined period of time. The data is saved in a data file for analysis by the computer.

10.5 Output devices

After a computer has processed data it needs to output the results, and there are several different devices that can be used for this.

10.5.1 Monitor

Be careful in exam answers: monitors are not the same as televisions.

CRT monitors are curved and bulky. LCD monitors are flat and thin.

The most commonly used output device is a **monitor**: a screen used to display information. A monitor was once often referred to as a Visual Display Unit (VDU). The size of a monitor is measured diagonally from corner to corner.

Older types of monitor use Cathode Ray Tube (CRT) technology and they are bulky devices that take up a lot of room on the top of a desk. Monitor Liquid Crystal Display (LCD) technology has advanced rapidly in recent years and much smaller and thinner types of monitor are now available.

The **resolution** of a monitor is a measure of the number of pixels that can be displayed. (A pixel is the smallest amount of the screen display that can be changed by the computer.) Modern monitors can display millions of different colours.

Figure 10.20 *Old CRT monitors are much bulkier than the thinner LCD monitors.*

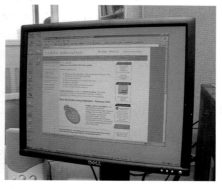

PIXEL: Short for *picture element*. The smallest amount of information displayed graphically on a screen. A single coloured dot.

LCD monitors are used in laptops because they have flat screens, but they are also used for desktop computers as they are much thinner than CRT monitors, use less power and are kinder on the eyes because they do not flicker.

Another monitor technology is the **plasma screen**, which are bright screens that can be manufactured in large sizes (up to 84 inches). They are also used for TVs but they are very expensive.

The visual output from a computer can be projected onto a screen using a video projector (sometimes this will be an interactive whiteboard).

10.5.2 Printer

HARD COPY: A document that has been printed on paper. Some people like to have a hard copy of their data as a security measure in case their hard drive fails. It is also sometimes more convenient to have a paper copy of a document to read away from a monitor, and some people find it easier to read on paper than on-screen.

People used to think that ICT would mean that business offices would operate without paper, but in fact it seems that computers generate more paperwork, not less! The paperless office was being talked about 20 years ago, but it still has not happened yet. One of the reasons is that paper is a very reliable medium for storing information. Hard disks and floppy disks fail eventually: paper lasts much longer if it is properly stored.

A printer is the device that outputs data onto paper, and the printed output is called 'hard copy'.

There are several different types of printer, distinguished by the technology they use, the quality of their print and the cost of buying and running them.

Dot-matrix printer

Some old types of printer such as dot-matrix printers use inked ribbons that are hammered onto the paper by a print head consisting of a number of pins. Their main advantage is that multi-part stationery can be used, where the output is printed on several pages at once, or continuous stationery where the paper comes on one long reel.

These printers are very noisy, especially in offices where there may be several of them running at the same time (often they need to be used in soundproof housings). The quality of print is poor so they are not as popular as they used to be and have generally been replaced by laser printers or inkjet printers.

Dot-matrix printers are cheap to buy and useful for multi-part stationery.

Thermal printer

A thermal printer uses heat to 'burn' an image onto specially treated paper. They may be found at some POS terminals.

Laser printer

Laser printers use a process similar to a photocopying machine where toner, a very fine powder, is transferred to the paper and fused onto it using heat and pressure.

Some laser printers are monochrome, and use a single cartridge of black toner while others print in colour and may use a number of cartridges of toner of different colours.

> 197
> A laser printer produces high quality print but may be expensive to run.

Advantages of laser printers:

● Very high quality of print, giving a professional look to documents and graphics.
● Almost silent running: ideal for busy offices.
● Some can be set to print both sides of a page.
● Large input trays for paper.

Figure 10.21 *A laser printer has large input trays for paper.*

Disadvantages of laser printers:

● Laser printers can be expensive to run because toner cartridges are expensive.
● Laser printers can be quite large.

Some laser printers are incorporated with a photocopier, scanner and fax machine.

Mainframes sometimes have high-speed laser printers for high-volume work such as printing bank statements, electricity bills or marketing mail.

Inkjet printer

An inkjet printer forms text and images by spraying dots of different coloured ink from nozzles on a print head that moves repeatedly across the paper. As each pass is completed, the paper is fed through a little bit more, ready for the next pass.

Most inkjets use four colours: yellow, magenta, cyan and black.

In recent years, the price of inkjet printers has come down and the quality of the print has improved, making them a cheap alternative to laser printers in situations where high quality is not so important, such as for the home user or in schools.

> 198
> Special paper can be used in inkjet printers to produce high quality printouts of photos.

Figure 10.22 *An inkjet printer.*

Advantages of inkjet printers:

● Cheap to buy (but, be careful, ink cartridges can be expensive!)
● Small, light (they can be put on a desk top).
● Easy to operate.

Disadvantages of inkjet printers:

● Print quality is not as good as laser printers.
● Small input trays for paper.
● Inkjet printers can be slow to print colour images.

■ Activity 10.2 Internet research and database

- Create a database with a single table called Printers. The data structure table for this is as follows:

Fieldname	Type	Comment
PrinterID	Number	The key field
PrinterName	Text	
Type	Text	Codes – 'I' for inkjet, 'L' for laser, 'O' for other.
Price	Currency	Price in £ (formatted to two decimal places).

- Use the Internet to find 20 printers of differing types, and enter the details into your database. Make sure that you select a wide variety of printers from a number of different companies.
- Create a query that outputs all the fields **sorted** in descending order of price.
- What do you notice?

10.5.3 Computer output on microfilm

Computer output on microfilm (COM) is a technique of reducing documents in size and photographically printing them so that they can be read using a special magnifying machine. Anything that can be printed or photographed can be placed on a microfilm or microfiche.

Figure 10.23 *Microfilm needs to be read using special magnifying readers*

Microfilm is a roll of film and **microfiche** is a rectangular sheet of film on which many frames (pages of information) can be stored.

Libraries use COM to archive documents such as newspapers, magazines or catalogues that may deteriorate with age or lots of use.

The advantages of COM are:

- Paper is bulky to store and microfilms take up **less space**.
- Microfilm **lasts longer** than paper, which discolours and fades with age.

A disadvantage of COM is:

● Microfilm cannot be read by eye, so a special reader is needed.

10.5.4 Graph plotter

Applications such as CAD use a graph plotter rather than a printer to output a finished design. They are slow but can draw continuous curves accurately and in a variety of colours.

On a flat-bed plotter the paper is held on a flat surface and the pens move across it, guided by a moving mechanical arm, which itself moves up and down the page.

Some blueprint designs are drawn on very large sheets of paper (the size is measured in metres rather than centimetres!). Large designs can include a lot of detail that would be difficult to see if the printout was too small.

If very long sheets of paper are needed then a drum plotter is used. The paper is held on a drum, which rotates as a pen moves up and down a fixed bar.

COMPUTER-AIDED DESIGN (CAD): A software drawing tool utilising computers to assist designers create graphic designs of objects. CAD can be used to design cars, houses, kitchen layouts, aircraft, bridges, electronic circuit boards, etc.

Figure 10.24 *A drum plotter is used for very large designs.*

10.5.5 Sound

Sound and music are output using speakers. Sound cards need to be installed in microcomputers to obtain good quality sound for music, software or games, but one of the most recent developments in sound output is that of **speech synthesis**: the artificial production of the human voice. Old attempts at speech synthesis produced robotic sounding voices but recently, they have become more natural and pleasant to listen to.

Text-to-speech systems create a spoken sound version of text in a document. This is useful for people with visual handicaps. Personal messages can be sent across the Internet using a recorded voice. The recipient plays the message in a similar way to receiving an email.

Some cars use voiced warnings (maybe a passenger has not

fastened their seat belt). Children's toys may have voices, and educational games that teach spelling may speak a word and ask the child to press keys to spell it.

On fast networks, microphones and speakers can be used for real-time speech where two users can hold a conversation, or as part of a videoconferencing system.

10.5.6 Control interface

Actuators are devices that are able to control machinery. They convert electrical signals into mechanical actions such as moving a robot arm, turning a tap or opening a ventilator.

Output signals from a computer are sent to a control interface, which can operate a number of different actuators. For example, in a computerised greenhouse, sensors input regular measurements to a computer that analyses whether they lie within allowed limits. If action needs to be taken, output signals are sent to a control interface that controls actuators that turn on a heater, open the ventilator and turn on a water sprinkler.

The control interface is needed because of the different operating characteristics of the computer and the devices being controlled.

10.5.7 CNC devices

CAD/CAM systems use computers to design and then manufacture items. The design is created using CAD software and, when finished, it is converted into digital form (numbers) and output to a CNC device. This then converts the numerical instructions into a sequence of actions.

Some of the main CNC devices used are discussed in Section 5.11.

Summary

01 A mainframe is the largest and most powerful type of computer, with many processors, large memories and backing storage.

02 A microcomputer is built around a single processor.

03 Laptops and PDAs are small microcomputers that are portable and can run off batteries.

04 An embedded computer has a processor built in and a stored program which operates it (e.g. washing machine, microwave ovens, etc.).

05 Memory is used for storage of data and programs.

06 RAM is used for temporary storage and is volatile.

07 ROM is used for permanent storage and is non-volatile.

08 Storage capacity is measured in bytes.

09 Backing storage is non-volatile storage and stores more data than memory.

10 A hard disk is a magnetic storage medium in a sealed unit to protect it from dirt.

11 Floppy disks are portable but do not store as much as hard disks.

12 CD-ROMs are optical backing storage devices. A CD is portable, and can store about 650 MB of data.

13 DVD-ROMs are optical backing storage devices, but a DVD can store more data than a CD.

14 Magnetic tape is often used for making back-ups of large amounts of data.

15 Removable storage media include Zip drives, Rev drives and USB memory sticks.

16 A keyboard is the most common input device. Concept keyboards have overlays.

17 A mouse is an input device that controls a pointer on the screen.

18 Tracker balls, joysticks, touchpads, graphics tablets and light pens are all input devices.

19 A scanner can digitise graphics or can be used to input text to a word processor using OCR software.

20 Digital cameras and video cameras are input devices which are used for photos and video clips.

21 Musical instruments with MIDI interfaces can be connected to computers.

22 Sound is input using a microphone but is sampled at regular intervals to convert it into numbers.

23 Control systems and datalogging systems use sensors for input.

24 A monitor is the most common output device.

25 CRT monitors are cheap but bulky. LCD monitors are thin and can be used in laptops.

26 There are three main types of printer:
- Dot-matrix printer (cheap and can be used for multi-part stationery but noisy).
- Laser printer (more expensive but good quality print).
- Inkjet printer (cheap but slower than laser).

27 Graph plotters are used to output designs created using CAD software.

28 A speech synthesiser converts text to spoken words.

29 Control systems output signals to actuators that control mechanical devices.

30 In CAD/CAM systems, output is sent as a sequence of numbers to CNC devices such as drills, lathes, milling machines or embroidery machines.

Practice questions 10

1 **a)** Name two types of magnetic backing storage. [2]

  b) Name two types of optical backing storage. [2]

2 A microcomputer is advertised as having:

32 GHz processor

512 MB RAM

17 in monitor

80 GB hard drive

16 × CD/DVD burner

Laser printer

  a) What does RAM stand for? [1]

  b) What is RAM used for? [1]

  c) What is the other type of memory? [1]

  d) What output devices are mentioned in the advertisement? [2]

  e) What backing storage devices are mentioned in the advertisement? [2]

  f) The size of memory is measured in bytes. How many bytes in a kilobyte? [1]

  g) Arrange in order of size (smallest first): gigabyte; kilobyte; byte; megabyte. [1]

  h) The microcomputer advertised has no floppy drive. Give one advantage of a hard disk over a floppy disk. [1]

  i) Give one advantage of a floppy disk over a hard disk. Why does the advertised microcomputer not need a floppy drive? [2]

Can you remember...?

1 What is the largest type of computer called?

2 What is an advantage of a laptop over a PC? What problem might arise when using a laptop?

3 What does COM stand for? Why is COM used to store images of newspapers?

4 Why are USB memory sticks useful? What advantages do they have over floppy disks?

5 Give two ways of getting a photo into a computer.

6 What input devices are used in control systems?

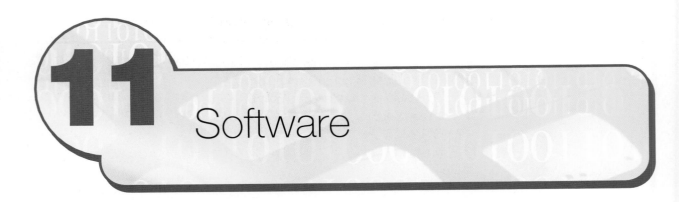

11 Software

11.1 Introduction

> **SOFTWARE:** The programs (i.e. the instructions) that a computer executes.

> **20 1**
> Generic programs (like spreadsheets) can be used for a wide variety of purposes.

A program is the set of instructions that tells a computer what to do. Software is defined to be all the programs that run on a computer system.

Software is generally divided into two main types:

- **Systems software:** programs that help a computer system to work (e.g. operating system, disk defragmenter, compiler, etc.).
- **Applications software:** programs that perform a specific task or generic programs that can be used for general purpose tasks (e.g. word-processing program, stock control program, computer game, etc.).

11.2 Operating systems

The most important program run on any computer is the operating system. A computer will not work without an operating system, as it is the program that controls the running of the computer. Every computer has one, from the smallest palmtop to the largest mainframe.

When a computer is switched on, the first thing that happens is that the operating system is loaded into memory. The computer is designed, with software on a ROM chip, to make this process happen automatically. The process is called **booting**.

What does the operating system do?

- **It loads and runs programs**. For example, when an application icon is clicked on the desktop, the corresponding program is loaded from the hard drive and stored in memory. The operating system will then start the program running.
- **It maximises the use of the memory**. For example, think of the operating system as a car park attendant showing a car where to park. The operating system will make sure that a program is stored in the best place in memory when it is loaded. It must not interfere with other programs and it must make efficient use of memory space.
- **It handles inputs and outputs from peripheral devices**. For example, when a key is pressed on a keyboard, a signal is sent to the operating system which outputs a signal to the monitor to display the character pressed.

- **If interrupts occur, then it deals with them**. For example, an interrupt is a signal from a device that needs attention. A printer may run out of paper, so it sends an interrupt to the processor. The operating system will output an error message to the monitor.
- **It maintains the security of the system**. For example, a user must log on to the computer using a name and password. The operating system only allows access if the password is correct.

Examples of operating systems include MS-DOS, Windows, Linux and UNIX.

Applications software may be specific to a particular operating system and so cannot run under another one. For example, a Windows program can not be run on a computer running a UNIX operating system.

There may be a number of utility programs stored separately that are only loaded into memory when they are run. Examples of utility programs are a virus scanning program, a disk defragmenter or a program that takes a back-up of a disk.

Different types of operating system

Many different types of computer system exist in schools, offices and organisations. Each different type of system needs an operating system and the characteristics of these will vary, depending on how the computers operate.

11.2.1 Single program

On some simple computers the operating system will only work on one program at a time. When one program has completed its processing, then the next program is loaded up and run. This sort of operating system is much slower than multi-programming systems and is not found much these days.

11.2.2 Batch processing

JOB: A program and the data it needs.

BATCH: A number of similar jobs.

> Batch processing is usually done at off-peak times such as nights or weekends.

A program, together with any data it needs, is called a **job**. For example a job may consist of an electricity bill program and the data about how many units of electricity a customer has used.

In a batch-processing system, jobs that are waiting to be run are collected and stored in a job queue and then they are all processed together.

Batch-processing systems are often found in businesses where there is no urgency that jobs are processed. An example is a monthly payroll system for a company. The jobs are collected together at the end of each month and run at night to calculate the wages of each employee and produce pay slips.

Advantages of a batch-processing system:

- Processing can be done at off-peak times when the computer is not needed for other processing tasks. Batch processing is often done at night or at the weekend.
- No human intervention is required once the batch has been started.

11.2.3 Multi-programming

The computer holds more than one program in its memory and gives each one a small amount of processing time in turn. This happens so fast that it seems to the user that the computer is running more than one program at a time.

It is the job of the operating system to share the resources such as processing time so that each program eventually gets completed successfully. The operating system will decide the order in which to run the programs, and will make sure that no program gets ignored completely.

The advantage of multi-programming systems is that more programs will be processed in less time than in an operating system that will only process one program at a time.

On a microcomputer, multi-programming is often called **multi-tasking**.

Figure 11.1

Multi-tasking on a microcomputer gives the appearance that the computer is running more than one program at the same time.

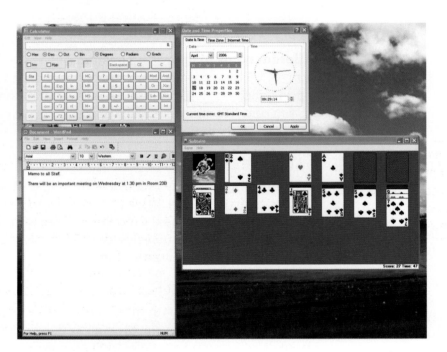

11.2.4 Multi-access

MULTI-ACCESS SYSTEM: Many users are able to work on the same computer at the same time.

A large mainframe computer may have a number of workstations connected directly to it. For example, hundreds of workstations may be spread out in different rooms and floors of a large office block, and the mainframe may be in the basement.

The workstations will consist of input devices such as a keyboard and a mouse, as well as a monitor, but there will be no computer unit. This is because the user of the workstation is actually using the mainframe computer.

Each user works **interactively**, even though the computer they are using may not be nearby. The operating system of the mainframe has to organise the inputs from all the workstations and make sure the outputs go back to the right user. It also has to make sure that each user's program gets processed quickly, and it will allocate resources such as processing time to each user in turn. The speed of the processor will give the impression to each user that they are the only person using the computer.

Figure 11.2 *Diagram of a multi-access system.*

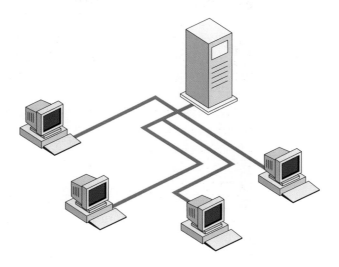

Networks are now replacing many multi-access systems.

11.2.5 Distributive

In a distributive system the processing and resources are shared between a number of different computers. It is the operating system that has to make sure that each of the computers in the system communicates properly. The user will feel that a single computer is being used, but in reality processing may be shared between several computers in the system and the user will be unaware of which ones are being used.

For example a user on computer A may run a program on computer B that uses data stored on computers C and D. The operating system will make sure that the correct connections are made and that processing is completed.

11.2.6 Real-time process control

Data is processed as soon as it is input.

A process control system is an example of a real-time system. Sensors monitor a process by taking environmental measurements and sending them to the computer as input. The computer processes the data immediately and takes action if necessary. This system can react fast enough to be able to take actions in abnormal situations such as a machine breaking down or even a fire.

REAL-TIME SYSTEM: A system in which input data is processed immediately.

The computer monitoring a process control system is a dedicated computer (i.e. it is not used for anything else).

Another example of a real-time system is a flight simulator being used to train pilots. If a rudder pedal is moved, a signal is input to the computer, which immediately analyses it and adjusts the attitude of the simulator accordingly.

Figure 11.3 *A flight simulator would use a real-time operating system.*

Real-time operating systems can be found in embedded computers. The operating system is stored in a ROM chip and runs and manages a single program that operates a device such as a washing machine or a digital camera. It handles simple input and output and makes sure the controlling program runs without problems. (See also Section 5.1.)

> 204
> Even small embedded computers need an operating system.

11.2.7 Real-time transaction processing

> **REAL-TIME TRANSACTION SYSTEM:** A sequence of transactions is processed in the order they are input, and each one is completed before the next begins.

Another type of real-time system involves transactions. Every time an item is sold or bought, or a booking is made, the data from the user is processed immediately. This may involve updating some data held in a record of a database. The transactions are processed in the order they are received, and each transaction is completed before the next one is processed.

An example of a real-time transaction system is a theatre seat booking system. Each time a user makes a booking, the data is processed and the seats requested are marked as being taken. This system should make sure that no two people can book the same seat in the theatre at the same time! (See also Section 5.8.)

The important thing about a real-time system is that it is always up-to-date. If an enquiry is made, then current data is immediately available to be searched.

11.2.8 Parallel processing systems

> 205
> Large tasks are shared between several processors in parallel processing systems, and so are completed faster.

Some larger mainframe computers have more than one processor. There are large mainframes with hundreds or even thousands of processors. Large tasks are completed faster if they are shared between a number of processors (the more people digging a ditch, the faster it will be finished!).

Special computer programming languages have been developed to write applications for parallel processing systems and complex operating systems are needed to share out the tasks to the processors and coordinate their activities.

Computers that process large quantities of data such as for a weather forecasting system use parallel processing.

11.2.9 Interactive systems

A user inputs a command to a computer, which may then respond with a request for further input of data. This is interactive computing: it is similar to a conversation between a user and the computer.

An example of interactive computing can be found when you take cash out of an ATM. The first thing you need to do is enter your PIN, and then the computer will ask you what service you require. You select the option for withdrawing cash, and it will ask you how much you want, and you enter the amount before it gives you the money.

11.3 System security

One of the tasks of an operating system is to maintain security. This means protecting the system from malicious or accidental damage by users. Damage may involve changing a data file or even deleting it.

Security on single-user systems is different to that on multi-user systems. Single-user system security involves protecting files of data from accidental change or deletion, and there is less need for protection from unauthorised users than there is on a multi-user system or a network.

Some of the security measures that might be taken by the operating system:

> The operating system may put in place some security measures to protect files form damage.

- On a multi-user system, the username and password will be checked every time a user logs on to make sure that they are authorised.
- A log is kept of computer usage. The time when a user logged on and how long the user used the computer are recorded.
- The time and date that a file was last changed are recorded. This means that if a file has been deliberately changed, it may be possible to track down who was using the computer at the time.
- The attribute of a file can be set to 'read only'. This would make it impossible to accidentally change or delete an important file.
- If a file is deleted, it may be put into a 'recycling bin' and if the user discovers that a mistake has been made then the file can be recovered.
- Tasks such as taking back-ups can be scheduled to occur at regular times.

Other software may be installed which protects the files on a computer from being changed by viruses.

In practice a combination of security measures needs to be in place, and it is worth remembering that the security of a system is only as strong as its weakest link. For example, it would be no good having a really strong protection against viruses if the protection against hackers is weak. (See also Section 8.8.)

11.4 User interface

HUMAN–COMPUTER INTERFACE (HCI): The way a user gives instructions to the computer and the way the computer displays information back to the user. It depends on the operating system being used.

The Human–Computer Interface (HCI) is the way a user interacts with the computer. This has already been discussed in Section 2.4.10, but it is worth mentioning the three main types of interface again, and the features and advantages of each.

11.4.1 Command line interface

The user types in a command at a prompt character. The operating system then executes this command. This way of telling a computer what to do is used with the MS-DOS operating system, and was used often in the early days of computing.

Some of the commands may have 'switches' to provide options for each command. For example, in MS-DOS, the command for listing the files in a folder called 'DOCS' on drive C, is:

DIR C:\DOCS

If the filenames are to be printed across the screen instead of down, then the instruction that needs to be entered at the command prompt is:

DIR C:\DOCS /W

Some instructions may have a number of switches, and the commands can become quite complex.

?o ?
Command line interfaces operate fast, but the instructions can be complex and need to be learned.

Figure 11.4 *The user has to remember text commands for a command line interface.*

```
Command Prompt                                                    _ □ ×

C:\>dir c:\docs /w
 Volume in drive C has no label.
 Volume Serial Number is E88F-FE95

 Directory of c:\docs

[.]             [..]                  compress.bat    LogiSetup.log    makeskt.bat
overflows.txt   test.txt
                5 File(s)             3,810 bytes
                2 Dir(s)       321,458,176 bytes free

C:\>_
```

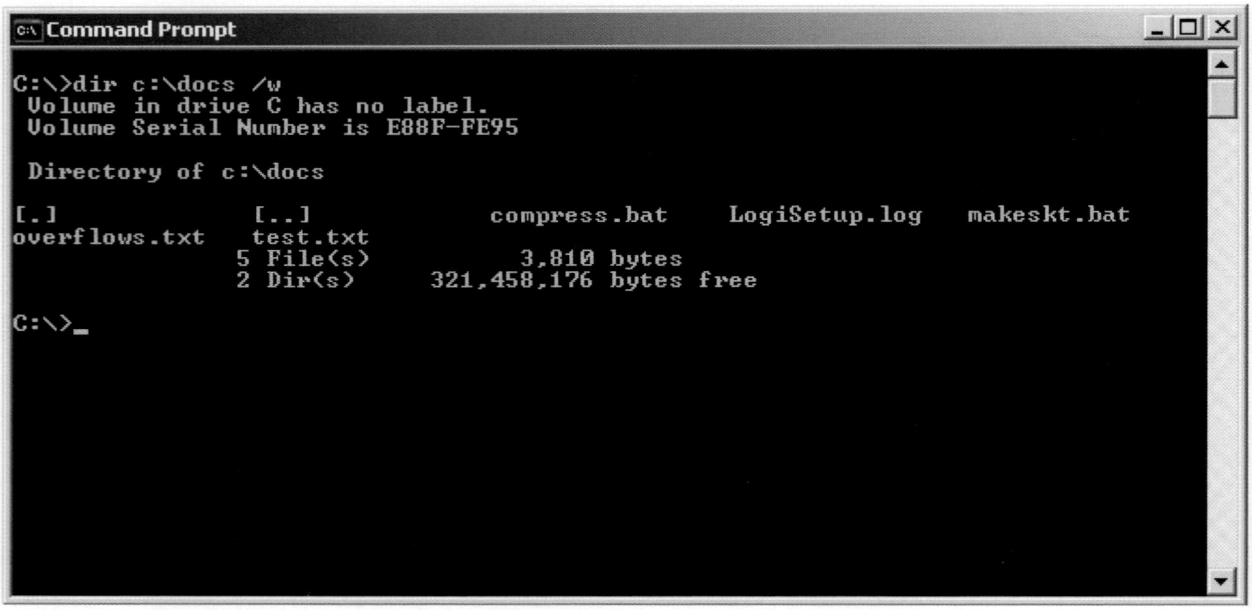

Advantages of a command line interface:

- The instructions execute quickly.
- The instructions are versatile. This means that the user can select a large number of options for each instruction.
- Operating systems that use command line interfaces are smaller when they are loaded into memory.

Disadvantages of a command line interface:

- You need to learn the special instructions used.
- If you mistype an instruction or spell it wrong, then it will not be executed.
- Some commands and their options can be very complex so high-level ICT skills are needed.

11.4.2 Menu-driven interface

A list of options available to the user is displayed and the user then selects one of them usually by clicking the mouse button with the mouse pointer on the option required or by pressing a key on the keyboard.

Several menus may be available to the user and are normally organised into groups of similar options. Selecting one menu option may open another menu (a sub-menu), and some sub-menus may have further sub-menus, etc.

Advantages of a menu-driven interface:

- Simple navigation to find the option required.
- You do not need to learn what instructions are available. They are displayed for you in the menu.

Disadvantages of a menu-driven interface:

- Some options in a menu may not mean anything to the user.
- It is sometimes difficult to find options if there are too many menus and sub-menus.

11.4.3 Graphical User Interface

Most modern computer operating systems use a Graphical User Interface (GUI). Small meaningful pictures called icons represent instructions that are available to the user, and each one is selected by selecting it with a mouse pointer and clicking the mouse button. For example an icon may be a small picture of a printer, and when the user clicks on this icon, the file that is open is printed.

Modern operating systems use WIMP environments:

- **Windows**: A window is a rectangular area of the screen within which an application is run.
- **Icons**: Small meaningful pictures.
- **Menus**: Lists of options.
- **Pointers**: A pointer is moved across the screen by the mouse.

Menus are easy to use but it is sometimes hard to find the option you want.

GRAPHICAL USER INTERFACE (GUI): An easy-to-use and intuitive interface that uses icons to allow the user to communicate with the computer. People with poor ICT skills should be able to use it with little difficulty.

Figure 11.5 *Applications running in Microsoft Windows use a WIMP interface.*

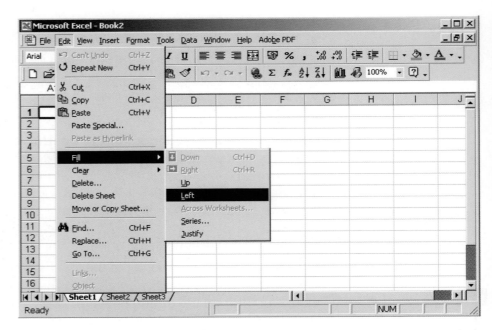

Most GUIs will provide help if users have difficulty. The purpose of a command button is often displayed if the mouse pointer hovers over it, and a help menu should provide a searchable database that will explain how to perform various tasks. Sometimes the help provided is a link to a website on the Internet.

Advantages of a GUI:
● Low level ICT skills are needed. A GUI is an easy-to-use intuitive interface.
● There is no need to learn any instructions.
● Pictures are more meaningful than words, so small children or people with reading problems can use this sort of interface.

Disadvantage of a GUI:
● They are large and complex and can use up a lot of a computer's resources, and may run slowly.

It is helpful to the user if features that are common to different applications running within a GUI can be found in similar places or look the same. For example, a button that is used for printing in one application should have the same icon, have the same colour and be in a similar position in another application.

Menus in all applications should have similar options so that users can become familiar with the layout and are able to find options easily. This will make them more confident about using the computer.

209
The **File** menu in Windows applications always has the Open, Save and Print options.

11.4.4 Sound and speech interfaces

Some user interfaces accept spoken commands. A microphone is used as an input device, the sound is analysed and the command is carried out. This type of user interface is useful if the user is handicapped or has no hands free to operate other input devices such as keyboards or mouses. For example, a surgeon in an operating theatre may use a computer with a speech interface while performing an operation.

Advantage of sound/speech interface:
- It can be used without needing hands.

Disadvantages of sound/speech interface:
- People speak with different voices. The tone of the voice may be high or low, or they may speak at different speeds.
- The interface may not be usable for someone with a broad accent. And people within and across countries speak with many different accents.
- People in different countries speak different languages. The interface may only be able to understand one of them.

220

Interfaces using speech are useful for people with no available hands to use keyboards or mouses, but they must work for people with different accents and ways of talking.

■ Activity 11.1   Integrated software

Microsoft Office is an example of integrated software: it includes the major types of application.

Using the three main programs in Office or a similar set of integrated software (word processing, spreadsheet, database), make a note of the similarities between each program.

Pay careful attention to:

- icons and buttons;
- menus;
- position;
- colour.

Summary

01 A program is a sequence of instructions for a computer.

02 The programs that run on a computer are called software.

03 Systems programs help in the day-to-day running of a computer.

04 Applications programs perform a specific task.

05 An operating system is a program that runs a computer.

06 Booting a computer loads the operating system into the memory.

07 Single-program operating systems load and run one program at a time.

08 Batch-processing systems collect similar jobs together and run them at off-peak times.

09 Multi-programming systems have more than one program loaded into memory. Each program is allocated a time-slice of processing time in turn.

10 In a multi-access system many users are directly connected to a single computer.

11 A distributed system has resources on a number of different computers. The user is not aware of using more than one computer.

12 Real-time systems process input data immediately.

13 Process control systems are examples of real-time systems.

14. In a real-time transaction processing system, the transactions are processed in the order they are input. Each transaction is completed before the next is processed.

15. Data in a real-time system is always up-to-date.

16. Parallel processing systems share the processing between a number of processors.

17. Interactive systems involve a two-way communication between the user and the computer.

18. An operating system puts in place some security measures to make sure data is not accidentally or maliciously changed or deleted.

19. The user interface is the way the user communicates with the computer.

20. A command line interface requires the user to type in instructions. The user needs to learn the instructions and what they do.

21. A menu interface displays a list of options and the user selects one of them.

22. A GUI uses icons (small pictures) to represent options to be selected.

23. A WIMP environment uses Windows, Icons, Menus and Pointers.

24. A GUI provides an easy-to-use and intuitive interface for people who have low ICT skills or are not confident in using computers.

25. Speech interfaces are useful for people who are unable to use keyboards or mouses, but they may have problems if the user speaks with an accent or in a foreign language.

Practice questions 11

1 Decide which of the following operating systems are most applicable for the applications listed: real-time; real-time transaction; batch-processing; multi-access. In each case, say why it is the most applicable.

  a) An on-line theatre booking system. [2]

  b) A computer-controlled traffic light. [2]

  c) Preparation and printing of electricity bills. [2]

2 Which of the following tasks are carried out by an operating system?

  a) Load a computer game.

  b) Display an error message about a printer running out of paper.

  c) Put more paper in a printer.

  d) Save a data record into a database stored on hard disk. [3]

3 If you were to design an integrated package of software that runs under a GUI, how would you make sure the programs were easy to use? [3]

Can you remember…?

1 What is an operating system?

2 What are the two main benefits of running a batch-processing system?

3 What is the main advantage of parallel processing?

4 What is a computer program?

5 What does GUI stand for?

6 What does WIMP stand for?

7 When deciding on a user interface, what factors might influence your decision?

8 Give an example of where a speech interface may be used.

9 Give three tasks an operating system might perform to maintain security of a computer system.

12 Networks

12.1 Introduction

When two or more computers are connected together to allow them to exchange data, this is called a **network**. A computer that is not connected to a network is called a **stand-alone** computer. For example, an organisation might have a number of offices in different towns. If their computers are networked then a worker in one office can view and use the data that is stored on one of the computers in another office.

The advantages of networks are so great that nearly all businesses, schools and other organisations that have more than one computer use a network. Some networks consist of many thousands of computers linked together, but some, for example in a home, may only have two.

The largest network is the **Internet**, which is really thousands of networks all connected together, covering the entire world.

A **server** is a computer on the network that has a resource that is shared and can therefore be used by any other computer on the network. There are different types of server:

- A **file server** has programs and data files stored on its backing storage. It probably has a large capacity hard disk.
- A **print server** has a printer that is shared. Jobs can be printed from any computer on the network.
- A **database server** stores a large database, which can be searched or maintained by any authorised user on the network.
- A **mail server** may manage the email traffic for all users on a network.

The resources may have permissions set so that only authorised users can access and use them.

> Computers on a network are connected together and can exchange data.

> **SERVER:** A computer that has some shared resource that can be used by any computer on the network.

12.2 Types of network

Networks can be simple, perhaps consisting of two computers linked together in a house, or they can be very complex. The design of a network is very important if it is to operate efficiently.

223

12.2.1 Peer-to-peer network

In a peer-to-peer network all the computers are equal in status: no computer is more important than any other. The computers on a peer-to-peer network will probably have similar specifications and be such as you might find in an office environment.

A peer-to-peer network is the opposite of a client/server network.

12.2.2 Client/server network

A client/server network is organised so that one computer acts as a server and all the other computers are clients that use the resources shared on the server. The server will probably be a larger and more powerful computer with more memory and backing storage capacity than the client computers.

12.2.3 Local Area Network

LOCAL AREA NETWORK (LAN): The computers are on the same site and linked by cable.

Where all the networked computers are in the same building or the same site, the network is called a Local Area Network (LAN). Examples may be found in the home, in an office or even in several buildings of a school or college.

There will be direct links connecting the computers using cabling.

12.2.4 Wide Area Network

WIDE AREA NETWORK (WAN): The computers are large distances apart and linked by phone or satellite connections.

If the computers to be connected are geographically distant from each other, the network is called a Wide Area Network (WAN). Computers anywhere in the world can be connected in a WAN. An example of a WAN may be a business that has branch offices in a number of different countries round the world. The computers in these offices may be linked using a WAN so that data can be exchanged between them.

The connections are made using the telephone network and satellites.

The most well-known example of a WAN is the Internet.

12.3 Network topologies

The way in which a network is configured is called a network topology. There are three main types of network topology:

- bus network;
- star network;
- ring network.

12.3.1 Bus network

A bus network is simple and cheap to install but data communication is slow.

The simplest type of network is where each computer is connected to the next computer in a line.

Figure 12.1 *A simple network.*

Bus networks are cheap, but if one computer in the line breaks down or one of the cables is damaged, the network will be split into two parts that will be unable to communicate. The speed of data communication in a bus network is slow.

A better way of setting up a bus network is to link each computer to a common cable called a bus. If this set-up is used then it will not matter if one computer breaks down. The rest of the network will be unaffected.

Figure 12.2 *A bus network.*

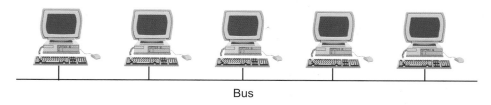

Bus

12.3.2 Star network

All the computers in a star network are connected to a central hub, which directs the flow of data, or to a central computer that acts as the file server. Each computer has its own connection to the hub so, if one computer or cable breaks down, it will not affect the rest of the network. However if the hub or file server at the centre of the network fails, then all computers will be affected.

Working on a computer in a star network is fast because of the direct link to the file server, and each computer only has two links of cable to another computer.

Star networks can be quite expensive to install because of the amount of cabling used.

> **213**
>
> A star network is more expensive than a bus network because of the amount of cabling but is faster and more reliable.

Figure 12.3 *A star network with a file server.*

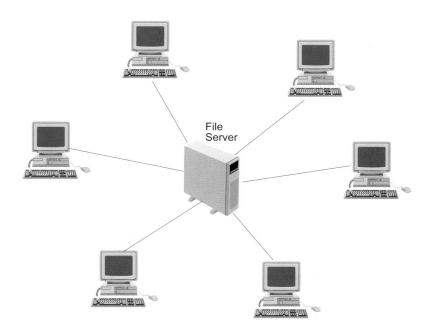

File Server

12.3.3 Ring network

The computers in a ring network are connected to each other in a loop. This topology is often used in a peer-to-peer network because there is no need for one computer to be more powerful than the rest, as there is in a star network.

Computers on a ring network communicate by sending data round the loop, always in the same direction, each one passing it on to the next, until it reaches the receiving computer.

A ring network is similar to a bus network but the last computer is linked back to the first, so it also has the problem that if one computer or cable breaks down then the whole network will be affected.

> **214**
> Ring networks are often used in peer-to-peer networks. They are inexpensive but can be affected by breakdowns.

Figure 12.4 *A ring network.*

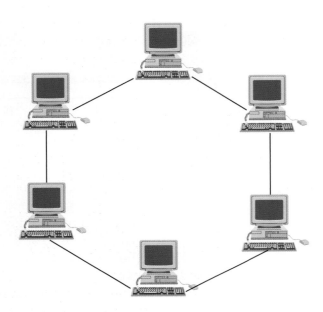

In reality large networks are combinations of several of these topologies.

12.4 Network security

Security on networks is taken seriously. No organisation wants its data files damaged or deleted, and measures are taken to protect them from problems caused by accidents or malicious misuse. There may also be a problem if data is disclosed to the wrong people.

Threats to networks may include hackers, viruses, hardware breakdown or simple human error.

A network **security policy** will set out what actions are allowed and the people who are authorised to perform them. These actions are:

- Access: viewing the data stored.
- Modification: changing data in any of the files.
- Deletion: removing data or even whole files.

> **215**
> Data and files stored on networked computers must be protected from damage or deletion, whether it is accidental or malicious.

Passwords

Every authorised user of a network is given a username and a password. These will need to be entered whenever a user logs on to the network, and the operating system will only allow access to the network if the password is correct.

Networks are prone to hackers (people gaining unauthorised access to data and possibly causing damage) and passwords should make it more difficult for them to access files.

There may be resources that are accessible only by some people, and different levels of security may be used.

Encryption

If data stored on a computer is encrypted, then it will be meaningless to someone who is not authorised to access it. The data is coded using a special key known only to authorised people, who are able to decode it when it needs to be used.

Back-ups

It is essential that data stored on a network is backed-up regularly. This is easier to do on a client/server network where all the files are stored on a file server. A back-up of all the files can be scheduled at regular times such as every night. The back-up copy of the files is best stored in a different location to the original in case of disasters such as a fire.

If there is a problem with the original data files then the back-up of the files is loaded, and all changes made since the back-up was created need to be done again.

It is easier to schedule regular back-ups if all files are stored on a file server.

File access rights

It may be possible to limit the access rights of a file. This means that only certain people are allowed to access the data in that file.

A user may have:

● no rights to access a file at all;
● the right to view but not change a file;
● full control so the file can be viewed and altered.

Permissions can be set on files or folders, and may only apply to certain groups of users.

Transaction logs

If there is a major problem with a computer it is important that any lost files of data can be re-created. A back-up may have been made of all the files of data the previous night but all the transactions that a business has conducted on the following day need to be recorded so that they can be processed again on any restored back-up if necessary.

This is the **transaction log**. All the transactions are recorded as they occur. Any action that caused a change in the data is added to the log.

GATEWAY: A computer that links two network segments.

Firewall

A firewall is software that runs on a gateway computer linking two networks. For example, it may be run on a computer that connects a school network to the Internet to prevent hackers from gaining access to the school's network of computers.

Virus protection

Computers on a network connected to the Internet may have a problem with viruses being introduced on downloaded files or on emails. To protect all the computers on the network, the Internet server, the computer linked to the Internet should run virus-protection software to prevent any attempted attack by viruses.

12.5 Advantages of networks

Networks allow computers to share resources.

Computers on a network can share:

Computers on a network can share hardware, software and data. It is also easier for them to communicate.

- Hardware: For example, a printer connected to a print server can be used by any computer on the network. Other hardware can be shared such as scanners and CD-ROM drives.
- Software: Programs installed on one computer can be run over the network on another computer. This is normally not a good idea because it slows down the speed at which the program runs.
- Data: A database can be saved on the backing storage of a file server, but users on the network can access and use the data.

Another important feature of networks is that it allows computers to communicate with each other. Users can send messages, data files or emails to each other whether the network is a LAN in an office or a global WAN.

There is also better control over the usage of the computers on a network. The network manager can allocate permissions to users to restrict their actions, or limit the amount of storage space they can use.

If data files accessed by users on a network are stored on a file server, then it is easier to make scheduled back-ups than if the files are stored on several different computers.

The advantage of a stand-alone computer is that it is not as prone to attack by viruses or hackers.

12.6 Data transmission

Data in a network can be transmitted by:

- **Cable:** Each computer has a network card installed (see Figure 2.25). On the card is a socket where the connecting cable is inserted. Network software (drivers) must be installed before the network card can be used.

There are two main types of cable: metal copper wire (twisted pair or coaxial) and fibre optic. Fibre optic cables have much higher capacity than copper wire cables and can carry thousands of times more information with little or no interference. They are also smaller and do not corrode like copper cables. (See also Section 2.4.1.)

- **Telephone:** A computer is connected to a network such as the Internet using a modem (see Section 2.3.2).
- **Wireless (microwave, infrared, radio):** To avoid the inconvenience of a lot of cables, networks are sometimes set up using wireless technology. Each computer needs a wireless network card together with software drivers installed.

A wireless hub transmits radio signals that are received by the network cards in each of the computers. An example may be a home network where a wireless hub is connected to a broadband Internet connection. The hub transmits radio signals to any other computer in the house fitted with a wireless network card. Laptops can be carried around and used anywhere in the house, or even sitting outside on the patio (but be careful of sunstroke!).

Businesses need to be aware that wireless networks present a potential security risk as hackers can 'tune in' to the transmitted data.

- **Satellite:** Some networks incorporate satellites orbiting in space. Geosynchronous satellites orbit at the same speed as the spin of the earth so they are effectively stationary, allowing a constant signal to be transmitted. Networks using satellites can cover vast distances, but special satellite dishes are needed to receive the signals.

2.1.8

Data transmission **speeds** may vary according to the type of cabling. Fibre optic cables are more reliable and carry more data than copper wire cables.

2.1.9

Home networks might use wireless technology to beam data to laptops that can be used anywhere in the house.

Figure 12.5 *A wireless hub.*

Summary

01 Two or more computers connected together so they can exchange data is called a network.

02 A server is a computer on a network that has a resource that can be used by other computers on the same network (e.g. a file server has shared files).

03 In a peer-to-peer network all computers are of equal importance.

04 A client/server network has a larger computer acting as a file server.

05 A LAN is a Local Area Network. Computers on the same site are connected with cables.

06 A WAN is a Wide Area Network. Computers geographically distant are connected using the telephone system or wireless technology using satellites or microwave signals.

07 Network topologies may be bus, star or ring configurations.

08 Files on a network must be protected from malicious or accidental damage. A network security policy lays down rules for what users are allowed to do.

09 Users of a network will have usernames and passwords which they must enter when logging on.

10 Data files may be encrypted.

11 Back-up copies of important data files must be regularly made.

12 Firewalls will protect computer networks from hackers.

13 Transaction logs record all changes made to data files.

14 Virus protection software will protect computers from viruses.

15 Computers on a network:
- can share hardware;
- can share software;
- can share data;
- can communicate.

16 Network cable can be copper or fibre optic.

17 Fibre optic cable can transmit data much faster than copper cable.

18 Wireless networks need a wireless hub that transmits signals to network cards installed in other computers.

19 Wireless networks need no cables.

20 Data in wireless networks is transmitted using radio, microwave or infrared signals.

Practice questions 12

1 Many businesses use a computer network in their office.
   a) What is a network? [1]
   b) Give three advantages of using a computer network rather than stand-alone computers. [3]

2 a) What is a LAN? [1]
   b) What is a WAN? [1]
   c) Explain the difference between a LAN and a WAN. [2]

3 Security of a network is the responsibility of the network manager.
   a) Give two ways in which the network could be protected from unauthorised access. [2]
   b) Give two ways in which the network could be protected from viruses. [2]

Can you remember...?

1 What is a file server?

2 What is the difference between a client/server network and a peer-to-peer network?

3 What are the three main network topologies? Can you draw them?

4 What are the two main types of network cable? Which is cheaper? Which is faster?

5 What cables does a wireless network use?

6 What is a transaction log?

13 Systems analysis

13.1 Introduction

ICT is always changing. New hardware is developed all the time and new devices are invented. Computers contain faster and more powerful processors, and backing storage devices increase in capacity. Software developers bring out new versions of software regularly, and new programs come on the market. Operating systems change to be able to operate with new hardware and networking demands.

Businesses spend a lot of money installing the latest computer system, only to find, after a few years, that it is out of date and needs upgrading. New businesses, or ones that do not have a computer system, may need to design one from scratch.

The process of designing new computer systems is called systems analysis, and the person who carries out this design process is a systems analyst.

> **SYSTEMS ANALYSIS:** The process of designing and making a new computer system.

13.2 The system life cycle

Every computer system goes through a system life cycle (Figure 13.1).

Figure 13.1 *The four stages of the system life cycle.*

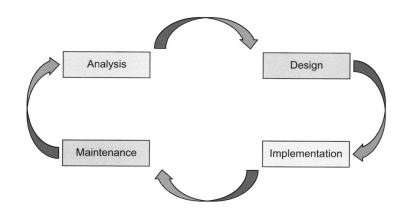

13.2.1 Analysis

The first stage of developing a new computer system involves an investigation into what the new system needs to do. The systems analyst may not work for the business and will need to find out how it works and which parts of it are suitable for computerisation.

There are four ways to carry out this investigation:

- **Interviews:** The systems analyst may interview the managers and other members of staff, and ask them questions about the way the business operates.
- **Questionnaires:** Employees may be asked to fill in questionnaires.
- **Observation:** The systems analyst wanders around the business looking at the jobs that people do and who does them.
- **Documentation:** If there was an old computer system, then there will be documentation about it, which can be read in order to understand the existing system.

The analysis will try to answer the following questions:

- What data does the business store?
- How does the data get collected in the first place. Are there any data capture forms?
- How is the data stored: in a computer system or a filing cabinet?
- What data is needed as input for processing in the existing system, even if the data is processed manually?
- What results are output, and how are they presented. Are they printed on paper, written by hand or is there another method?
- Who is involved in carrying out each of the above processes?
- What problems is the current system experiencing?

The systems analyst will gather all the findings of the investigation together, and analyse them. The way the current system works and the problems of the system should now be fully understood, and the parts of the system suitable for computerisation should have been identified.

A **feasibility report** will be produced which will consider whether a new computer system is a reasonable course of action to take. Costs and the effect on the existing employees will be considered.

There is no point in going ahead with a new system if it is going to cost more to create and run than the extra money it would generate, and it may not be a good idea if it involves sacking most of the workforce.

The feasibility report will weigh possible benefits against the costs, and will be presented to the management of the business, who will then decide whether to go ahead with developing the new system.

13.2.2 Design

Assuming the management has given the go-ahead for the new system to be developed, the next stage is the design of the new system.

2.20
You will be carrying out an **analysis** of a system for your coursework project.

2.21
Computerisation means changing work from being done by hand to being done on computers.

2.22
Good design should result in an error-free system that works well.

The objectives for the new system will need to be declared. These are the targets the new system will be required to achieve such as:

Reduce by 50 per cent the time it takes to process a customer's order.

The design specification of the new system will include:

- **Hardware requirements:** What new computers or devices need to be bought and installed. Will the computers be stand-alone or networked computers?
- **Software requirements:** What new software needs to be bought and installed. Will the programs need to be installed on every computer or only on a network server? What version of which operating system will be used?
- **Data control:** What data needs to be stored? How will this data be collected? If data capture forms are used, then they will need to be designed. What verification or validation checks will be put in place to make sure there are no errors in the data?
- **Input designs:** Screen displays will need to be designed.
- **Output reports:** What output will be produced and how will it be presented (screen or paper, text or graphics)?
- **Security:** What security measures will be put in place to make sure the data is not maliciously or accidentally damaged or deleted? What physical measures for securing the system will there be, such as locking the computer rooms and allowing access only by fingerprint scan devices?
- **Testing:** Decisions need to be made at this stage about how the new system will be tested.
- **Documentation:** All systems need documentation. This will enable people not involved in creating the system to understand how it works, in case it needs changing at a later date.
- **Evaluation criteria:** How will the new system be judged in terms of how effective it is? Standards will be set by which the success of the new system will be measured.

The systems analyst also needs to take into account the social implications of the new system and what effects it might have on the workforce. Will there be anybody made redundant, or will there be the need for any training of the staff to tackle new jobs?

Effects on health may also be considered. Will the staff spend too much time sitting at computers and not get enough exercise?

13.2.3 Implementation

This stage involves the creation of the new system and then getting it working. The old system will be stopped and all employees will start using the new system.

Implementation
means getting the new system up and running.

- **Hardware:** Any new computers and equipment will be bought and set up.
- **Software:** New programs will be bought and installed on the computers. If any programs need to be written, then programmers will code, test and debug them.
- **Data:** Data from the old system will need to be transferred to the new system. This may involve transcribing the data into a new database, or importing data from old databases.

- **Testing:** The new system must be systematically and fully tested. There could be real problems for a business if the new system does not work properly. Sequences of test runs are made using valid data, invalid data, missing data or extreme data such as very large numbers. Any problems arising from failed tests must be solved.
- **Changeover:** Changing over from the old system to the new system. This can be done by:
  - **Direct changeover:** The old system is stopped and the new system started straight away. This could be disastrous if there are errors in the new system.
  - **Parallel running:** The new system is started but the old one keeps running at the same time. This is a safer way of introducing the new system, but there is a lot of extra work as all jobs have to be done twice.
  - **Pilot study:** The new system is tried in only one part of the company, such as one branch of a large business, to see if it works. If all goes well then the rest of the company can start using the new system.
  - **Phased conversion:** Parts of the new system are introduced at a time. If there are no problems then another part can be introduced and so on, until eventually the entire new system is implemented.
- **System evaluation:** The new system must be checked to see if it achieves all of its objectives and all the design requirements have been satisfied. The impact of the new system on jobs (redundancies or re-training) and any social problems such as possible isolation of workers will also be investigated.

13.2.4 Maintenance

All computer systems need some maintenance. Businesses change: they expand or grow smaller, they open new branches or start selling new goods. Any computer system being run will need to adapt to these changes.

> **224**
> The needs of businesses change all the time, so their systems have to be adjusted. **Maintenance** is making changes in the system.

- **Data:** This needs to be kept up-to-date. New records may need to be added or changes may need to be made to existing data.
- **Hardware:** New hardware is being produced all the time and it may be desirable to upgrade it. Hardware that breaks down will need to be replaced.
- **Software:** Errors may come to light that were not picked up when the system was being tested. Changes in the programs may need to be made to solve these problems.
- **Perfective maintenance:** This means improvements are made to the existing system to make it better in some way such as improving the speed of performing one of the tasks.

Whenever any changes are made to a system, the documentation must be updated. Any differences in the way the system is used must be recorded in the user documentation and any changes to the hardware or software must be included in the technical documentation.

When a program is changed it is often rewritten by a programmer who was not the one that wrote the original code. The technical documentation will show how the program works and will need to be consulted if changes are to be made successfully. This is why it is so important to keep the technical documentation up-to-date and well-written.

> **225**
> Programmers often change code that another programmer has written.

If any changes are made to a program then it will need to be tested again to make sure no errors occur.

Summary

☐1 A computer system consists of hardware, software, people and processes.

☐2 All computer systems need upgrading from time to time.

☐3 Systems analysis is the process of designing a new computer system.

☐4 There are four main stages in systems analysis:
- Analysis: Investigating the old system and the requirements of the new system.
- Design: Planning the new system.
- Implementation: Getting the new system working.
- Maintenance: Making adjustments to the system.

☐5 Four methods of investigation used in analysis are questionnaires, interviews, observation and reading existing documentation.

☐6 Testing of the new system will take place at all stages.

☐7 Documentation of the system consists of:
- User documentation: Information on how to use the system.
- Technical documentation: Useful for programmers who need to make changes.

☐8 Changeover can be made in four ways:
- Direct changeover: Stopping the old system and starting the new one straight away.
- Parallel running: Running both systems and dropping the old system when the new system works perfectly.
- Pilot study: Trying out the new system in part of the business first.
- Phased conversion: Implementing parts of the new system gradually.

☐9 Evaluation of the system assesses whether the new system achieves its objectives.

Practice questions 13.1

1 A systems analyst is employed to design and implement a new computer system for a library. Describe the steps to be followed in each of the stages:

a) Analysis of the current system. [2]

b) Design of a new system. [2]

c) Implementation of the new system. [2]

d) Maintenance. [2]

An important part of a new system is the documentation.

e) What are the two main types of documentation? [2]

13.3 Information systems in society

The progress of ICT has been rapid over the past thirty years and society has been forced to make many changes because of it. However, some of these changes happen slowly, such as the changes in the legal system and there are many areas in law that are rather vague when it comes to applying them to ICT systems.

There have been a number of notable laws passed that apply to computer users and we will study three of them here.

13.3.1 The Data Protection Act

The first Data Protection Act was passed in 1984, but a revised version was introduced in 1998. It was introduced because so much data about people was being stored on computer systems and existing legislation was not appropriate.

The Act deals with **personal data**: data held about a person. There are many organisations and businesses that hold personal data on each of us. Here are some examples:

- The Tax Office;
- A doctor or a dentist;
- The Driver and Vehicle Licensing Agency (DVLA);
- The police;
- and many more.

> **DATA PROTECTION ACT:**
> UK legislation that states some obligations for a company storing personal data and some rights of the data subject: but there are some exemptions.

The Act states that the data subject (the person whose personal data is stored on a computer) has certain **rights**, and the organisation that stores the data has certain **obligations**.

When an organisation needs to store personal data, it needs to register with the Data Protection Act, and state the purpose for which they need the information.

The obligations of the organisation storing the data are:

- Data must not be stored or processed other than for a lawful stated purpose.
- The data must be collected and processed fairly and lawfully.
- The data must be adequate, relevant and not excessive for the stated purpose.
- The data processing must meet the rights of the data subject.
- The data must be accurate and kept up-to-date.
- The data must not be kept longer than necessary.
- The data must be kept secure.
- The data must not be sent abroad, other than to EU countries.

The rights of the data subject are:

- The right of access: data subjects are entitled to view the personal data stored about them.
- The right of correction: if incorrect data is stored, the subject has the right to have it changed.
- The right of compensation: if unlawful processing of the data leads to damage or distress, the subject is entitled to compensation.

> Incorrect data could lead to you being refused a loan, not given a job or even arrested.

The Act also defines 'Sensitive Personal Data', which must not be disclosed or processed without the subject's knowledge and permission, unless it is necessary for other legal reasons.

Sensitive Personal Data includes data about the subject's:

- racial or ethic origin;
- religious beliefs;
- political opinions;
- trade union membership;
- physical or mental health;
- offences and convictions.

Not all organisations have to register their use of personal data. Exemptions from the Data Protection Act are:

- Data held for purposes of national security.
- Data which helps in the detection of crime.
- Data for home use (household or recreational).
- Data used for calculation of wages, pensions or tax.
- Data used for the distribution of literature, information or advertisements.

13.3.2 Copyright law

Computer software companies have a big problem. People obtain illegal copies of their software without paying for it, either by making a copy of somebody else's or by downloading it from the Internet. Developing and testing of software is an expensive business, and software piracy is costing the companies a lot of money.

The **Copyright, Designs and Patents Act 1989** makes software piracy illegal. It is a criminal offence to steal or copy software without the permission of the copyright holder or the owner of the software. It also states that it is an offence to run pirated software on your computer.

Some software requires the user to enter a special licence number when installing the programs. This licence number is given to the purchaser of the software, or included in the documentation and is an attempt to prevent software piracy.

Some companies buy site licences for software. This means they are legally allowed to run the programs on a given number of computer on their site, which may be an office a school, or a college campus.

The problem for the software companies is that this law is very difficult to enforce. Software piracy is very common, but it is difficult to detect and even harder to prove.

SOFTWARE PIRACY: The illegal stealing or copying of software without permission of the copyright holder.

13.3.3 Computer Misuse Act

New laws have been necessary to combat new crimes that have emerged with the development of ICT. The **Computer Misuse Act 1990** is a law that makes it illegal to:

COMPUTER MISUSE ACT: UK legislation that makes hacking, as well as creating or planting viruses, illegal.

- Gain unauthorised access to files stored on a computer system, including viewing and copying the files. It is an offence to try to hack into a system even if you fail!
- Gain unauthorised access to files and use them for criminal activities such as fraud or blackmail.
- Change or delete any files unless authorised to do so. This includes creating or planting viruses as they may alter or delete files.

Summary

01 The Data Protection Act (DPA) deals with personal data.

02 The DPA imposes some obligations on the organisation storing data:
- Data must be stored and processed for a good reason.
- Data must be collected fairly and lawfully.
- Data should be adequate, relevant and not excessive for the stated purpose.
- Processing of the data must not infringe the rights of the data subject.
- Data must be accurate and kept up-to-date.
- Data must not be kept longer than necessary.
- Data must be kept secure.
- Data must not be sent abroad to countries outside the EU.

03 The DPA imposes some rights for the data subject:
- The subject is entitled to view the data stored on them.
- The subject can have the data stored on them corrected if it is wrong.
- If processing of the data causes distress the subject is entitled to compensation.

04 Exemptions from the DPA include data for national security, the prosecution of crime, household and recreational data, data for tax purposes or the distribution of information such as mailshots.

05 The Copyright Law makes it an offence to copy a file without the permission of the owner or copyright holder.

06 The Computer Misuse Act makes it illegal to hack into a computer system, use data files for purposes such as fraud or blackmail, and to create or plant viruses.

Practice questions 13.2

1 A doctor's surgery stores personal information about its patients on its computer system.

    a) Name three fields of personal data other than name, address and telephone number, that might be stored by the surgery. [3]

    b) What would the surgery have to do to comply with the Data Protection Act? [2]

    c) Why could the surgery not pass on the data to an insurance company? [1]

    d) A patient is unhappy about the data stored about him on the surgery's computer, and he demands to see it. The surgery refuses to show him. Who is in the right? [1]

    e) Name three types of data that are exempt from the Data Protection Act. [3]

2 What crimes are highlighted by the Computer Misuse Act? [3]

SECTION  3

Portfolio

14 Introduction: What is expected of the pupil

The assessment of the GCSE is in two parts:

- The **written exam(s)**: this is **40 per cent** of the total marks.
- The **coursework**: this is **60 per cent** of the total marks.

This applies to both Full and Short Course.

> ???
> Coursework is the main part of the exam so you must make a good job of it!

14.1 Short course

There is only **one** written exam (Paper 1), and it is offered at two levels:

- Foundation Level: 1 hour.
- Higher Level: 1 hour 30 minutes.

Those sitting at the Foundation Level will be awarded grades C–G.
Those sitting at the Higher level will be awarded grades A*–D.
The coursework consists of a **portfolio** of work worth 60 per cent of the total marks.

14.2 Full course

There are **two** written exams (Paper 1 and 2), and they are offered at two levels:

- Foundation level: 1 hour.
- Higher Level: 1 hour 30 minutes.

Those sitting at the Foundation Level will be awarded grades C–G.
Those sitting at the Higher level will be awarded grades A*–D.
The coursework consists of:

- a **portfolio** of work worth 30 per cent of the total marks;
- a **project** worth 30 per cent of the total marks.

The make-up of the total exam mark is displayed in the following table:

	Short course		Full course	
Written exam paper	Paper 1	40%	Paper 1	20%
			Paper 2	20%
Coursework	Portfolio	60%	Portfolio	30%
			Project	30%
		100%		100%

ICT is designed to be a practical course and this is reflected in the fact that most of the final marks are assigned to the coursework. Those pupils who can work well on the computers on their own, and who can concentrate on what they are doing and not be distracted by others will do well.

15 The portfolio

15.1 Introduction

> **2.28**
> The three portfolio tasks can be done in any order.

The portfolio consists of three parts:

- Information handling
- Spreadsheet modelling
- Communicating information

These three tasks may be handed in separately or presented as a single integrated task. The example portfolio in this book will treat the portfolio as three distinct separate assignments.

The three tasks can be done in any order.

15.2 Portfolio task 1: Information handling

> **2.29**
> No marks will be awarded for any task if you do not provide printed evidence.

This task will let you show off all the things you know about databases. You will design and create one of your own, and then use it to perform some searches and sorts.

With all of the portfolio tasks it is important that you keep your work organised and that plenty of evidence of the work you have done is displayed on printed documents.

Your target is **20 marks**. Use a checklist (see the Activity at the end of this section) to cross off each task as you finish it.

Your teacher will tell you what topic you will do for this portfolio task.

> **2.30**
> Let your imagination run wild: but keep it realistic!

1	
Use	Word processor (Microsoft Word)
Title	Background information
Task	● Describe the situation where the database is going to be used and explain what it is to be used for.
Marks	This task need only be a few paragraphs long, and is not worth any marks. Treat this as a warm-up exercise and hopefully you will think of some ideas.

The main requirement of this task is that you create a database and then use it to solve some problems.

The database may consist of any data of your choice.

The **planning** of the database is important and the first task will be to create a data structure table.

To do this you need to decide:

- What data is going to be stored and what names will be given to the fields?
- What type of data will be stored in each field?

2.3.1

Make sure there are a number of different data types: text, number, date, currency, etc.

2	
Use	Word processor (Microsoft Word)
Title	Data structure table
Task	● Write a short introduction about what data is going to be stored in your database and how the data will be collected. (You will be designing a data capture form later.) ● Create the data structure table. You will need to insert a table with three columns and a row for each field, and fill in the fieldname, the data type and add any comments about the field.
Marks	1 mark for the design of the data structure table.

For our example database, we may decide on the following data structure table:

2.3.2

It is important that fields are chosen with a variety of different data types: some text, numbers, currency and dates.

Fieldname	Data type	Comments
RideID	Integer	The key field for the database
Name	Text	Maximum length 30
DateOpened	Date	Formatted dd/mm/yy
PriceAdult	Currency	e.g. £1.50
PriceChild	Currency	
RidesTW	Number	Rides sold this week
RidesTY	Number	Rides sold this year
Category	Text	A code : 'F' for Family, 'A' for Adult only.

Text fields should have maximum lengths, and any formatting of numbers or currency fields should be specified.

3	
Use	Database software (Microsoft Access)
Title	Database creation

Task	● Create a new blank database.
	● Create a new table in design view and enter the details of each field. Make sure you:
	  ● set the key field;
	  ● save the table using a sensible name.

Marks	1 mark if you have used and set a key field.

2.3.3

It is a good idea to create a new folder to put all your coursework files in.

When you create a new blank database, make sure it is put in a folder that you can find easily. And give it a sensible name!

4	
Use	(a) Database software (Microsoft Access) and (b) Word processor (Microsoft Word)
Title	Validation
Task	(a) Set Validation Rules for some of the numeric fields (integer, real, currency or date), as well as appropriate Validation Text messages which appear when invalid data is entered. (b) Test the validation rules and provide proof that they work.
Marks	1 mark for design of validation rules. 1 mark for the validation tests using valid and invalid data.

Validation is checking the data to make sure that it is sensible data, and there are rules you can set for numerical fields (integer, real, currency or date).

These are the Validation Rules, and the data will be checked every time it is entered to make sure that it obeys the rules.

Inequalities are used to set the rules.

The error message that appears if the data is incorrect is called the Validation Text.

It is now time to test that your validation rules work. The best way to do this is by providing screenshots of the Validation Text (the error message that appears if you try to enter invalid data).

Open your table and try to enter invalid data. An error message should appear.

Use a word processor, put a heading 'Validation Tests', and:

> ⌐ᴶᴸ
> Run tests with both
> valid and invalid data.

- describe the validation rules that you have set;
- give details about the data that you are testing them with (one valid and one invalid).

Screenshots like the one below will provide proof that they work.

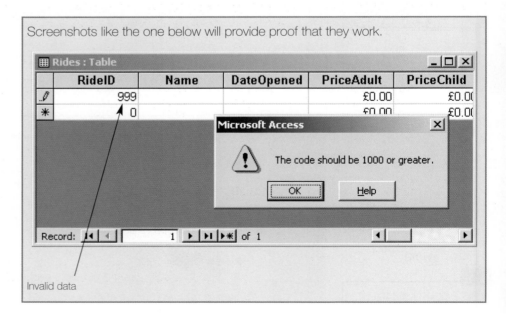

Invalid data

5	
Use	Database software (Microsoft Access)
Title	Data entry
Task	● Open your table in Datasheet view, and enter data. You need to make sure there are no mistakes and that the data you use is sensible.
Marks	1 mark if you use two different data types.
	1 extra mark if you use three or more different data types (text, integer, currency, date, lookup).
	1 mark if there are no mistakes.
	1 mark if the data is sensible and relevant.
	1 mark for the printout to show the table.

235

Save your table frequently in case your computer develops problems!

236

Make sure there are no mistakes on the printout of your table. If there are, correct them and print it out again!

You have done all the preparation work and the next step is to actually create the records in the database.

Open the table in Datasheet view and enter at least 10 records of data. You need to make sure there are no mistakes such as spelling mistakes, and that capital letters are properly used (e.g. proper names should start with a capital letter).

It is also important to make sure the data is plausible. This means that it must be realistic and not have any errors such as a person called 'Sally' whose sex is 'Male'.

When the table is finished, save it and print it out.

Study your printout carefully because it provides evidence of a number of things such as the different data types used in the fields. Make sure that it shows there are no mistakes such as spelling mistakes, and that the data is reasonable and realistic.

Rides : Table

RideID	Name	DateOpened	PriceAdult	PriceChild	RidesTW	RidesTY	Category
1000	Sliderama	12/04/2004	£2.00	£1.00	25	189	F
1001	Big Dipper	08/07/2005	£2.50	£1.50	18	241	F
1002	Skelemania	25/06/2002	£3.00	£2.00	39	398	A
1003	Mud Madness	08/04/2001	£2.00	£1.00	57	658	F
1004	Nerves of Steel	16/12/2000	£3.50	£1.50	19	169	A
1005	Spinning Tops	16/12/2000	£2.00	£1.00	12	89	F
1006	Devil's Dare	19/02/2001	£3.50	£2.00	25	204	F
1007	Rocket Adventure	08/04/2001	£2.00	£1.00	16	167	F
1008	Duck Shoot	16/12/2000	£2.00	£0.75	35	268	F
1009	Wall of Death	12/04/2004	£1.50	£0.50	39	359	A
1010	Slippery Slope	27/11/2003	£1.00	£0.50	57	685	F
1011	Starry Night Ride	16/12/2000	£3.50	£2.00	25	542	F
1012	Water Chute	16/12/2000	£2.50	£1.50	102	980	F
1013	Aviator	25/06/2002	£2.00	£1.00	69	710	F
1014	Wild West Train	08/04/2001	£2.00	£1.00	34	544	F
1015	Insanity City	25/06/2002	£2.50	£1.50	98	898	A
0			£0.00	£0.00	0	0	

Record: 16 of 16

6	
Use	Database software (Microsoft Access)
Title	Sorts
Task	● State a reason for sorting the data and present a printout of the sorted database. ● Repeat for a second different sort.
Marks	1 mark: Sort with a valid reason.
	1 mark: A second different sort with reason.

NOTE: If your database software allows it, you can create a graph of some of the data instead of one of the sorts. There must be a sensible reason for making the graph.

Sorting data means putting it in numerical or alphabetical order of one of the fields. The sort may be ascending (smallest first) or descending (largest first).

If you are using Microsoft Access, then you must create a Query for each sort, giving the fields you want to display, and setting the field to be sorted by, as well as whether it is to be in ascending or descending order.

Use a word processor to create a document with a heading 'Sort 1'.

Give details about your sort and explain the **reason** for it.

In the database, create a query that performs the sort and include the grid design as well as the results of the sort. These can be copied and pasted into the document.

You now need to repeat the process for another different sort, but you must make sure there is a different reason for it, and different fields are displayed.

You will not get the marks for these sorts if you do not give a realistic reason for them.

7	
Use	Database software (Microsoft Access)
Title	Simple searches
Task	● Give a reason for and carry out a simple search. ● Carry out a second simple search with a reason.
Marks	1 mark for simple search with reason.
	1 mark for second simple search with reason.

A **simple search** is a search on one field only.

Think of a reason why the search needs to be done, but make sure that it is a realistic reason. Set up the Query and carry out the search.

Print out the grid showing the **search criteria** you used, and the results of the search. Copy and paste each into a word-processed document that explains what you have done.

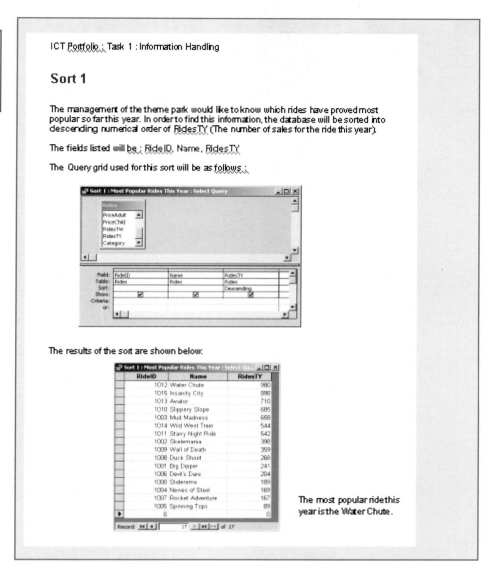

ICT Portfolio : Task 1 : Information Handling

Sort 1

The management of the theme park would like to know which rides have proved most popular so far this year. In order to find this information, the database will be sorted into descending numerical order of RidesTY (The number of sales for the ride this year).

The fields listed will be : RideID, Name, RidesTY

The Query grid used for this sort will be as follows :

The results of the sort are shown below:

The most popular ride this year is the Water Chute.

The reason, search criteria, grid and results should be pasted into a word-processed document titled 'Simple Search 1', and printed out.

You now need to do another different simple search, with a different realistic reason and different fields. Repeat the above process and print out a document titled 'Simple Search 2'.

8	
Use	Database software (Microsoft Access)
Title	Complex searches
Task	● Give a reason and carry out a complex search. ● Carry out a second complex search with a reason.
Marks	1 mark for complex search with reason.
	1 mark for second complex search with reason.
	1 mark for explaining the search criteria.

A complex search is a search which uses two or more fields, combining them with the logical operators OR, AND or NOT.

The reason, search criteria, query grid and results should be pasted into a word-processed document called 'Complex Search 1', and printed.

A **second** and completely different complex search needs to be done. Make sure the fields displayed and the search criteria are different to the first one.

> **239**
> Note that units of measurement are not used in the search criteria.

9	
Use	Word processor (Microsoft Word)
Title	Data capture form
Task	● Draw the design of your data capture form.
Marks	1 mark for designing a data capture form.

A data capture form is a paper form that is filled in whenever a new record is to be added to the database file. The form is then handed to someone who inputs the data.

The fields on the data capture form must match the fields in the database table.

Open a new word-processing document and put a heading 'Data Capture Form', and describe how the data in your database is collected. Where can the data capture form be found? Who fills in the forms? Where are they taken when they are completed? Who inputs the data?

Make sure there is plenty of blank space on the page and print out the document.

Draw by hand the design of the data capture form on the same sheet, indicating colour schemes.

10	
Use	Word processor (Microsoft Word)
Title	Data storage
Task	● Print out details of where the files are stored.
Marks	1 mark for details of file storage.

Create a new word-processing document with a heading 'Data Storage'.

Give details of the names of your files and where they are stored. This can be done by copying and pasting a screenshot of the files.

11	
Use	Database (Microsoft Access)
Title	Advanced processing
Task	● Describe any advanced processing used.
Marks	2 marks for evidence of any two of the list below.

240
You only need to do two of these, but do more if you can!

There are **two extra marks** available if you include any of the following in the task:

- Import or export of data.
- Headers/footers.
- Use of forms for data entry.
- Command buttons on forms.
- Hyperlinks on forms.
- Design and output of a report.
- Use of formulae or calculations in files.
- Input masks.
- Use of a parameter query.
- Use of a macro.
- Use of a sub-form.
- Mail merge.

For each option, you will need to open a word-processing document, describe what you have done and provide evidence that it was completed satisfactorily by copying and pasting screenshots.

12	
Use	
Title	Front Cover / Bind
Task	● Create a front cover, collect and bind all documents.
Marks	

Make sure the printed sheets of your portfolio task are in the correct order, and properly bound or placed in a file cover.

Activity 15.1 gives a checklist of the tasks.

Activity 15.1   Checklist for Portfolio Task 1 (Spreadsheet)

Create a new spreadsheet and copy the table below into the cells.

Task no.	Task	Done	Marks
1	Background information		
2	Data structure table		1
3	Database creation		1
4	Validation rules		1
	Validation tests		1
5	Data entry (2 data types)		1
	Data entry (3 or more data types)		1
	Data entry (no mistakes)		1
	Data entry (sensible and relevant data)		1
	Data entry (print out)		1
6	Sort 1		1
	Sort 2 (or graph)		1
7	Simple search 1		1
	Simple search 2		1
8	Complex search 1		1
	Complex search 2		1
	Explaining search criteria		1
9	Data capture form		1
10	Data storage		1
11	Advanced processing 1		1
	Advanced processing 2		1
12	Front cover / bind		
		Total	20

Save this spreadsheet and use it as a checklist. When you finish each task, colour the square in the 'Done' column green.

15.3 Portfolio task 2: Spreadsheet modelling

This task will allow you to show off all the clever things you can do with a spreadsheet.

Your target is 20 marks. Use a checklist (see the Activity at the end of this section) to cross off each task as you finish it.

Your teacher will tell you what topic you will do for this portfolio task.

1	
Use	Word processor (Microsoft Word)
Title	Background information
Task	● Explain the situation and describe what you are going to investigate using a spreadsheet.
Marks	This task need only be a few paragraphs long, and is not worth any marks. Hopefully, it will give you a clearer understanding of what you are going to do.

Use a word processor to create a new document with a heading 'Background Information', and describe the situation and the reason for your investigation and what you are going to use the spreadsheet for.

2	
Use	Word processor (Microsoft Word)
Title	Spreadsheet design
Task	● Create hand-drawn designs for each sheet of the spreadsheet.
Marks	None yet, but be patient!

Use a word processor to create a new document with a heading 'Spreadsheet Design'. Print this document: you are going to draw on it.

Sketch on this sheet, a rough outline of the spreadsheet you are going to create. You will need to do one of these designs for each sheet of the spreadsheet, and include details about colouring and formatting.

Indicate which cells will have formulae (calculations) in them, but there is no need for details of these because they will be explained later.

24.1

It is important to check the list of complex features and advanced processing (Tasks 12 and 13) to see if you can use any of them in your spreadsheet.

24.2

Try to include different data types: text, number, currency, dates, etc.

Note that the design should include information about:

● Labels
● Colours
● Fonts
● Formatting
● Alignment
● Formulae.

The other sheet used in this example is a sheet of the details of the rides and their prices.

This hand-drawn design can be rough but it is important that you show that your work has been properly planned.

In this example, only one sheet has been drawn: The Adult Ticket.
However, it is necessary to do a drawn design for each sheet you are going to use.

3	
Use	Spreadsheet (Microsoft Excel)
Title	Spreadsheet outline
Task	● Create an outline grid for each sheet of the spreadsheet.
Marks	1 mark for outline grid, labels and at least one row of data.

Using a spreadsheet program, create an outline grid for your spreadsheet.

Set up the grid lines, the labels, the fonts, the formatting and the formulae.

Only enter one line of data for now.

When it is finished print the completed outline grid.

In the example, the outline grid is shown. Note that only one line of data has been entered.

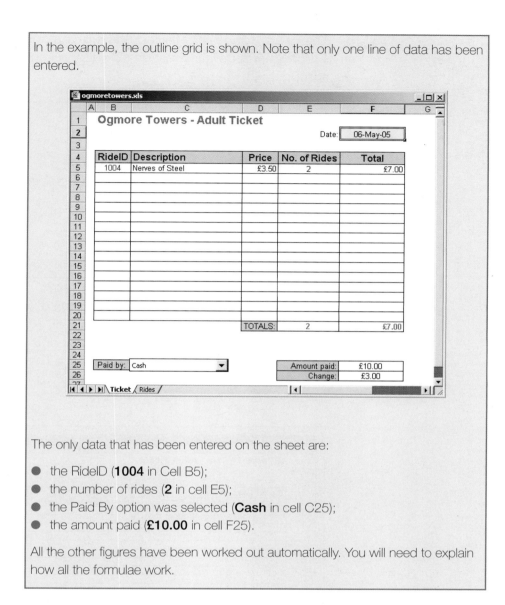

The only data that has been entered on the sheet are:

● the RideID (**1004** in Cell B5);
● the number of rides (**2** in cell E5);
● the Paid By option was selected (**Cash** in cell C25);
● the amount paid (**£10.00** in cell F25).

All the other figures have been worked out automatically. You will need to explain how all the formulae work.

4	
Use	Word processor (Microsoft Word)
Title	Explanation of formatting
Task	● Create a document and describe the formatting used on the spreadsheet.
Marks	1 mark for appropriate formatting.

This step is necessary because formatting of data is not always apparent from a print out.

Create a new document headed 'Formatting'. A detailed description of the formatting used in the spreadsheet should be given.
Formatting includes:

● **Alignment**;
● **Text formatting** (font and colour);
● **Cell formatting** (currency, numbers or dates).

The cell or range of cells should be given and the formatting used.

Formatting details must be given for all sheets used in the spreadsheet.

5	
Use	Word processor (Microsoft Word)
Title	Explanation of formulae
Task	● Create a document and explain the formulae used on the spreadsheet.
Marks	1 mark for design of correct formulae.
	1 mark for explanation of formulae.
	1 mark if you have used simple formulae to create new data.

Create a document headed 'Explanation of formulae', and explain all the formulae used on the spreadsheet.

This should be accompanied by print outs of all the sheets of your spreadsheet with the formulae showing. This provides proof that you have used formulae: it is not evident from a normal printout that formulae have been used.

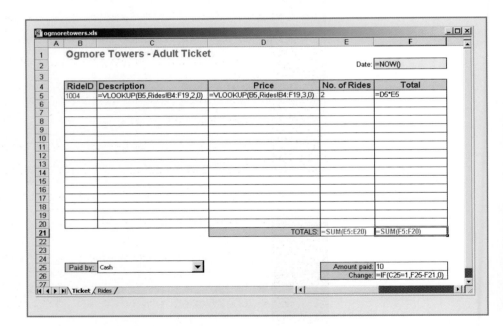

24.3
There are some clever formulae used in this example. Marks are awarded for these, so try to understand them and use them.

The formulae used in the above sheet are:

Cell	Formula	Explanation
F2	=NOW()	Inserts the date automatically.
C5	=VLOOKUP(B5,Rides! B4:F19,2,0)	Looks up the code in B5 in the table on the sheet 'Rides' and returns the description.
D5	=VLOOKUP(B5, Rides!B4:F19,3,0)	Looks up the code in B5 in the table on the sheet 'Rides' and returns the price.
F5	=D5*F5	Multiplies the price by the number of rides to give the total cost for that ride.
E21	=SUM(E5:E20)	Adds up the number of rides.
F21	=SUM(F5:F20)	Adds up the total costs for each ride to give the total amount due.
F26	=IF(C25=1,F25-F21,0)	If 'Cash' is selected in C25, then it works out the change by subtracting the total amount due from the amount paid.

6	
Use	Spreadsheet (Microsoft Excel)
Title	Spreadsheet data entry
Task	● Complete the spreadsheet by filling in remaining data.
Marks	1 mark for using labels and integers.
	1 mark for using at least two other data types (real, text, currency or dates).
	1 mark for using more than one sheet.
	1 mark if there are no obvious errors.
	1 mark if the data is sensible and suited to the purpose of the spreadsheet.

Enter the remaining data on all the sheets of the spreadsheet.

7	
Use	Spreadsheet (Microsoft Excel) and Word processor (Microsoft Word)
Title	Graph
Task	● Use the spreadsheet to create a graph. A valid reason for the graph must be given.
Marks	1 mark for a graph with reason.

24.4
Care needs to be taken over the title and the labelling of the axes to make sure the graph is meaningful.

A valid and sensible reason for creating a graph should be described, and the type of graph should be appropriate to this reason.

Create the graph and make sure that it is properly labelled and is meaningful to someone else who looks at it, and that it satisfies the reason that was described.

8	
Use	Spreadsheet (Microsoft Excel) and Word processor (Microsoft Word)
Title	Investigation 1
Task	● Use the spreadsheet to carry out an investigation involving the changing of data.
Marks	1 mark for an investigation, with a reason and a comment on the result.

It is now time to use the spreadsheet you have made. Decide on a realistic question that may need answering, and carry out an investigation that involves changing some of the data on the sheets.

An investigation should have:

● a question;
● evidence of the use of the spreadsheet;
● an answer.

Create a new document with heading 'Investigation1', and describe the investigation you are going to undertake.

Use the spreadsheet to carry out the investigation, printing out both a 'before' and an 'after' version of the spreadsheet.

This investigation must involve changing some of the data.

9	
Use	Spreadsheet (Microsoft Excel) and Word processor (Microsoft Word)
Title	Investigation 2
Task	● Use the spreadsheet to carry out an investigation involving the changing of formulae.
Marks	1 mark for an investigation with a reason and a comment on the result.

A second investigation must involve changing the formulae or the structure of the spreadsheet.

Again, describe a question, show how the investigation was carried out and provide an answer.

You will need to provide 'before' and 'after' printouts of the spreadsheet with the formulae showing, to prove that you have changed them.

10	
Use	Spreadsheet (Microsoft Excel) and Word processor (Microsoft Word)
Title	Investigation 3
Task	● Use the spreadsheet to carry out an investigation that involves the changing of the spreadsheet.
Marks	1 mark for an investigation, with a reason and a comment on the result.

A third investigation must be carried out using your spreadsheet. The formulae or structure of the spreadsheet need to be changed, but this investigation must be significantly different to your previous ones.

A customer comes in to the reception desk and asks:

Question: 'What is the most number of different rides I can go on if I only have £20 to spend?'

The spreadsheet shows that if a customer went on all rides, it would cost £35.50. Too much!

This printout shows the 'before' stage: a situation that does not answer the question.

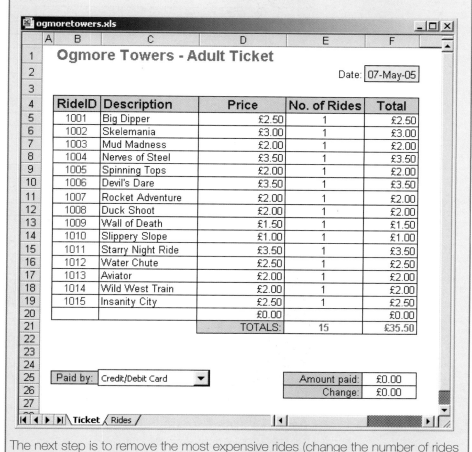

The next step is to remove the most expensive rides (change the number of rides from 1 to 0).

247

This printout is the 'after' stage, showing the solution.

Evidence:

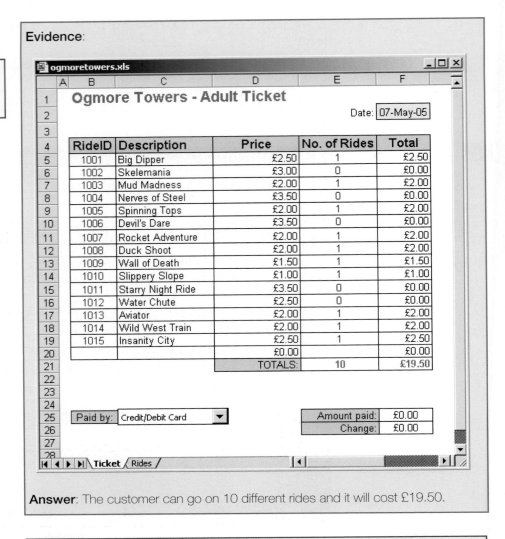

Answer: The customer can go on 10 different rides and it will cost £19.50.

11	
Use	Word processor (Microsoft Word)
Title	Data storage
Task	● Print out details of where the files are stored.
Marks	1 mark for details of file storage

Create a new word-processing document with a heading 'Data Storage'.

Give details of the names of your files and where they are stored. This can be done by copying and pasting a screenshot of the stored files.

12	
Use	Spreadsheet (Microsoft Excel) and Word processor (Microsoft Word)
Title	Complex features
Task	
Marks	3 marks for evidence of the use of any of features listed below.

248

Use at least three of these complex features on your spreadsheet.

There are three extra marks available if you have used any of these features in your spreadsheet:

- IF functions
- Absolute referencing
- Simple sorts
- Validation
- Referencing data on other sheets
- LOOKUP tables
- Protecting cells by hiding or locking
- Searches.

You need to use a word processor to create a new document with a heading 'Complex Features'. Explain which of the features you have used and describe where they can be found. Screenshots are useful here, as you need to provide proof that you have used these features successfully.

For example if you **sort** some of the data, make sure you provide screenshots of the data before they are sorted as well as after.

If you use **validation rules** on some of the cells, then you will need to provide screenshots of the error messages that appear when incorrect data is entered.

13	
Use	Spreadsheet (Microsoft Excel) and Word processor (Microsoft Word)
Title	Advanced processing
Task	
Marks	2 marks for evidence of the use of any of features listed below.

There are **two extra marks** available if you have used any of these advanced processing techniques in your spreadsheet:

- Import/export to a database or a document
- Multi-level sorts
- Multiple IF functions
- Macros
- Control buttons
- VLOOKUP or HLOOKUP across multiple sheets
- Data entry forms
- Headers and footers (include automatic features such as time and date)
- Pivot tables.

> 리 나
> Macros are useful for creating a template for each sheet of a spreadsheet.

Use a word processor to create a document with heading 'Advanced Processing', explain each of the processing techniques you have used, and provide proof that they have been successful by including screenshots.

Collect all your documents and bind them together or file them in the correct order.

Use the spreadsheet checklist below to make sure all tasks have been completed.

■ Activity 15.2   Checklist for Portfolio Task 2 (Spreadsheet)

Create a new spreadsheet and copy the table below into the cells.

Task no.	Task	Done	Marks
1	Background information		
2	Spreadsheet design		
3	Spreadsheet outline		1
4	Explanation of formatting		1
5	Explanation of formulae (design correctness)		1
	Explanation of formulae (explanation)		1
	Explanation of formulae (use)		1
6	Spreadsheet data entry (labels and integers)		1
	Spreadsheet data entry (2 additional data types)		1
	Spreadsheet data entry (more than one sheet)		1
	Spreadsheet data entry (no errors)		1
	Spreadsheet data entry (suited to purpose)		1
7	Graph		1
8	Investigation 1		1
9	Investigation 2		1
10	Investigation 3		1
11	Data storage		1
12	Complex features		3
13	Advanced processing		2
14	Front cover / bind		
		Total	20

Save this spreadsheet and use it as a checklist. When you finish each task, colour the square in the 'Done' column green.

15.4 Portfolio task 3: Communicating information

You may use any of the following for this task:

- Desktop publishing software (e.g. Microsoft Publisher);
- Multimedia presentation software (e.g. Microsoft PowerPoint);
- Website authoring software (e.g. Microsoft FrontPage Express).

You need to do two presentations for this task, but if you select two of the same type, then they must be significantly different in content and style.

1	
Use	Word processor (Microsoft Word)
Title	Background information
Task	● Describe the presentations that you are going to produce and how they will be used in your situation.
Marks	1 mark for suitable presentation of text-only document.

> **250**
> A good idea is to set up a template for each word-processed page of this task. It will look professional and get you an extra mark.

Decide what two presentations you are going to produce. Describe the situation and explain why the presentations are needed and how they will be used.

This is only an introduction, but you need to use some simple formatting techniques to make it look good. Use at least one of bold, italic, underline, indent or paragraphing.

> **251**
> There is no need for pictures here, but make sure you use some simple formatting (bold, italic, underline, etc.).

2	
Use	Word processor (Microsoft Word)
Title	Simple formatting
Task	● Describe the formatting used in the background information.
Marks	1 mark for use of one type of simple formatting (bold, italic, underline, text alignment, indent).

Create a new document with heading 'Simple Formatting' and explain what formatting you have used in the document in Task 1.

State the font and size of the text.

3	
Use	Word processor (Microsoft Word)
Title	Design of Presentation 1
Task	● State the purpose and sketch a design of your first presentation.
Marks	1 mark for sketching a design.
	1 mark for explanation of the features of the design.
	1 mark for explanation of where text and pictures come from.

Create a document with heading 'Design of Presentation 1'.

Explain in a short paragraph what Presentation 1 is, and what software you are going to use to create it.

Print out the sheet and draw a sketch of the design of the presentation.

Label the main parts of the design (the text and graphic), and explain what each consists of.

There must be only one graphic. Explain where the graphic has come from (e.g. a photo from a digital camera, a scanned image, a piece of clipart, copied from the Internet, or any other source).

In our example, the design of the leaflet may look like this:

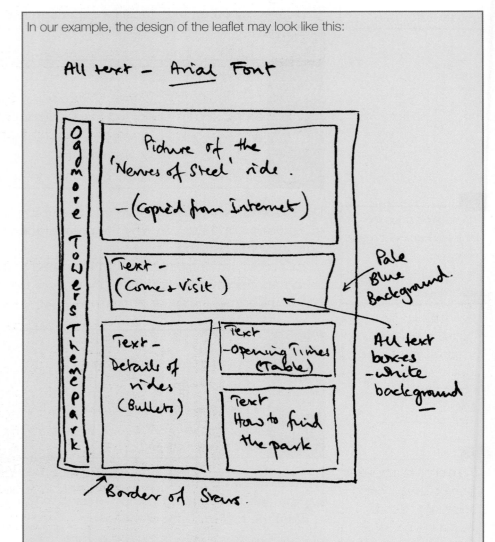

The **purpose** of the leaflet is to make the local people more aware of the attractions of the park, where it is and when it opens, and try to encourage them to visit.

The document is to be created on A4 page, with margins:
Left, Right: 1.5 cm
Top, Bottom: 2 cm

4	
Use	Word processor (Microsoft Word) or DTP (Microsoft Publisher)
Title	Presentation 1
Task	● Create and print out Presentation 1.
Marks	1 mark for a presentation which shows text and has one graphic, electronically imported. 1 mark for some text… . 1 mark for some more relevant text. 1 mark for even more relevant text with plenty of detail! 1 mark if there are no spelling mistakes. 1 mark if the text and graphic are relevant to the topic.

Use a word-processing or desktop-publishing program to create the presentation you have designed in the previous section.

Make sure you include at least one of these simple presentation techniques:

● Frame
● Border
● Fill effect
● WordArt.

Check the list of advanced formatting techniques and try to include some of them in your presentation.

252

Look ahead to Task 8 and make sure you include some of the advanced formatting techniques in your design.

253

There are a number of different formatting and presentation techniques used in this poster: a table, frames, bullet points and text orientation.

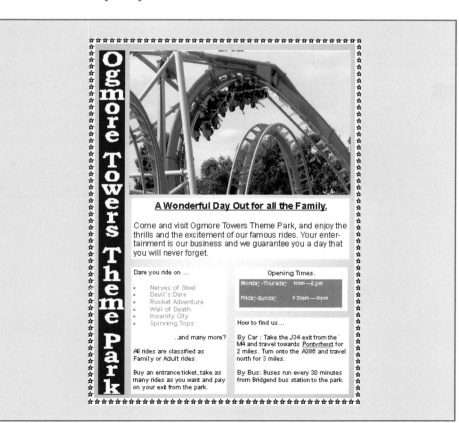

5	
Use	Word processor (Microsoft Word)
Title	Simple presentation techniques
Task	● Describe the simple formatting techniques you have used in presentation 1.
Marks	1 mark for one of the simple presentation techniques (frame, border, fill effect, WordArt).

Use a word-processing program to create a new document with heading 'Simple Presentation Techniques'.

Describe the presentation techniques used in your first presentation and where they can be found.

6	
Use	Word processor (Microsoft Word) or DTP (Microsoft Publisher)
Title	Design of presentation 2
Task	● State the purpose and sketch a design of your second presentation.
Marks	3 marks, but these are shared with 'Design of Presentation 1'.

2.5.4

Look ahead to Task 8 and try to include some of the advanced formatting techniques you did not use in the first presentation.

2.5.5

There may be things not apparent on a print out that you need to explain, such as use of sounds, animation, transition of slides, etc.

Your second presentation should be a different type of presentation to your first, and its purpose and content should also be markedly different.

Use a word processor to create a new document with heading 'Design of Presentation 2'.

Sketch the design and include detailed information about text and graphics or any other features that are to be included. Make sure that you include some of the advanced techniques listed in Task 8.

Sketch designs of all the parts of your second presentation. For example, if a multimedia presentation is going to be created then the design should include details about the contents of each slide and where the graphics come from, as well as details about animation and slide transitions.

Remember that some things are not visible when printed onto paper. The examiner will not be able to see your animation so you must describe it.

If a web page is to be created, then details about the hyperlinks must be given.

7	
Use	Word processor (Microsoft Word) or DTP (Microsoft Publisher)
Title	Presentation 2
Task	● State the purpose and sketch a design of your second presentation.
Marks	1 mark for a presentation that is suitable for the stated purpose. 1 mark if there is more than one form of electronically imported data (e.g. clipart, scanned from an image, copied from an Internet web page).

Create your second presentation and print it out.

8	
Use	Word processor (Microsoft Word)
Title	Advanced formatting
Task	● Describe any advanced formatting you have used on any of your presentations.
Marks	3 marks for any three of the advanced formatting techniques listed below.

Create a new document with heading 'Advanced Formatting', and explain where you have used any of the advanced formatting techniques.

The advanced formatting techniques are:

● Headers and footers
● Tables or spreadsheets included
● Producing and sticking to a plan which includes margins, gutters, orientation, etc.
● Complex use of frames (e.g. overlapping frames)
● Superscript or subscript
● Text orientation
● Text shaping
● Styles, tabs or indents
● Bullet points
● Line spacing
● Orphans and widows
● Graphs or charts
● Hyperlinks
● Hover buttons
● Command buttons
● Animated effects
● Imported sound or video.

9	
Use	Word Processor (Microsoft Word)
Title	Advanced and automated routines.
Task	● Describe the advanced and automated routines used in any of the documents.
Marks	2 marks for the use of any advanced and automated routines.

Create a new document with heading 'Advanced and Automated Routines' and explain where you have used any of the advanced and automated routines:

● Import or export of data from other applications or text files.
● Automated page numbering (not using a wizard).
● Templates.
● Using a formula in a document.
● Macros.
● Automatic contents production.
● Automatic index production.
● Use of script (JavaScript or VB Script) to enhance web pages.

You can get a mark under this section for setting up a template for each word-processed page of this task.

You could also do this using a recorded macro.

Automated page numbering can be done in the header or footer of each page.

10	
Use	Word Processor (Microsoft Word)
Title	Data storage
Task	● Print out details of where the files are stored.
Marks	1 mark for details of file storage.

Create a new word-processing document with a heading 'Data Storage'.

Give details of the names of your files and where they are stored. This can be done by copying and pasting a screenshot of the stored files.

11	
Use	
Title	Front cover / Bind
Task	● Create a front cover, collect and bind all documents.
Marks	

Collect all your documents and bind them together or file them in the correct order.

Use the spreadsheet checklist below to make sure all tasks have been completed.

■ Activity 15.3   Checklist for Portfolio Task 3 (Spreadsheet)

Create a new spreadsheet and copy the table below into the cells.

Task no.	Task	Done	Marks
1	Background information		1
2	Simple formatting		1
3	Design of presentation 1		(3)
4	Presentation 1		6
5	Simple presentation techniques		1
6	Design of presentation 2		(3)
7	Presentation 2		2
8	Advanced formatting		3
9	Advanced and automated routines		2
10	Data storage		1
11	Front cover / bind		
		Total	20

Save this spreadsheet and use it as a checklist. When you finish each task, colour the square in the 'Done' column green.

SECTION 4

Project

Only those doing FULL COURSE GCSE need present a Project.
The Project is **30 per cent** of your total GCSE mark, so it is important to make a good job of it!

The project consists of a report on the solution to a problem, and it must demonstrate all the ICT skills you have learned. It is a substantial piece of work and must be planned and organised well, otherwise you will either run out of time or present a Project which does not represent your capabilities in the subject.

The subject of the Project is your choice, but it must be different to your Portfolio work and presented separately. In fact the hardest part may be in deciding on the topic of your Project.

The steps involved in completing the Project are listed below, and you must make sure that none are missed out and all of them are completed in good time. If you present your Project early, it may be possible to improve it. If you present it on the day of the deadline, this cannot be done.

The topic should be a situation where a business or an organisation is having problems and you are the systems analyst who is going to help by designing and implementing a new computer system for them. There may be an existing computer system that is out-of-date or there may be none at all and the paperwork is done manually.

- All projects should be presented on A4 (or similar) paper in an envelope or flat file. (Ring binders are too bulky and are not acceptable.)
- The first page should be a title page and should include:
  - your name and examination number;
  - your school or centre name and number;
  - the title of the Project.
- The second page should be an index page. You will not be able to complete this until you have finished the Project.

Before you start...
You need to select a topic that you think will benefit from a computerised solution, preferably something that you are familiar with.

The topic should be investigated thoroughly so that you have a very clear idea of how the system operates at the moment. The

> **256**
> Complete the project early, and you will have time to improve it, and make sure it gets a good mark.

> **257**
> An index is important so that the person marking your Project can find everything easily.

problems with the system can then be identified and a solution designed and implemented (put into use).

Tips for the Project:

- Make your Project look professional by creating a document **template** and using it for every word-processed page. The template can include the name of the company, details such as its email address, a logo, dividing lines, etc., but make it small and stylish.

- Use **Headers and footers**. Include the title of the Project and your name, in case some of your pages go astray.

- Make sure every document has a clear **Heading**. The examiner will not be pleased with pages that are difficult to understand. If the examiner cannot see what you have done then you will get no marks.

- Use **Dividers**. These are pages at the start of each section.

- **Explain** everything. Remember some things are not apparent from printouts:
  - If you are using a spreadsheet the formulae used are not visible, so you must do another printout with the formulae showing.
  - The results of a database search do not show how the search was carried out, so you need to explain what search criteria were used.
  - Animations, slide transitions, sounds and videos in multimedia presentations are not visible.
  - Hyperlinks on web pages do not show where they link to.

- Make sure the work is your own work. Your teacher will need to see you working on your Project in class, even if you do a lot of the work at home.

- The most important tip! There is a lot to do and no time to waste. Concentrate and get on with it, and aim to finish it early so you will not have the pressure build-up at the end. Try to keep **ahead** of your friends doing the same project.

17 The project

17.1 Section 1: Statement of the problem and analysis

In this section, you will describe the topic you are intending to do and investigate the way the existing system works. The problems of the existing system need to be known and analysed before a new improved system can be designed.

Task Number	Description	Marks
1.1	**Title and Background** Describe the problem that you are going to solve. There is no need for great detail here – just a general discussion of the business, club, shop or organisation. Aim for about a page … you can let your imagination loose here a little. Give your Project a clear Title – which may be the name of the business.	2
1.2	**Analysis of the Current System** The first job a systems analyst does is to investigate the system being used at the present time. You will need to describe how you went about doing this. Remember there are four methods of investigation: **Questionnaire** – Include a questionnaire in this section. Print out two copies and fill one of them in. **Interview** – You could include a transcription of an interview you held with the manager of one of the staff. **Observation** – Describe what you saw when you paid a visit and watched the staff working for a day. **Documentation** – What documentation about the existing system did you read?	4

Describe in detail how the existing system works:

- How is the data collected?
- How is the data stored?
- How is the data accessed and used?
- Who uses the information?

Make sure that you investigate all aspects of your chosen topic. This investigation must be detailed and should not simply consist of a few general points.

1.3	**Problems with the Current System**	2

Describe the **problems** the staff are finding with the existing system. Here are some suggestions:

258

> Make sure the problems you discuss are appropriate to your topic.

General:

- The business needs to get more customers as sales are dropping.
- Customers are being lost because of poor stock control.
- There are problems hiring staff because of the nature of the work.

Data storage:

- Only one person can access the data at a time.
- Sorting is almost impossible with a large amount of data, especially if it is stored on paper.
- Searching is difficult and time consuming.

Documents:

- Storing large volumes of paper.
- Misplacing documents.
- There are difficulties in making changes to documents.
- It is not possible to make changes in the size of text or graphics.
- Documents have to be re-typed even for a minor change.

Spreadsheet:

- It is difficult to make any changes to paper-based spreadsheets.
- If any changes are made to the data, the calculations have to be done again.

1.4	**Aims and Objectives**	2

Describe the improvements that you intend to make to the system.

What are the **objectives** of the new system (relate these to the problems you mentioned in the previous section)? What do you hope to achieve?

Describe how you will measure whether the new system is an improvement on the old system.

17.2 Section 2: Design of the solution

In this section you will design a solution to the problems in the existing system.

Task Number	Description	Marks
2.1	**Alternative methods**	1

Describe the different ways you could solve the problems of the old system.

Here are some possible suggestions:

- If a manual system exists you could improve it by buying bigger filing cabinets.
- Re-organise the filing system
- Employ more staff
- Advertise the business on radio or television.
- If an old computer system exists you could upgrade the hardware – e.g. buy faster processors, more memory or hard drives with greater storage capacity.
- Computerise an existing manual system
- Buy specialised programs.
- Pay a programmer to write programs for the business or set up a database.
- Use integrated software packages like Microsoft Office.

Task Number	Description	Marks
2.2	**Software**	1

Describe the **software** that will be installed and used in your organisation. (Not the software you are using to do this Project!)

What operating system will you use? What version?

What applications software will be installed on the computers?

Will there be a need for Internet browsers or email programs?

Task Number	Description	Marks
2.3	**Information handling**	3

Design the **data structure table** for the database.

Use column headings: Fieldname, Type, Description.

Show which field is to be used as the key field.

Design and make a **data capture form**.

The fields on this form should exactly match the fields in the data structure table.

Print two copies of the finished form and fill one in by hand.

Data validation – Draw a table of the fields and describe the validation to be used to make sure the data entered is acceptable.

Use column headings: Fieldname, Validation Rule, Validation Text.

Not all fields need to be validated, but include them on the table.

The Validation Text is the error message that appears when incorrect data is entered.

| 2.4 | **Modelling** | 3 |

Do a **hand-drawn design** of the spreadsheet.

Include all sheets if there are more than one.

Make sure you include some of the more complex features such as:

- IF functions
- LOOKUP functions
- Referencing between different sheets
- Validation rules on cells
- Drop-down boxes

(These are examples and there are many more possibilities.)

Design of formulae:

Explain which cells will have formulae in them, and what the formulae will be calculating.

Use of more **complex designs or formulae**.

Explain the complex features of your spreadsheet and where they will be used. Remember that not all features are visible on printouts.

| 2.5 | **Communicating information** | 3 |

Do a **hand-drawn design** of the **first** presentation.

Make sure there is plenty of detail on the design about:

- Font types and sizes.
- Text colours and orientation.
- The subject of any text.
- What the graphics are.
- Frames, borders etc.

Do a **hand-drawn design** of the **second** presentation.

(Make sure the second presentation is of a different type to the first. Examples are leaflets or posters, multimedia presentations, web pages.)

Give **details** of where the text comes from. Is it original or does it come from an existing document?

Give details of where any graphics come from. Are they scanned images, copied from the Internet, downloaded from a digital camera?

Do this for both presentations.

| 2.6 | **Design of data flow** | 1 |

Design a document that you are going to use for a mail-merge.

Describe the reason you are going to do a mail-merge.

17.3 Section 3: Development of the solution

In this section you create the solution: the database, spreadsheet and presentations.

Task Number	Description	Marks
3.1	**User documentation**	4
	Describe the **hardware** setup of the new system.	
	How many computers are there going to be in your organisation?	
	What type of computers will they be, and what are their specifications?	
	Are they going to be networked?	
	Describe the **security** measures and how a user is going to access the system.	
	Will there be any protection against viruses, spyware or hackers?	
	Give **instructions** for use. (This does not have to be a large booklet!)	
	Give details of any **advanced features** that will be used such as: ● Macros ● Templates for new documents. ● Import or export of data. E.g. Importing data from your database into your spreadsheet. ● Data entry forms ● Parameter queries in your database. …and many more. (If you are planning on doing anything really clever – mention it here!)	
3.2	**Data flow**	2
	Use your design in Task 2.6 to create a **form letter** to be used in a mail-merge.	
	Print out this form letter with the field names showing.	
	Use a small database (3 records) to merge the fields into the form letter and print out the **final documents**.	
3.3	**Information handling**	8
	Set up the **database table** in Design View (use the data structure table in Task 2.3).	
	Enter a number of records (approximately 20 records).	
	Make sure you have used a **variety of field types** (text, integer, real, currency, date).	

Test Plan:	**Test 1: Change the data in a record** (or delete a record or draw a graph)

- Describe the change you are going to make.(E.g. a woman's surname has changed from 'Smith' to 'Jones' because she got married)
- Print out the record before the change.
- Edit the data and print out the record after the change.

Test 2: Simple search and sort

- Describe the test, which should involve a search on only one field, and sorting the result in order of one of the other fields.
- Name the fields that are to be displayed.
- Give the search criteria for this test. (Paste the Query Grid and explain.)
- Which field will the results be sorted by? Ascending or descending order?

Carry out **Test 2** and print out the results. Make sure your printout has a header/footer to explain what the printout is.

Test 3: Complex search

Describe fully the test, which should involve a search on more than one field.

Carry out **Test 3** and print out the results. Make sure your printout has a header/footer to explain what the printout is.

3.4	**Modelling**	8

Use your design in Task 2.4 to create your spreadsheet. Set up the grid and enter all the **formulae**.

Enter all the **data** and make sure there are no mistakes.

Print out the finished spreadsheet.

Print out the finished spreadsheet with the formulae showing.

Create a **graph** and explain the reason why it is needed.

Make sure all axes are labelled appropriately and that the graph is suitable for the stated reason.

Print out the graph.

Test Plan:	**Investigation 1**

Give details about a 'what if' investigation that involves changing the data on the spreadsheet.

Give the reason for the investigation – What is the **question**?

Print out 'before' and 'after' spreadsheets to provide **evidence** of the investigation.

What is the **answer** to the question?

Investigation 2

Give details about a 'what if...?' investigation that involves changing the formulae on the spreadsheet.

Give the reason for the investigation: what is the **question**?

Print out 'before' and 'after' spreadsheets to provide **evidence** of the investigation.

What is the **answer** to the question?

| 3.5 | **Communicating information** | 8 |

Create **Presentation 1** from the design in Task 2.5.

Create **Presentation 2** from the design in Task 2.5

Check that there are **no mistakes** in either presentation.

Make sure that one of the presentations has **text**.

Make sure that one of the presentations has a **graph** that has been copied and pasted…

…and a piece of clipart, or a scanned picture, or a downloaded photo from a digital camera.

Make sure there is one **advanced technique** used in one of the presentations:

- Table
- Overlapping frames
- Text orientation
- Text shaping
- Bullet points
- Hyperlinks
- Hover buttons
- Command buttons
- Animations
- Sound or video
- Macro
- Template

…and make sure there is a **second advanced technique**.

17.4 Section 4: Evaluation

This section is a discussion about whether what you have done is a suitable solution to the problems the organisation was having, and whether you think it is a good solution.

Task Number	Description	Marks
4.1	**Evaluation**	8

Create a document with heading '**Evaluation**'.

Evaluate the appropriateness of data in the database.

- Why was the data suitable?
- What differences are there to the data that was held in the old system?
- What does this new data enable you to do that you couldn't before?

Comment on how well the database system worked.

- Does the database allow you to find information easily and quickly?
- Were there any problems when using it, and have they been sorted out?
- Is it easy to print out sorted lists?
- Does the database solve the problems mentioned in Task 1.3?

Evaluate the appropriateness of data in the spreadsheet.

- Why was the data suitable?
- What differences are there to the data that was used in the old system?
- What does this new data enable you to do that you couldn't before?

Comment on how well the spreadsheet worked.

- Is it easy to use?
- Is it accurate?
- Does it save work with the automatic calculations?
- Does it save time? Why?
- Does it solve the problems mentioned in Task 1.3?

Evaluate the appropriateness of data in the presentation.

- Do the presentations have relevant information?
- Are the pictures relevant?

Comment on how well the presentation worked.

- Are the presentations informative?
- Will they attract the attention of viewers?
- Can they be used to solve the problems mentioned in Task 1.3?

Identify future modifications and developments for the system.

- Would any extra hardware be useful?
- Would any extra software be useful?
- Would the organisation benefit from its own website?

… or changes to the database, spreadsheet or presentations such as:

- Additional fields added to the database.
- Additional formulae added to the spreadsheet.
- Additional information added to the presentations?

AND FINALLY …

Bind all your work together using this checklist as a guide.

Add a '**Contents**' page and a front cover … Number the pages … and hand it to your teacher. Phew! Job done!

SECTION  5

The examination

18 Preparing for the examination

18.1 Revision

It is impossible to remember everything you learn in lessons, and you will need to spend some time on revision: refreshing your memory on the topics that you have covered in the course.

Revision for exams is your responsibility and it will not happen unless you make **some** effort!

The key to successful revision is planning and organisation.

You will have other exams to sit and your ICT revision will need to be planned as a part of your revision for all of your exams. Make sure you do not run out of time or leave too much work to be done in the last few days.

First of all, get yourself a checklist of all the topics. Either make it yourself or download one from the website for this book. If you make your own, a spreadsheet is an ideal tool.

As you revise, use a colour code to shade the square alongside each topic:

- Green: I understood this entire topic and it is easy.
- Amber: I may need to look at this topic again if I have got time.
- Red: Difficult. I did not fully understand and I must revise it again.

When you have read through all the topics, you will see the red and amber ones that need a second look. If you understand them better after a second revision, you can change the colour code.

If you are revising at home, do not work at it for too long at a time. Try to make revision an enjoyable task.

Revision tips

- Set yourself a time limit. About 20–30 minutes at a time is plenty. Several short sessions are better than one long one.

  'I will revise ICT for 20 minutes and have a break at 7.30 p.m.'

- Give yourself rewards.

  'When I stop revising I will have a chocolate bar and a drink and sit and watch *EastEnders*.'

> 259
> Always have a revision plan and set yourself daily targets… and rewards!

> 260
> In the right atmosphere, revision can be fun!

- If you are getting tired, take a break. Revision done when your brain is tired will not be effective: you will think you have revised a topic but it has not really been absorbed.
- Set targets for your revision session, and make a list of these. Cross them off when you achieve them.

'I will learn this list of 10 abbreviations and what they stand for.'

- Find a quiet place. It can be unsettling at the start if you are used to blaring music, but you will get used to the calm. If you have to play music, use calming music without words, and play it softly just for the atmosphere.

Good methods for revising include:

- **Write out**, or use a word processor, to make notes from a text book, or copy out notes that you have made. You will learn them by writing them out. Short notes are easier to learn, so pick out the key points and write them down.
- **Read** your notes out loud.
- **Make lists**. It is easier to learn from lists than from a lot of text. Bullet points like the ones in this paragraph are handy for making lists of important points.
- **Revise with someone else** who is doing the same exam. Discuss topics you are revising and test each other … but you need to agree first that you are going to revise and not discuss next weekend's party! Some discipline is needed here!
- Try to do **past exam papers**. If you can get a copy of the answers then this will be useful, but if you are unable to answer a question or you are unsure of the correct answer, then ask your teacher.

The important thing is that you are as prepared as you can possibly be when you go into the exam. Not everybody is going to get top grades and you need to be realistic about your capabilities. Make sure that you come out of the exam and can say to yourself …

'Well, I did the best that I could.'

18.2 Before the exam

Hopefully, with a good revision plan, you have not left too much to do in the days leading up to the exam. It is important that you ease back and undertake light revision only.

One big mistake made by pupils is to spend a long time revising on the day before an exam. Don't! This tactic will lead to mental exhaustion and you will not be able to perform to your best on the day of the exam. It would be better to go out in the fresh air and take some light exercise, take the dog for a walk, get your football out and go down the park, or stroll along the beach with some friends.

A brief review of your notes in the evening and an early night is the recipe for success. Make sure you get a good night's sleep, and you will wake up refreshed and ready to tackle the exam.

So remember:

- Late night cramming sessions the night before the exam are definitely out!
- Blow the cobwebs away with some light exercise in the fresh air the day before an exam.
- Try not to get too stressed! It is important but it is not the end of the world.

There is one other important thing you need to do before the exam takes place. Find out exactly what time it starts and where you will be sitting it. You may be given a room and a seat number. It can be very stressful just before an exam if you go to the wrong place at the wrong time!

18.3 Sitting the exam

You are sitting there with the exam paper in front of you and the invigilator tells you that you can start.... Help!

You have done all the easy bits like filling in your name and exam number on the front cover, and now the work begins....

You open the exam paper and see lots of questions and diagrams. You try to read the first question, but you look up and see that everybody else seems to be writing already. You try reading it again. It makes no sense. Your mind is a blank. Panic begins to set in!

What you need are:

Tips for success in ICT exams

- **Do not rush**. There is plenty of time for the written exam papers. It is not a race!
- **Read the question**... read the question again... and keep on reading it until you understand fully the situation and what is being asked.
- **Answer the question**. Make sure you give an answer to the question written in the paper and not a question of your own!
- **Cover up** the other questions. If you have a spare sheet of paper, cover up the questions you have not reached yet, and leave visible only the question you are working on. The whole paper will seem much easier.
- **Think before you write**. Once you have read a question and know what is being asked, take time to stop and think: 'What is the best way of explaining my answer?' Too many pupils rush through the written exams and fail to make their answers clear.
- **Banned words**. Never use words like 'thing', 'something' or 'stuff'.
  BAD: A thing for reading stuff on shopping items.
  GOOD: A device for reading barcodes on shopping items.
- **Explain**. Always make sure the examiner can understand your answer. Try to avoid using the word 'it'.
  BAD: It is faster.
  GOOD: Serving customers is faster.
- **Answer all questions**. Blank paper does not score, so it is always worth having a guess: you never know, you just might be right.
- **Avoid one-word answers** (unless it is obviously needed). Use full sentences if space allows it.

26.1
Three Golden Rules:
1 Read the question.
2 Read the question.
3 Answer the question.

26.2
Your teacher could probably add more words to this list of words not to use.

- **Use the mark scheme**. The number of marks awarded to each question shows you how much to write. If a question has two marks, for example, then you need to write two different points. Also keep an eye on how much space there is for the answer.

Above all, make sure you are properly prepared for the exam. Revise the work thoroughly and you will enter the exam with confidence, … but not too much!

After the exam, … forget it! Relax or prepare for the next one!
Good Luck!

SECTION  6

Practice questions: Answers

Chapter 1

1 a) Documents can be stored and re-used so there will be less typing; less time searching for documents; many copies of one document can be printed, saving typing time.

b) Fewer staff need to be employed in the office; faster processing of documents will lead to happier clients.

c) The cost of the computer equipment may be high.

d) Regular back-ups of the documents should be made and stored in a different place to the originals.

2 a) Data may be filled in incorrectly on the form; data may be incorrectly transcribed (copied from the form and typed into the computer).

b) Better design of the form or careful checking of the data; data verification (proofreading or double-entry).

Can you remember…?

1 GIGO stands for Garbage In, Garbage Out. If incorrect data is input then incorrect results will be output.

2 Data verification checks for transcription errors.

3 Data validation checks that data is 'sensible' and acceptable.

4 Range check: making sure data falls within an acceptable range.
Presence check: making sure no data is missing.
Format check: making sure data is the correct type and format.
Check digit: extra calculated digit added to numerical data.

5 A virus is a program that can copy itself. Install virus-protection software.

6 A hacker is a person that gets unauthorised access to data. Protect against hacking with a system of user names and passwords.

Chapter 2

Practice questions 2.1

1 a) At the checkout.

b) Barcode reader, keypad, magnetic stripe card reader.

c) LED screen (monitor); speaker; receipt printer.

d) Faster service so less queuing; fewer mistakes are likely to be made.

e) Automatic stock system, so less chance of running out of goods; fewer staff need to be employed as there is no need for staff to collect stock details.

2 a) Money-off vouchers mean cheaper shopping bills.

b) Customers may be encouraged to return and not go elsewhere.

3 a) ● At POS, the item being bought is identified (barcode, machine-readable tag) and details sent to the main computer.

● The computer adjusts the stock level on the stock database.

● Items whose stock levels fall lower than their re-order levels are automatically re-ordered from the suppliers.

b) Overstocked items may not be sold, and may be perishable; understocked items may run out.

Can you remember…?

1 OMR stands for Optical Mark Recognition.

2 OCR stands for Optical Character Recognition.

3 a) OCR is used for scanning a typed document.

b) OMR is used for a lottery ticket.

4 PDET devices are portable (they can be carried around).

5 Touch-sensitive screens are less likely to be stolen or damaged.

Practice questions 2.2

1 a) PIN (Personal Identity Number); the amount of money he wants to withdraw.

b) They are open 24 hours a day, every day; they are readily available; service is fast so there is not much queuing.

c) The ATM might not read your card if it is damaged; the ATM might have run out of money.

d) There are fewer customers in the banks so they need employ fewer staff.

e) Print out a bank balance; print out a mini-statement; change a PIN; order a cheque book.

2 a) MICR stands for Magnetic Ink Character Recognition.

b) Bank sort code; bank account number; cheque number.

c) MICR is faster than other methods at reading data off cheques; spoilt cheques can usually be read; difficult to use forged cheques.

Can you remember…?

1 The date; the person/company being paid; the amount in words; the amount in figures; signature.

2 A list of the most recent transactions.

3 The amount of money left in the account.

4 ● Credit card: credit company lends you the money and you have to pay it back.

● Debit card: money is moved directly from your account to the account of the company being paid.

5 Electronic Funds Transfer. Money is transferred by computer from one account to another.

6 PIN stands for Personal Identity Number

7 You should not tell your PIN to anyone else; you should not let people see you entering it at an ATM or on a 'chip and PIN' device.

Practice questions 2.3

1 a) The signal may not be strong enough; the battery may run flat.

b) A mobile phone can be used anywhere (provided there is a signal).

c) Sending a text message; taking and sending photos or videos; sending emails; playing games; listening to music.

2 a) Electronic mail. A system for sending messages between computer users on a network.

b) Emails arrive within seconds; emails can be used from home (no need to go to a post box); there is no need to buy a stamp (but there may be a phone connection charge); one email can be sent to a number of different people.

c) You cannot send physical objects; open an email attachment and you may receive a virus.

3 a) Internet Service Provider: a company with computers linked to the Internet.

b) Set up a website.

c) Reaches a wider and global market.

Can you remember...?

1 Uniform Resource Locator: used to identify a web page.
2 Pay a bill; transfer money between accounts; print a statement; open new accounts; set up standing orders or direct debits.
3 Advantage: you can telebank from home at any time.
  Disadvantages: telebanking may not have all the services that banks provide; security worries; lack of the personal touch.
4 Holding meetings over the Internet between people who are not physically in the same place.
5 Never give out personal details on a chat line.
6 An Internet browser is needed.
7 Email; home shopping; chat lines; search engines to find information; radio broadcasting; on-line databases; home banking; web publishing.
8 Interactive viewing (e.g. viewing a sports event from different angles); surveys; shopping; viewing selection; email.

Practice questions 2.4

1 **a)** A network consists of a number of computers linked together so they can communicate with each other.
  b) Networked computers can share hardware (e.g. a printer); networked computers can communicate with each other (data files or messages can be sent between them).
  c) Networks may spread viruses; hackers may use networks to gain unauthorised access to data.
  d) Username and password.
  e) There is no need for cabling.
2 Text alignment (centring); change in font size (in title 'Fame'); bold formatting; use of colour; use of border.

Can you remember...?

1 Command line interface; menu interface; GUI (Graphical User Interface).
2 Eye strain; neck or back strain; RSI (Repetitive Strain Injury).
3 WYSIWYG stands for 'What You See Is What You Get'.
4 Bitmap; vector.

Practice questions 2.5

1 **a)** Preparing a monthly household budget.
  b) Computer-controlled burglar alarm system or heating system.
  c) Preparing a news-sheet for a leisure club.
  d) Creating a database of all music CDs in the home.
2 **a)** They may help with relaxation or provide a break between uninteresting tasks.
  b) They can be addictive, and may prevent a pupil completing important tasks.
3 **a)** Home learning can be done at any time; students can progress at their own speed.
  b) There may be distractions such as small children or pets.

Can you remember..?

1 CAL stands for Computer-assisted Learning.
2 Movement sensor; light sensors; pressure sensor.
3 A device with a dedicated microprocessor in it.
4 Microwave oven; washing machine; video/DVD player; central heating controls; mobile phone; dishwasher.

5 An ADC is an analogue-to-digital converter.

6 Analogue signals received from a sensor will need to be converted to digital before a computer can process them.

Practice questions 2.6

1 a) Braille keyboard; concept keyboard; speech recognition system; head-tracking mouse; touch screen.

  b) Use plenty of colourful screens; use sound, videos or animation.

2 Use the Internet by using a search engine and a browser; send emails to experts or friends who may know about the topic; use encyclopedias on CD or DVD.

Can you remember…?

1 Automatic data readings are taken at regular intervals by sensors and input to a computer.

2 The overall length of time to take readings; the time between each reading (the frequency of readings).

3 Greater accuracy of readings; less chance of missing a reading; no human intervention necessary, and readings can be taken over a long time; readings can be taken in dangerous situations (e.g. radioactive, extremes of temperature, etc.).

4 Users can leave messages on a forum, communicating with other users with the same interest.

Chapter 3

1 a) There is no need to provide office space or facilities such as a canteen or toilets; the employers do not have to pay travel expenses.

  b) Work can be done when it is convenient and in flexible hours; there is no need for commuting to work.

  c) There may be a loss of social contact; loneliness.

2 Communications are done through emails rather than using letters and the postal service; buying goods is often done over the Internet, instead of travelling to shops; extended working hours due to the portability of laptops; mobile phones are frequently used instead of landline phones, allowing communication from almost anywhere.

3 a) Filing clerk; shop assistant to take stock; many conveyor belt jobs in manufacturing industry; bank tellers.

  b) Systems analyst; computer or robotic programmer; robot maintenance; ICT technician; computer hardware designer.

  c) Hacking; programming or planting viruses; identity theft; software piracy.

Chapter 4

1 a) 5 records.

  b) 7 fields.

  c) A simple query could be run (Preference = "Lighting").

  d) A complex query could be run (Preference = "Acting") AND (Sex = "M").

2 a) ii) B4–C4.
   b) ii) SUM(B2:B7) or iv) B2+B3+B4+B5+B6+B7.
   c) D3; C8; D8.

Chapter 5

1 a) anemometer; thermometer; barometer; hygrometer.
   b) Sea ferry operators need to know when there are going to be high winds or rough seas; farmers need to know when the weather is going to be fine so they can gather in their harvest.
   c) Mainframes (supercomputers).
2 a) Paint spraying; assembling; welding; fetching and carrying.
   b) They work 24 hours a day every day; they do not need paying; consistency of work quality.
   c) Initial costs of installation may be high; their use may cause some unemployment; they may not respond well to crises.
3 a) Heart beat (pulse); temperature; blood pressure. (Also breathing rate, blood pressure, blood gases.)
   b) Continuous monitoring; automatic alarm system; hospital staff are released to perform other duties; no chance of human errors due to tiredness.

Can you remember…?
1 CAD stands for Computer-aided Design. CAM stands for Computer-aided Manufacture.
2 A knowledge-based computer system that takes the place of a human expert.
3 Large database of knowledge; expert systems never get facts wrong; computer experts don't retire or give up work like humans.
4 Theatre booking system: on-line real-time transaction system.
Billing system: batch processing.
Process control in car manufacturing: real-time system.
Payroll: batch processing.
5 Barcodes.
6 CAL stands for Computer-assisted Learning.
Pupils can learn at their own speed; better motivation for learning; immediate feedback from assessments; difficult topics can be repeated as often as necessary.

Chapter 6

1 Input: reading instructions.
Processing: building the chest of drawers.
Output: the finished chest of drawers; showing off to wife.
2 Input: reading from sheet of music.
Processing: pressing stops on trumpet; playing the tune.
Output: the noisy tune.
3 Input data: the fixtures and dates.
Processing: sorting the fixtures into order of date.
Output: the printed fixture list.

4 Input data: readings from sensors (movement, sound, breaks in infrared beams, etc.).
Processing: analysing whether a break-in has occurred.
Output: alarm; call to police.

Chapter 7

1 a) Reading data from bank cheques: MICR.
 b) Reading data from lottery tickets: OMR.
 c) Scanning text into a word processor: OCR.
 d) Recording details of book lending in a library: barcodes.
2 a) Range check: the value must lie in the range 1 to 12.
 b) Batch total: the total mark should be included as a batch total.
 c) Check digit.
3 John Ssmith: data verification. 12/99/85: data validation (range check).

Can you remember…?

1 Check digit.
2 Proofreading and double-keying.
3 Check to make sure that data is not missing.
4 Optical Mark Recognition.
5 Optical Character Recognition.
6 Magnetic Ink Character Recognition.
7 Parity is used to check for errors when data is transmitted over a network. Even parity: every binary number has an even number of 1 bits in it.
8 Many questionnaires can be used at a time; interviews can only be done one at a time.

Chapter 8

1 a) Artist: Text (String); Stock: Integer (Numeric); Cost(£): Currency.
 b) Code is the key field.
 c) Reorder Level; No. Sold This Month.
 d) A new CD is released which the shop owner decides to sell.
 e) The shop owner decides to no longer sell one of the CDs.
 f) The cost of one of the CDs may be changed (e.g. in a sale).
 g) Fixed length fields are processed faster.
 h) Variable length fields mean the file is smaller and uses less storage space.
2 a) Locking the doors of the computer room; access only by cards or biometric systems.
 b) Access only by using passwords; encryption of the data.

Can you remember…?

1 A field is a single data item. A record is a collection of related fields. A file is an organised collection of related records.
2 A master file is a permanent file of all data. A transaction file is a temporary file of some of the data.
3 An archive file is a file saved for long-term storage.

Chapter 9

1 ● A formal font would be used on the letter, whereas a more outrageous or 'fun' font could be used on the invitation.

   ● The layout would be more formal on the letter, with a standard letterhead and format, whereas the invitation might be displayed in a more haphazard way with, for example, writing that is rotated or shaped.

   ● The invitation may be more colourful than the letter.

   ● Graphics are more likely on the invitation than on the letter.

2 ● The advertisement could be printed on paper. This could be displayed in places where people could see it, or may be posted to prospective clients (mailshot), or used as inserts in newspapers or magazines.

   ● The advertisement could be displayed on screen as a television advert. The advantage here is that sound or animation and video clips can be used.

   ● The advertisement could be displayed as a web page on the Internet. The advert could be seen by people anywhere in the world: a global audience.

Chapter 10

1 **a)** Magnetic disk (hard disk, floppy disk); magnetic tape.

   b) CD; DVD.

2 **a)** RAM is Random Access Memory.

   b) Temporary storage of data and programs.

   c) Read-only Memory (ROM).

   d) Monitor; laser printer.

   e) Hard drive; CD/DVD burner.

   f) 1024 bytes in one kilobyte.

   g) byte – kilobyte – megabyte – gigabyte.

   h) A hard disk can store much more data than a floppy disk.

   i) A floppy disk is portable. Data can be saved on CD or DVD and carried around.

Can you remember…?

1 Mainframe (supercomputer.)

2 A laptop can be carried around (it is portable). The battery may become flat.

3 Computer Output on Microfilm (Microfiche). Smaller storage space needed and film lasts longer than paper.

4 USB sticks are portable. Data can be saved on them and carried to a different computer. They hold more data than a floppy disk.

5 Scanning a photo or downloading from a digital camera.

6 Sensors.

Chapter 11

1 **a)** Theatre booking system: real time transaction. Data must be kept up-to-date to avoid double-booking.

   b) Traffic light: real time. The system must react immediately to traffic conditions.

c) Electricity bills: batch-processing. There is no urgency and the bills can be run off when they are all ready, at off-peak times of computer usage.

2 An operating system carries out (a), (b) and (d).

3 Use meaningful and recognisable icons to represent the applications; use consistent command buttons on each program (make sure that buttons that perform the same task look the same in each program); make sure the buttons are in the same position on each program; make sure the menus are similar wherever possible on each program, and in the same order (e.g. the File menu is always first).

Can you remember...?

1 A program that controls the running of a computer.

2 A batch-processing system can be run at off-peak times of computer usage; there is no need for human interaction.

3 Faster processing.

4 A sequence of instructions for a computer.

5 GUI stands for Graphical User Interface.

6 WIMP stands for Windows, Icons, Menus, Pointers.

7 The IT skills of the users; the power and resources of the computer.

8 In a fighter plane (where the pilot is using hands to fly the plane).

9 Check user names and passwords; keep a log of computer usage; scheduled back-ups.

Chapter 12

1 a) A network consists of two or more computers connected together so they can communicate.

b) Computers on a network can share hardware such as a printer; computers on a network can share data (they can all access the same database stored on one of the networked computers); Computers on a network can communicate (transfer data or messages between them).

2 a) Local Area Network.

b) Wide Area Network.

c) A LAN connects computers on the same site usually using cables. A WAN connects computers which may be geographically distant, usually by the telephone network.

3 a) A system of usernames and passwords could be used; a firewall could be installed.

b) Install virus-protection software; install an email filter which blocks unwanted emails (spam) or files with attachments from unknown senders.

Can you remember...?

1 A file server is a computer on a network where files are stored. The files can be accessed by any computer on the network.

2 A client/server network has a more powerful server acting as a file server. A peer-to-peer network has no server (all the computers on the network are of equal importance).

3 Bus network; ring network; star network. (See diagrams in text book.)

4 Metal and fibre optic. Metal cables are cheaper. Fibre optic cables transmit data faster.

5 No cables are used in a wireless network.

6 A transaction log is a record of all the transactions that have caused a change in data files.

Chapter 13

Practice questions 13.1

1 **a)** ● Investigate the old system using questionnaires, interviews, observation and reading existing documentation.
   ● Define the problems of the old system and set objectives for the new system.

b) ● Designing the new hardware set-up.
   ● Deciding on the software to be installed or the new programs to be written.
   ● Deciding on database structures.
   ● Input and output designs need to be created.

c) ● Writing, testing and debugging new programs.
   ● Creating the database and entering the data.
   ● Buying new hardware and installing new software.

d) ● Troubleshooting any problems that arise.
   ● Keeping hardware up-to-date.
   ● Making adjustments to the software or database if there are any changes in the library.

e) ● User documentation: a non-technical explanation of how to use the system.
   ● Technical documentation: for other programmers, so they can make changes to the system.

Practice questions 13.2

1 **a)** Ilnesses suffered; vaccinations received; date of birth.

b) The surgery needs to register with the DPA and state the purpose for which they are holding personal data.

c) The data would no longer be stored for the stated purpose.

d) The patient is right.

e) Exemptions include data for tax, data for detection and prevention of crime, data for household use or recreational clubs.

2 Virus creation or planting; hacking; using computer data for extortion or blackmail.

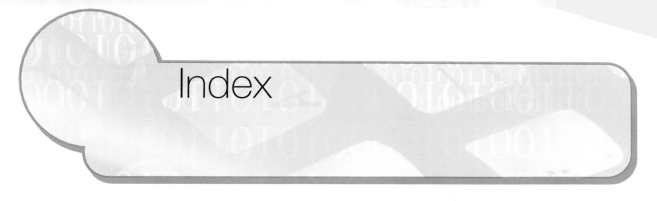

Index

Entries in **bold** refer to items which are defined on the **page** which is **emboldened**.